THE CATHCART CIRCLE

Station, Mount Florida.

Cathcart station in the first decade of the twentieth century. The Lanarkshire and Ayrshire Railway, to the right, has only recently been constructed. NIALL FERGUSON COLLECTION

THE
CATHCART CIRCLE

Second Edition

JACK KERNAHAN

LIGHTMOOR PRESS & THE CALEDONIAN RAILWAY ASSOCIATION

CR '439' Class 0-4-4T No. 468 at Glasgow Central. Built in 1905, it is in the Caledonian light blue which had become the standard for all passenger engines. It became British Railways No. 55201 (see page 13).

J. MacIntosh collection

First published in 1980 by The Scottish Railway Preservation Society.

This expanded edition published by LIGHTMOOR PRESS
in conjunction with the CALEDONIAN RAILWAY ASSOCIATION.

First edition © Jack Kernahan 1980
Second edition © Lightmoor Press, the Caledonian Railway Association and Jack Kernahan 2011.

Designed by Nigel Nicholson.

British Library Cataloguing-in-Publication Data. A catalogue
record for this book is available from the British Library.

ISBN 9781899889 52 5

LIGHTMOOR PRESS
Unit 144B, Lydney Trading Estate, Harbour Road, Lydney, Gloucestershire GL15 5EJ
www.lightmoor.co.uk
Lightmoor Press is an imprint of Black Dwarf Lightmoor Publications Ltd.

Printed by TJ International, Padstow, Cornwall.

CONTENTS

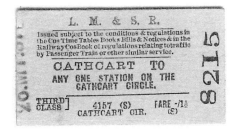

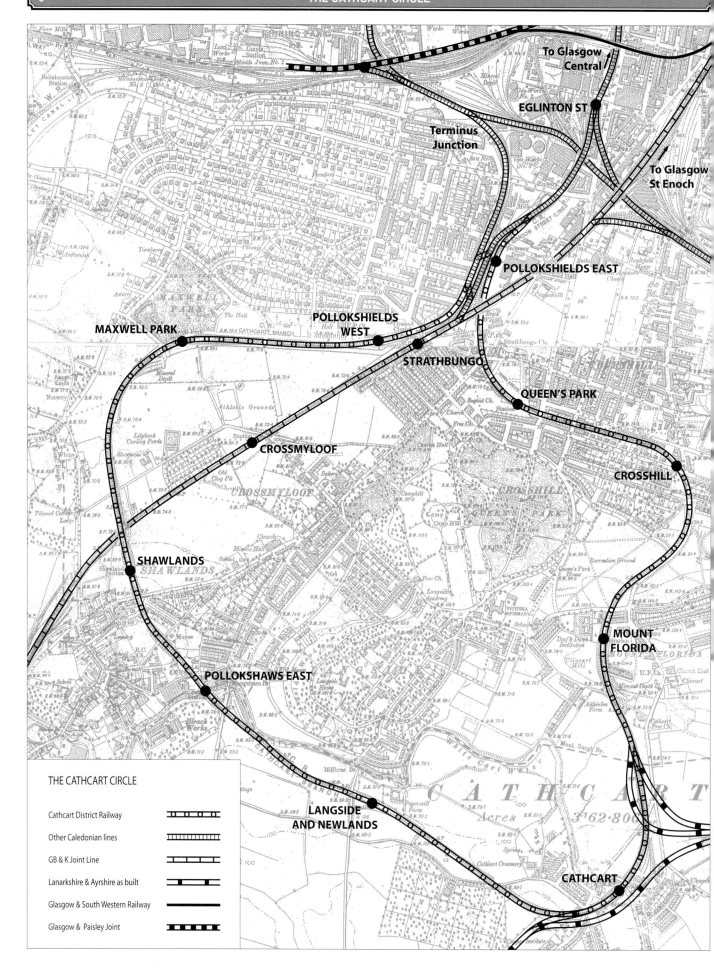

To Glasgow
Central

EGLINTON ST

Terminus
Junction

To Glasgow
St Enoch

POLLOKSHIELDS EAST

POLLOKSHIELDS
WEST

MAXWELL PARK

STRATHBUNGO

QUEEN'S PARK

CROSSMYLOOF

CROSSHILL

SHAWLANDS

MOUNT
FLORIDA

POLLOKSHAWS EAST

LANGSIDE
AND NEWLANDS

CATHCART

THE CATHCART CIRCLE

Cathcart District Railway

Other Caledonian lines

GB & K Joint Line

Lanarkshire & Ayrshire as built

Glasgow & South Western Railway

Glasgow & Paisley Joint

INTRODUCTION

'God made the country, man made the cities and the railways made the suburbs.' This introduction to *Snooker Tam of the Cathcart Railway*, R. W. Campbell's fictional tale of life on the Cathcart Circle first published in 1919, goes on to state that the railway is 'as famous as the Grand Trunk Road or Watling Street and to be ignorant of the Cathcart Circle is akin to saying that the Thames is in Germany and the Tweed in Alaska!' These days neither the Grand Trunk Road nor Watling Street are particularly famous and the Cathcart Circle is not the railway line of character that it was in the first half of the twentieth century.

It is now thirty years since the first edition of my short history of the Cathcart Circle was published. I am delighted to have been asked to bring the history of the Circle up to date and, as it is now over forty years since the days when I spent my teenage years at Maxwell Park station in an early unofficial version of the 'adopt a station' scheme, and some interest has been shown from both railway and non-railway friends in these activities, a new chapter is included about the station. The opportunity has also been taken to include some additional information which has come to light in recent years, particularly in respect of the development of the Muirhouse Junction area, to incorporate additional photographs and to append a few chapters of *Snooker Tam* which give a wonderful picture of life around the Circle about the time of the First World War.

Researching the history of the line has been most enjoyable and rewarding. The Circle was a local enterprise which retained at least nominal independence from the Caledonian Railway until the grouping of 1923. This alone was an indication that it had an interesting history, and so it proved. Three schemes promoted to cover the same territory on the same day, the bankruptcy of the contractor building the original line and the decision to build an extension through open country in the hope that building would follow. These and many more fascinating facts were unravelled, often from plans and documents unopened since the nineteenth century. The real character of a railway often lies not in its company's history, but in the little daily events and the people who make it alive. I have

only personal recollection of the line since British Railways days, but the local newspapers provided an enthralling insight into the day-to-day happenings a century ago.

Much has changed in the last fifty years. Leisurely steam trains, where schoolboys skylarked and businessmen had their own specific seats, are gone, while station gardens and neat signalboxes are things of the past. Only four of the original station buildings remain, three modernised and the fourth, Maxwell Park, unstaffed but preserved, while at four of the stations only simple passenger shelters are now provided.

I am grateful to the staff at the Mitchell Library in Glasgow, National Archives of Scotland in Edinburgh and the National Archives at Kew for assistance in locating further information on the line, and to Paul Aitken, Godfrey Croughton, Niall Ferguson, Albert Greig, Jim MacIntosh, Willy McKnight, Gordon Murray, Fiona Sinclair and David Stirling for material and information supplied. My thanks are also due to my former colleague from Maxwell Park days, Hamish Stevenson, for providing further photographs from his own collection and that of his late father, James L. Stevenson. It would have been impossible to adequately illustrate the period of steam operation in the 1950s and early 1960s without the photographs of the late W. A. C. Smith and G. H. Robin, whose photographs are now in the care of The Transport Treasury, Insch, and the Mitchell Library, Glasgow. I am grateful to Barry Hoper of The Transport Treasury and the staff of the Mitchell Library for assistance in supplying the additional photographs by these gentlemen who expertly recorded scenes now gone forever.

Finally, I am pleased to record the encouragement and assistance of the Caledonian Railway Association in the publication of this second edition, and my thanks to Nigel Nicholson and Neil Parkhouse of Black Dwarf Lightmoor Publications for making this a much more professional production than the first edition.

Jack Kernahan
Stornoway Isle of Lewis
November 2010

Class 303 electric multiple unit 048, restored to original Caledonian blue livery, on display at the Scotrail Open Day held at Maxwell Park on 20th June 1993.

THE CATHCART DISTRICT RAILWAY COMPANY,

Incorporated by "The Cathcart District Railway Act, 1880."

Agreement for Maintenance and Working by Caledonian Railway Company sanctioned and confirmed by "The Caledonian Railway (Additional Powers) Act, 1881."

AUTHORIZED CAPITAL, £175,000.   BORROWING POWERS, £58,330.

ISSUE of one-half of Company's Capital in 8,750 Shares of £10 each, at par, payable as follows:—

10s. on Application; 10s. on Allotment; £1 on 16th January, 1882;

And the remainder by instalments at such periods as may be found necessary, having regard to the progress of the Works, in amounts not exceeding £2 each, at intervals of not less than two months; but the aggregate amount of Calls in any year not to exceed £6 per Share.

The other half of the Company's Capital to be taken by the Caledonian Railway Company on the Shares now offered being subscribed for, and £2 per Share paid thereon.

The liability of Shareholders is limited to the amount of their Shares.

===

DIRECTORS.

PROVOST BROWNE, Crosshill, *Chairman.*

T. R. J. LOGAN, Esq., of WM. DIXON, LIMITED, Ironmasters, Glasgow.

R. G. SOMMERVILLE, Esq., Ex-Provost of Port-Glasgow.

A. F. STODDARD, Esq., of A. F. STODDARD & Co., Manufacturers, Glenpatrick.

By the Act of Parliament incorporating the Company the number of Directors is limited to FOUR.

BANKERS.

THE BANK OF SCOTLAND.

BROKERS.

MESSRS. GRAHAMES, CRUM, & SPENS, 12 St. Vincent Place, Glasgow.

GEORGE MORTON, Esq., 104 West George Street, Glasgow.

MESSRS. BELL, BEGG, & COWAN, 8 North St. David Street, Edinburgh.

ENGINEERS.

MESSRS. WHARRIE, COLLEDGE & BRAND, C.E., Bath Street, Glasgow.

SOLICITORS.

MESSRS. J. M. & J. H. ROBERTSON, 44 West Regent Street, Glasgow.

SECRETARY.

J. M. ROBERTSON, Esq.

TEMPORARY OFFICE.

44 WEST REGENT STREET, GLASGOW.

CHAPTER 1

THE ORIGINAL LINE

Early in the morning of the 25th of May in 1886, John McGaw, the local postmaster, trudged up the cobbled incline to the new station, and purchased the first ticket to Glasgow. The railway had come at last to Cathcart, and what was later to become a Glasgow institution was born.

Cathcart is said to owe its foundation, and its name, to a twelfth-century castle standing on the 'cart', or fertilising stream. The industrial revolution did not bypass the village, and by the time of the opening of the railway several industries had been established, mostly attracted by the flowing waters of the Cart. The earliest was a paper mill operated by Nicholas Deschamp, a Huguenot refugee from France, at Millholm, while the Lindsays manufactured snuff and cardboard at their mill near the Old Bridge. These mills, together with the dye-works, creamery and carpet factory, were the main sources of employment before the coming of the railway. It was in 1886 that George and James Weir opened a small factory, known locally as the 'Pump Factory', later to expand into Weir Pumps Limited.

Until 1879 the railway had avoided Cathcart, promoters having concentrated on routes linking large centres rather than on suburban traffic. In 1879 the new Central terminus had opened, and on 15th November of that year three separate schemes for lines to Cathcart appeared in the parliamentary notice columns of the newspapers. Two schemes were promoted by the Glasgow South Suburban Railway

Company, and the third by the Cathcart District Railway Company. Of these lines, two were 'circles', while one basically was a branch line. These were locally promoted companies, but access was required to one of the two large terminals which now existed for south-bound traffic from Glasgow, the Central station of the Caledonian Railway, or its rival, the Glasgow & South Western Railway's St Enoch station, which had opened in 1876. The plans of all three lines permitted running into either station over existing lines.

The South Suburban Company's proposed circle commenced with a junction with the Glasgow Barrhead & Kilmarnock line, which was owned and operated jointly by the Caledonian and Glasgow & South Western Railways, immediately south of their station at Strathbungo, which had opened on 1st December 1877. The line then headed due south for 171 yards before turning east to pass under Pollokshaws Road which was to be raised 3 feet 3 inches where it dissected the recreation grounds and bowling greens. It then passed across Govanhill Road and turned south towards Cathcart. At Cathcart the line crossed the Cart 18 feet above water level before swinging west towards Pollokshaws. Between the river and the Kilmarnock Road the line swung north again, crossing the Cart 34 feet above water level, parallel with and to the east of the Kilmarnock Road. The line was to cross Regent Street (now Regwood Street), which was to be lowered 2 feet 1 inch, on an arch 14 feet high with a 20-foot

ABOVE: CR '171' Class 0-4-4T No. 228 at the original Cathcart station, possibly on opening day, 25th May 1886.

FACING PAGE: The front sheet of the Prospectus for the original line.

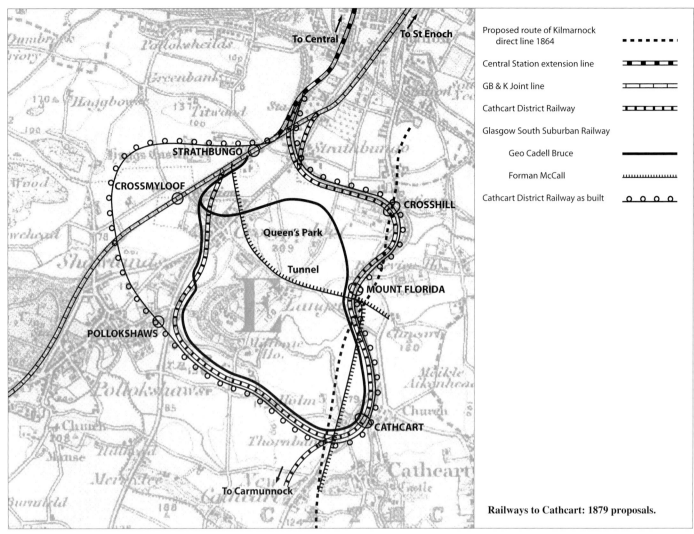

Proposed route of Kilmarnock direct line 1864 ....

Central Station extension line

GB & K Joint line

Cathcart District Railway

Glasgow South Suburban Railway

Geo Cadell Bruce ————

Forman McCall ....

Cathcart District Railway as built o o o o

To Central   To St Enoch

STRATHBUNGO

CROSSMYLOOF

CROSSHILL

Queen's Park

Tunnel

MOUNT FLORIDA

POLLOKSHAWS

CATHCART

To Carmunnock

Railways to Cathcart: 1879 proposals.

span, resulting in the road having a 1 in 20 gradient on either side of the railway. The line continued north, passing under the roadway at Shawlands Cross, to complete the circle, although the tightness of the curves resulted in the line looking more like a square, with a junction with itself near Titwood Road.

Running powers were sought into both Central and St Enoch stations, as well as to Alexandra Park on the City of Glasgow Union and Parkhead on the North British Railway, thus providing a service between districts on the south side and the north and east of the city. The engineer for the line was to be George Cadell Bruce and Messrs Gordon, Smith and Lucas were the solicitors. No major engineering features were required.

The South Suburban Company's less ambitious alternative proposal was engineered by Messrs Forman and McCall and envisaged a branch from a similar point south of Strathbungo station, although 29 yards further away from that station than the circular route. The line ran to the north of the road from Battlefield to Crossmyloof (the present Langside Avenue), and necessitated a tunnel 310 feet in length with a maximum depth of 66 feet under the hill at Battlefield. Near Battlefield the line turned south to Cathcart, crossing the river on a bridge 27 feet above the water level before terminating at New Cathcart. At the point where the line turned south, a branch one furlong in length was to continue east to a terminus just north of Battlefield East Church. Running powers were sought into Glasgow Central and St Enoch stations, but not to Alexandra Park or Parkhead.

The third proposal was by the Cathcart District Railway Company and was the most comprehensive, embracing aspects of both the other

schemes with about 7 route miles. The line was circular, but differed slightly in its course from the South Suburban line. It was to leave the Kilmarnock Joint line 342 yards north of the bridge carrying the Titwood Road over the line, and run south to Shawlands Cross, which it was to burrow under, and follow a similar course to the Suburban line to the east of the Kilmarnock Road, although passing underneath Regent Street, which required to be raised 8 feet 6 inches. The bridge over the Cart at this point was to be 10 feet 6 inches above water level, the footpath on the north, which is today Holmbank Avenue, being shut up. The line then swung east towards Cathcart crossing the river 31 feet above water level. The route back to Glasgow ran via Mount Florida, Crosshill and Govanhill, to the north of the GSSR line, and from Queen's Park diverged, with spurs permitting operation to St Enoch station and to Central station by connecting with the GB&K line and the Central station line respectively.

Another feature of the District Railway Company's proposals was a branch 2 miles 165 yards in length which was to run south from Cathcart for about a mile and turn east to terminate at Netherton, bringing, as contemporary newspaper reports stated, railway facilities to the 'singularly picturesque and beautiful valley'. The line was to cross the Cart at the Netherlee Print and Dye Works on a viaduct 120 yards in length and a height of 67 feet 11 inches from rails to water. The bill also sought authority to construct a road 670 yards in length from the terminus at Netherton to the road to Carmunnock. The road was to have a basic gradient of 1 in 46, although short sections were to be as steep as 1 in 10. Running powers were sought into Central and St Enoch stations.

The success of all three schemes depended on one of the two

Mount Florida early in the life of the Circle, showing a train composed of nine four-wheeled coaches which formed most of the services at that time.

established large companies taking them up. The Glasgow & South Western was interested in none of them, and Mr Peter Clouston, the G&SWR Chairman, told Provost Browne of Crosshill, the principal promoter of the District Railway scheme, that his directors had gone into the matter very carefully and had arrived at the conclusion that it was a line which would never pay. He was surprised that the Provost should have anything to do with the promotion of the Cathcart Railway, and, as an old personal friend, recommended that he drop the scheme. As this conversation was not regarded as private, the Cathcart District promoters had been informed of the G&SWR opinion and put their proposals only to the Caledonian, which at that time was also considering the rival schemes.

On 9th December 1879 the Caledonian Board considered a letter from Gordon Smith & Lucas, the solicitors, with reference to the GSSR's 'circle' line, but this was not approved, and, indeed, nothing further was heard of this line, possibly due to the sum of £2,000 received by its promoters from the District Railway promoters in an effort to dissuade them from advancing the scheme. The South Suburban company's simpler scheme, the basic branch line to Cathcart with the diminutive spur at Mount Florida, fared slightly better in the Caledonian court. On 23rd December 1879 the Caledonian Board decided that it did not approve of the scheme, submitted in a letter from Messrs H. & R. Lamond, the solicitors for the line, but this did not prevent the proposed line going to Parliament, the required 5 per cent guarantee as to costs being deposited during January 1880. On 2nd March, Messrs Lamond again wrote to the Caledonian requesting an interview but this was promptly declined. The prospects of the line succeeding without Caledonian support were bleak, and on 18th March the Caledonian received intimation that the promoters of the Bill had abandoned it.

The Cathcart District Railway Company was successful, possibly solely because it was always one step ahead of the GSSR in its negotiations with the Caledonian. On 4th March 1880 the Caledonian suggested to Mr Robertson, the CDR law agent, that it would be prepared to work the line at cost price on condition that the G&SWR running powers be struck out of the Bill. At about this time the Glasgow and Kilmarnock Joint Line Committee lodged objections against the GSSR and the CDR Bills, but, on the promoters of the CDR undertaking to abandon their running power clauses and insert additional clauses for the protection of the Joint Line, the Committee withdrew its objection on 29th June 1880, leaving the Bill unopposed.

On 22nd June the Caledonian had decided to apply for a Bill enabling it to subscribe 50 per cent of the Capital of the Cathcart District Company, provided the remaining 50 per cent was subscribed by the public and the management and working of the line was vested in the Caledonian. During August 1880 the questions of the connecting spur with the G&SWR, Railway No. 3 in the plans, and power being allowed in the Bill for the G&SWR to make working arrangements which had been earlier deleted at the Caledonian's insistence were raised by the promoters. The Caledonian Board decided at a meeting on 16th August that under these circumstances it could no longer proceed with the Bill, and Messrs Robertson and Colledge, the CDR engineer, together with Provost Browne were informed accordingly. They argued that the Caledonian might enter into an agreement whereby it would be placed in as favourable a position as it would have been had the provisions not been restored, and retired to give the directors an opportunity for further consideration. The Board's decision was rather guarded, and two directors, Messrs Jackson and Gibson, were despatched to London to consult with Mr Alex Graham,

LEFT: Queen's Park station shortly after opening, showing the bookstall opened by F. W. Wilson in 1892.

BELOW: The original (1886–94) station building at Cathcart shortly after the opening showing Mr John Cowper, the first station master, his three members of staff, retired gamekeeper Hugh McLachlan and a few passengers.

who was absent from the Glasgow meeting, on the subject. On 24th August the draft agreements, which had received certain minor alterations at the London meeting, were finally approved. On the last day of the 1880 Session of Parliament, 7th September of that year, the Cathcart District Railway Act was passed.

The promoters met formally in the offices of the law agents on 16th December and appointed George Browne, Provost of Crosshill, William Giffen Lindsay, Accountant of Glasgow, and Robert Galbraith Sommerville, ship owner and ex-Provost of Port Glasgow as the first directors. Mr Browne was appointed Chairman and Mr J. M. Robertson Secretary. The only business transacted was the approval of the agreement with the Caledonian.

No move to raise finance was made until the agreement with the Caledonian was approved. On 18th July 1881, despite G&SW objections, House of Lords approval was given to the agreement in the Caledonian Railway (Additional Powers) Act, which 'confirmed an agreement for the maintenance, working and management of the undertaking of the Cathcart District Railway by the Caledonian Railway and for enabling the Caledonian Railway to contribute to, and hold shares in, that undertaking'. Messrs Grahames Crum & Spens, stockbrokers, were consulted regarding the best means of raising the 50 per cent of the Share Capital which fell to be raised by the promoters, as the Caledonian had agreed to subscribe 50 per cent of the £175,000 authorised Share Capital when the subscriptions had been received by the CDR for the remainder, and £2 per share paid up. On 15th November Mr Lindsay resigned from the Board and Messrs T. R. J. Logan and A. F. Stoddart were appointed. This brought the number of directors to four, the maximum prescribed by the 1880 Act.

On 7th December 1881 the Prospectus was published, inviting public subscription for 8,750 shares of £10 each at par, payable 10 shillings on application, 10 shillings on allotment, £1 on 16th January 1882, and the remainder by instalments at such periods as may be found necessary having regard to the progress of the Works, in amounts not exceeding £2 each at intervals of not less than two months, although the aggregate amount of calls in any year were not to exceed £6 per share. The prospectus explained the background to railway communication in the area and the financial prospects of the company, and is worth recording:

The routes of Railways centering in Glasgow have hitherto been fixed exclusively with reference to their suitability for

connecting the City with places at a distance. Hence large masses of its suburban population, most of whom require to travel daily to and from the City, and to whom Railway connection with it would be of the greatest importance, derive no advantage from the present Railways, simply because none of the routes selected for main lines or through routes happen to pass through the District in which they reside.

The Cathcart District is a striking example of this. Possessing every condition necessary to make it a pleasant and healthful place of residence, its popularity has been attested by a rate of increase of its population without parallel in the history of Glasgow. Already it contains as many inhabitants as are often to be found along the route of Railways many miles in length; and though the great majority of them are necessarily daily travellers, it is entirely destitute of Railway accommodation.

The Cathcart District Railway has been designed to meet this pressing public want. Commencing at a point equally convenient for the villages of Old Cathcart and New Cathcart, it passes through the populous districts of Mount Florida, Crosshill, Govanhill, and Strathbungo, and joins the Central

Station Line of the Caledonian Railway immediately adjoining Pollokshields.

Twenty years ago the whole of the district thus traversed was practically green fields. Now, along its whole length, the land is either built on, or laid out for building.

The population in the district in 1861, was 3,000; in 1871, 8,000; and in 1881, 26,000 (according to the recent Census), thus showing a rate of increase in these twenty years almost without precedent. The Rental during the same period increased from £5,000 in 1861, to £37,600 in 1871, and £101,400 in 1881.

Within the same period the means of conveyance in the district has increased from 20 daily runs by Omnibuses in 1861, to 144 in 1871, and (including Tramway Cars) to 962 in 1881.

The present means of conveyance only partially accommodate the district, and are not to be compared, in speed and comfort, to what would be afforded by a Railway worked as a Suburban or Omnibus Line. It is, therefore, confidently expected that not only would such a line receive a large proportion of the existing traffic, but ensure a rapid increase of it, by promoting the development of the district.

As the Railway skirts the Queen's Park – the most attractive of the Glasgow Public Parks – and passes in close proximity to several Volunteer, Bowling, and Football Club grounds, it will not only, by providing speedy communication between these places and the centre of the City, confer a benefit on the public, but obtain a considerable addition to its revenue.

The Finance Committee of the Town Council of Glasgow, in reporting to that Corporation of the Scheme, state that they 'were of opinion that the proposed Line would be advantageous to the district, and that the arrangements which the Directors have made for the working of the Line afford the prospect of its being also financially successful.'

The prospectus continued by explaining that an alliance had been effected with the Caledonian, which undertook to work and maintain the line for 45 per cent of the gross earnings, and that the balance remaining after costs of management should be sufficient to pay a dividend of four and a half per cent. This figure was based on estimated receipts from the existing population and could only rise with the anticipated increases in population following the opening of the line.

The first five hundred shares were issued on 9th December 1881 to the major parties interested in the promotion of the railway.

Shares		
1–100	George Browne	Director
101–150	Thomas R. J. Logan	Director
151–250	Robert G. Sommerville	Director
251–300	Arthur F. Stoddard	Director
301–350	Thomas Wharrie	Engineer
351–380	Francis S. Colledge	Engineer
381–400	James Brand	Engineer
401–450	John M. Robertson	Secretary
451–500	James H. Robertson	Partner of Secretary

After number 500 the shares were issued principally to small investors. The shareholder appearing before the mighty Caledonian Railway in the Share Ledger was the proud owner of one share. Investments came from all over Scotland and England, although

CR '439' Class 0-4-4T No. 55201 at Queen's Park hauling the 4.30pm Outer Circle on 16th May 1956.   W. A. C. Smith/Transport Treasury

perhaps the most fascinating entry in the Share Ledger is that of 'Patrick Fraser, Oriental Club, Hanover Square, London.'

The first half-yearly meeting on 12th April 1882 heard that the 8,750 shares had been taken up, 1,000 of these by the Corporation of Glasgow, but many by the prospective passengers along the route to Cathcart. This was duly reported to the Caledonian together with a request for its subscription under the 1881 Act. £16,500 was received, this being £2 on 8,750 shares less £1,000 already advanced to cover Parliamentary promotion costs.

The directors reported to the second half-yearly meeting that there was nothing now to hinder contracts being advertised, although the preparation of working drawings had taken longer than they anticipated. This was followed within a month by a radical alteration in the company's proposals being submitted to the Caledonian.

On 22nd November a letter was sent to the Caledonian secretary asking if the Caledonian concurred with the suggestion that the line be terminated meantime on the east side of the River Cart due to a relative lack of support in the district. A week later this was approved.

A total of seventeen tenders for construction of the line were received, the highest by Messrs R. B. Stewart at £131,307:14/8, and the lowest by Messrs Alex Coghill & Co., who had not previously been involved in railway contract work, at £85,553:17/-, with the proviso that this could be reduced to £76,571:11/9 if certain amendments were incorporated, principally the alteration of the site of the first station from the north to the south side of Albert Road. Wharrie, Colledge & Brand, reporting on the tenders on 6th December, 1882, estimated that an additional £15,000 would be required for permanent way materials and stations. The Abstract for the cost of the railway was as follows:

Capital		£175,000: 0: 0
Borrowing powers		58,333: 0: 0
		233,333: 0: 0
Cost of works tendered for	£76,571:11: 9	
Cost of works to be tendered for	15,000: 0: 0	
	91,571:11: 9	
Land per Parliamentary estimate	122,778: 1: 3	
Less: savings by proposed alterations	3,117: 0: 0	
	119,661: 1: 3	211,232:13: 0
To the Credit of the Company		22,100: 7: 0

The contract with Messrs Coghill was signed on 10th January 1883, and ten days later on Saturday the 20th, the first turf was cut with the usual ceremonies by Provost George Browne, who was presented with a suitably inscribed full sized silver spade to mark the occasion. The spade, still contained within a glass case, remained in the Provost's family until the twenty-first century. At the end of the month a further call of £2 per share was made. Operations commenced at three different places on the line; an inspector of works, who was given the use, free of rent, of an unlet house at Crosshill belonging to the company, being appointed in lieu of a resident engineer.

ABOVE: CR '439' Class 0-4-4T No. 15265 entering Crosshill with an Outer Circle train on 24th April 1948.   G. H. ROBIN

FACING PAGE: Undertaking given by the Cathcart District Railway Company to the Caledonian relating to the working of the temporary single line between Crosshill and Mount Florida.   THE NATIONAL ARCHIVES

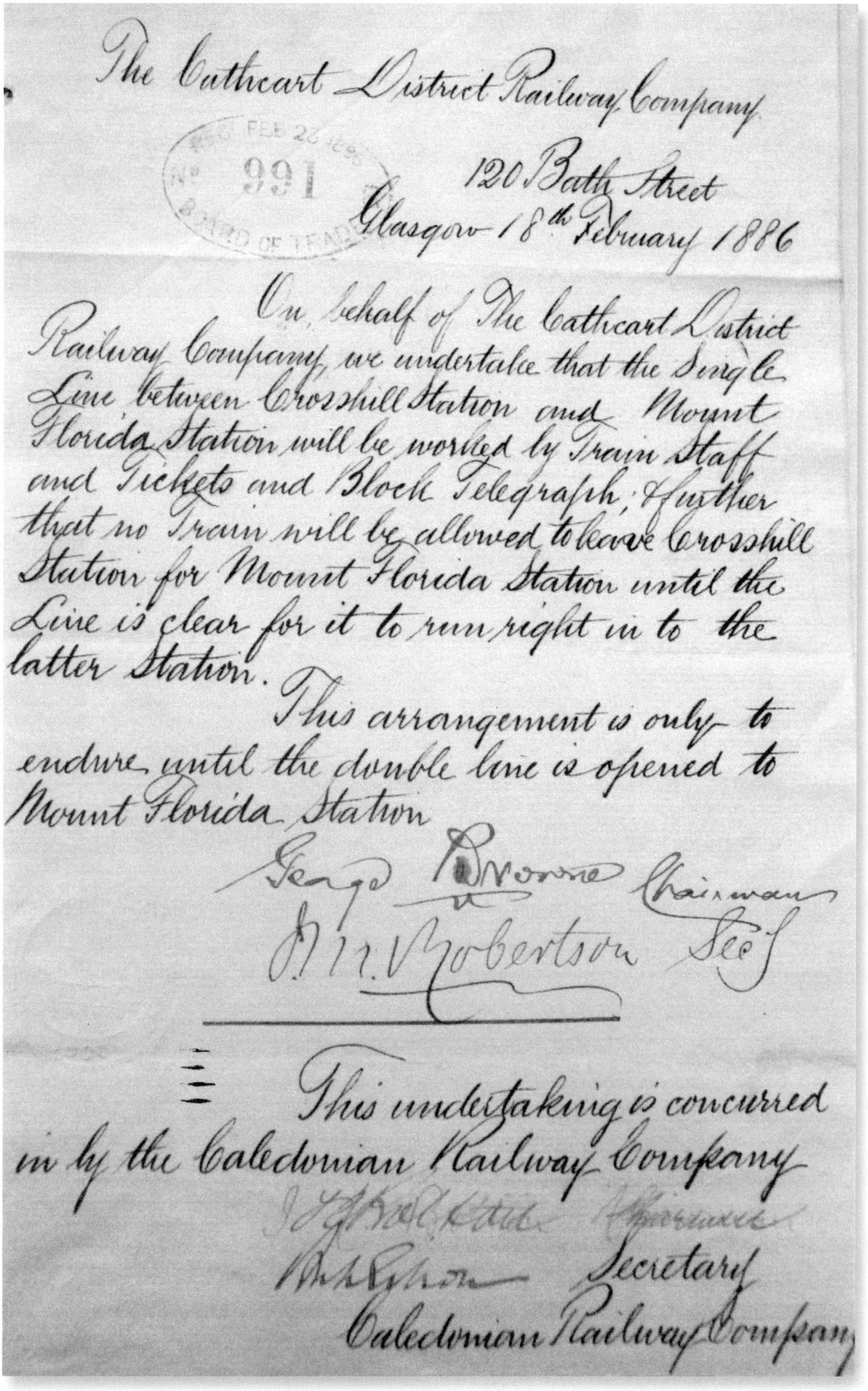

The Cathcart District Railway Company.

120 Bath Street
Glasgow 18th February 1886

On behalf of The Cathcart District Railway Company, we undertake that the Single Line between Crosshill Station and Mount Florida Station will be worked by Train Staff and Tickets and Block Telegraph, & further that no Train will be allowed to leave Crosshill Station for Mount Florida Station until the Line is clear for it to run right in to the latter Station. This arrangement is only to endure until the double line is opened to Mount Florida Station

George Browne Chairman

Jno. Robertson Secy

_____

This undertaking is concurred in by the Caledonian Railway Company

J.C. Bolton Chairman

Jas. Thompson Secretary

Caledonian Railway Company

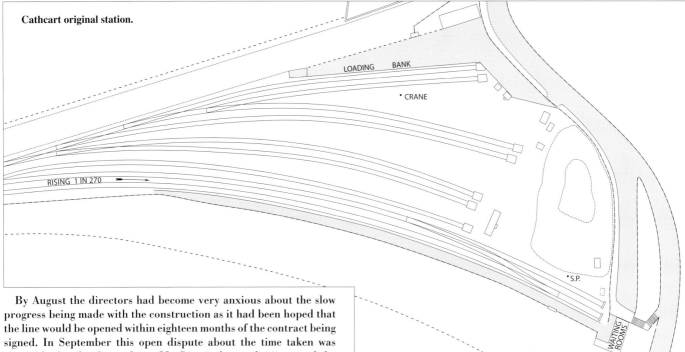

Cathcart original station.

LOADING BANK

• CRANE

RISING 1 IN 270

• S.P.

WAITING ROOMS

By August the directors had become very anxious about the slow progress being made with the construction as it had been hoped that the line would be opened within eighteen months of the contract being signed. In September this open dispute about the time taken was put in the hands of an arbiter, Mr Cunningham, who inspected the works on 11th October. He pointed out that there was an immediate danger of ground slipping at the Eildon Villas at Mount Florida, and, indeed, a week later a report was made to the Procurator Fiscal that there was a likelihood of a house falling down at this point. By mid-November two actions had been raised against the company by house owners, and complaints were received regarding the quality of the mortar being used in constructing the retaining walls.

The inevitable confrontation between the directors and the contractors came, surprisingly, at the instigation of the contractors. On 12th November the directors had approved the instalment for work completed and certified by the engineer, and the contractors had accepted the payment. Within an hour, however, Mr Coghill called personally at the company's office demanding an additional £1,000 beyond the amount certified, and threatening that, unless it was paid immediately, he would stop all operations on the line. He refused to put his demand in writing but agreed to attend the Board meeting on the 14th and ask in person. His demands were refused, although the directors suggested that if Mr Coghill thought that the engineer's calculations were wrong he should appeal to the arbiter.

The following day a letter was received from the contractors intimating that 'they had decided on stopping in the meantime further operations under their contract'. This action was followed, within two days, by a letter from two of Coghill's cautioners withdrawing the cautionary obligations which they had undertaken, the Board immediately replying that it denied the cautioners' powers to make such a withdrawal and indicating that it would enforce the obligations should the circumstances arise.

On Friday 16th November, as threatened, operations ceased, the workmen dispersed, and in the course of the following week the various stores on the line were sold off by the contractor. The Board immediately applied to Mr Cunningham for authority to take possession of the works and plant abandoned by the contractors and take all precautions necessary for the protection of the buildings which had been endangered. An exact measurement of the work executed and an inventory of all the abandoned plant were also sought and, finally, the arbiter was asked to consent to notice being given by the company of its intention to relet the works so far as unexecuted. One week later an order was granted in the above terms, during which time the company employed its own labour force to protect the dangerous works.

Meanwhile the contractors had lodged a summons in the Court of Session against the CDR for £18,000, being the balance which they alleged was due to them as a consequence of the 10 per cent retentions in monthly payments on the engineer's certificates, and, incredibly, for damages for breach of contract. Several actions followed against the company for damage caused to property due to the contractor's operations. Except for essential protecting works, notably the completion of the massive retaining walls at Eildon Villas, Mount Florida, which had been undertaken under the control and direction of the engineer and on the order of the Sheriff, no work was done on progressing the line and the works lay idle. On 9th January 1884 the secretary was instructed to readvertise for tenders, Mr George Graham, the Caledonian chief engineer, was asked for his opinion on the tenders. This time the tight purse strings did not rule the situation and the lowest tender, namely that of Messrs Short and Devlin, was not accepted, due to their complete lack of experience in railway construction. The contract went to Messrs Morrison and Mason, who specialised in railway construction, and whose tender, at £76,407 exclusive of ironwork, was the second lowest. At the half-yearly shareholders meeting on 30th April the directors were able to report that the works were now being 'vigorously prosecuted' by the new contractors and there was every prospect that the line would be completed within the time prescribed by the Company's Act.

In June 1884 Lord Lee found that the grounds of action stated by Coghill raised questions which properly fell within the arbitration clause in the contract and the matter was therefore remitted to Mr Cunningham to determine these questions. The company appears to have anticipated the arbiter's decision, for on 2nd September there appeared in the Glasgow Herald an advertisement to the effect that on the following day there would be an auction of the plant and machinery left by Messrs Coghill on the railway works which the CDR maintained had become its property under the contract. The sale was stopped in time.

The arbiter's decision was that Coghill was entitled to terminate the contract and be paid for the work executed at contract rates, but not to loss of profit on work unexecuted, nor to damages. The amount payable by the CDR, exclusive of interest or expenses, was £5,498:2/2, subject to certain deductions for injury to properties for which, in the opinion of the arbiter, the contractors were liable. The amount included £1,819:9/1 representing the value of the plant taken over by the railway company on the contractors suspending operations, the balance consisting mainly of the 10 per cent retentions. The CDR's cheque in final settlement was paid to the Trustees of Messrs Coghill & Company's Sequestrated Estate, as the railway contract had crippled the firm.

On 4th August 1884 the directors examined the works. A masons' strike during that month resulted in delays and the new contractors were requested to speed up progress. By November it was seen that the line would not be completed within the statutory time, and an Act authorising a two year extension was obtained. By March 1885 steady progress was being made. Plans of the station buildings, which were most likely designed by Francis Colledge the line's engineer rather than the architect, were sent to the Caledonian for approval.

In April an informal verbal approach was made by the factor of the Pollok Estates, asking whether the company would be interested in extending the line beyond Cathcart to the west, and beyond the GB&K line, on the understanding that the ground required would be given at full agricultural rates. The directors accepted the proposal,

but reserved full rights to reconsider the matter on its merits when exact details were submitted.

By 1885 work was nearing completion, and, following the Caledonian's approval of the design of the station buildings, with the minor proviso that the stationmaster's room be increased to 10 feet square, tenders for these buildings were advertised and that of Messrs Miller and Murray at £5,818, being the lowest, was accepted. During June, in an attempt to reduce costs, it was decided to increase to nine weeks the time permitted for completion of the station buildings from the date when possession was given of the platform in a condition ready for the contractor to begin operations. Five stations were built, instead of the six originally proposed. One station with two entrances replaced the two designed to serve Pollokshaws Road and Victoria Road. This station, Queen's Park, was consequently the longest on the line. The names chosen by the Cathcart Company's directors were submitted for Caledonian approval. These were Pollokshields East, Queen's Park, Myrtle Park, Mount Florida, and Cathcart. All were approved with the exception of Myrtle Park, which Mr Thompson, the Caledonian General Manager, thought should be Crosshill.

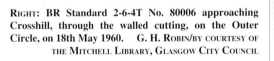

RIGHT: BR Standard 2-6-4T No. 80006 approaching Crosshill, through the walled cutting, on the Outer Circle, on 18th May 1960. G. H. ROBIN/BY COURTESY OF THE MITCHELL LIBRARY, GLASGOW CITY COUNCIL

BELOW: Fairburn 2-6-4T No. 42171 leaving Mount Florida on the Outer Circle, with a Metropolitan-Cammell diesel multiple unit on the Inner Circle. The engine is passing the high retaining wall at Eildon Villas, which caused difficulties during construction.

G. H. ROBIN

Winter once again slowed progress. During the laying of the permanent way, the contractors were allowed to use the junction with the Caledonian line at Albert Road, on the provision of a set of catch points to protect the main line. The retaining wall at Crosshill constructed by Coghill was showing signs of yielding and the engineer was asked his opinion on the practicability of opening the line as far as Crosshill while this reconstruction was taking place. On 13th January, 1886 a request was sent to the Board of Trade to have the line inspected to permit opening on 30th January as far as Mount Florida. On the 27th Major General Hutchinson wrote to say that he would attend on 5th February for the inspection and on the 1st the directors met at Pollokshields East station to walk the line. Unfortunately the works were snowbound and the Major General was informed that it would be advisable for him to postpone his inspection for a few days.

The inspection took place on 11th February and the report stated that the line could be opened to Mount Florida for passenger traffic, subject to certain requirements which could easily be effected prior to 1st March. In particular, no train was to leave Crosshill until it could run right into Mount Florida. The Secretary was instructed to write to the Caledonian intimating the directors' earnest desire that the line be opened on 1st March.

A public opening ceremony was dispensed with, but the provosts and chairmen of the local authorities of the area through which the line passed were invited to accompany the directors at the inspection of the line on Saturday 27th February prior to the opening on the following Monday. The inspection train, which was composed of six first and third class carriages and a wagon packed with goods addressed to the various stations, ran of course only as far as Mount Florida. After the train's return to Glasgow, Provost Browne presided over a substantial luncheon at the Central Hotel, where the warmest wishes were expressed for the success of the line. It was probably just as well that there was no formal ceremony, as it was in the middle of a spell of the worst weather known in the area for many years that, on Monday 1st March 1886, more than six years after the first proposals, the first 1¼ miles of the Cathcart Railway opened to passenger traffic.

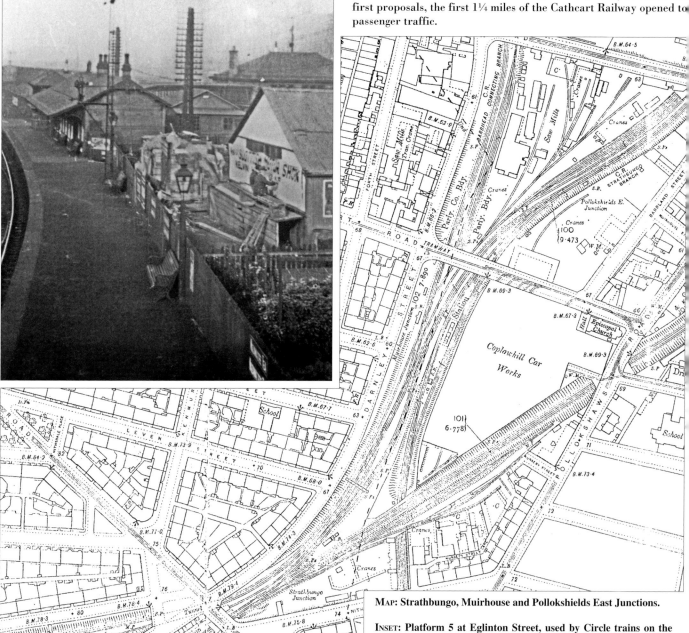

MAP: Strathbungo, Muirhouse and Pollokshields East Junctions.

INSET: Platform 5 at Eglinton Street, used by Circle trains on the outward journey from Glasgow Central. H. STEVENSON COLLECTION

CHAPTER 2

THE EXTENSION LINE

The line proved popular immediately and, a few days before the opening, Peter Craig, omnibus proprietor at New Cathcart applied to the Cathcart Railway directors, offering to sell the company his plant, which consisted of two horse-drawn buses, with a view to avoiding competition on the road, but this offer was politely refused. During the first month of operation, 93,083 passengers travelled on the line, excluding season ticket holders, thirty-two trains being operated in each direction daily, except Sundays, the first leaving Glasgow at 7.25am and the last at 11.10pm.

On Thursday 20th May, Major General Hutchinson returned and passed the remainder of the line for opening. This involved the section of line between Crosshill and Mount Florida being opened as double line instead of single, and the continuation to Cathcart being opened as a new stretch of double track. Monday 24th May proved to be a day of anxiety for the directors. The company was poised for its opening on the following day when a telegram was received from Mr Thompson, the Caledonian General Manager, expressing doubts as to the condition of Cathcart station which was far below the standards of the intermediate stations on the line in terms of passenger facilities, despite the fact that it was the terminus. The directors met in the forenoon as the arrangements for the opening

had been suspended, pending a decision from Mr Thompson. Nothing was heard during the meeting which was adjourned until 3pm. At that time Mr Kinghorn, assistant General Manager of the Caledonian appeared with the expected telegram from Mr Thompson:

Mr Thompson to Mr Kinghorn.
Your telegram. I agree to the Cathcart line being opened tomorrow provided that Neave gets it arranged that the present Cathcart station is not to be looked upon as a permanent one and that the position of the Caledonian Company is not prejudiced in any way.

24th May 1886

Trains started to serve Cathcart the following day as planned, although it was to be nearly eight years before anything was done about the Cathcart station.

For most of its length the CDR ran through the high-walled cuttings which had caused such trouble during the lengthy period of construction. Leaving the Central extension line at Cathcart Junction the line almost immediately reached the first station at Pollokshields East, serving the nearby Albert Road after which it was originally to have been named. After passing under the GB&K line to St Enoch, a

Cathcart station in 1947, with the Lanarkshire & Ayrshire line from Cathcart East to West Junctions on the right.   G. H. ROBIN

ABOVE: Fairburn 2-6-4T No. 42127 passes Pollokshields East Junction signalbox on 5th August 1952 with an Inner Circle train.   G. H. ROBIN

MAXWELL PARK

POLLOKSHIELDS WEST

STRATHBUNGO

CROSSMYLOOF

N

SHAWLANDS

POLLOKSHAWS EAST

To Cathcart

GB & K Joint line

Cathcart District extension line

Proposed deviation

1887 – Proposed deviation of extension line at Shawlands.

BELOW: CR 'Jumbo' 0-6-0 No. 57292 starts a freight train from the gasworks sidings at Muirhouse Junction on 7th April 1957.
G. H. ROBIN/BY COURTESY OF THE MITCHELL LIBRARY, GLASGOW CITY COUNCIL

deep cutting brought the line to Queen's Park station where there was a short respite from the walls, as the northern boundary was a grass slope, this having been approved very late in the construction timetable in an effort to reduce costs and speed the works. Immediately after Queen's Park station, the line passed under Victoria Road where by underpinning the railway was excavated under an existing tenement building which thus came to stand on a bridge over the railway, steel girders supporting the walls. The grass slopes gave Queen's Park a much more open outlook than the next station, Crosshill, which very rarely saw the sun. In addition, Crosshill was a very narrow station and did not permit the spacious platform buildings which the other intermediate stations possessed. After Crosshill, a short open space followed before the final major cuttings at the Eildon Villas, adjacent to Mount Florida station, where the retaining walls reached a height of 60 feet. It was at this site that the incident of the dead donkey occurred during construction. The course of the line ran near to the Institution for the Deaf and Dumb who for many years had possessed a donkey whose final resting place was never discovered until, some time after its demise, its remains were uncovered by one of the three steam navvies excavating the new railway.

Mount Florida was, of course, a residential area before the coming of the railway, the Eildon Villas having been constructed in the 1870s. Mount Florida House used to stand on the hill later occupied by the Eildon Villas, and was in the 1820s occupied by a family from Florida in the U.S.A. This, however, is unlikely to be the derivation of the area's name, as earlier reports in the nineteenth century quote Mount Florindon and Mount Floradale.

Beyond Mount Florida, open country stretched to Cathcart, with fields on either side, Steen's farm lying to the right of the line, near to the site later occupied by the Tramway depot. At Cathcart, the station, on the north bank of the Cart in a former field to the west of the Manse, consisted of a long single platform with a building at the buffer end at right angles to the platform. The simple building consisted solely of a booking office, next to the gate, and a waiting room, and contrasted strongly with the fine, glass-canopied buildings provided on the island platforms at the intermediate stations. The first stationmaster at Cathcart was Mr John Cowper. He was succeeded on 25th August 1888 by Mr W. J. Munro, who was to remain at the station for twenty-eight years.

During Mr Cowper's short stay at Cathcart, two interesting innovations occurred at the station, both suggested by his friends. The first was at the instigation of Mr Preece, who installed a telephone link between the station and the nearby signal box, to avoid the time-consuming procedure of sending staff back and forward with messages.

The 'telephone' consisted of zinc plates with holes in the centre through which the connecting wire passed. This allowed Mr Cowper to speak to the signalmen, Sandy Robertson and Tom Graham. An early photograph of the station shows Mr Cowper (with his dog) and his assistants, Joe McNay, Alex Gray and Alex Lennox. Hugh McLachlan, a retired gamekeeper is also in the picture, which is reproduced on page 12.

The second innovation was that of electric lighting. Mr Rankine suggested that this would be a vast improvement on the original oil lamps, and permission was granted for power to be brought from the recently opened Weirs' factory. In the winter of 1887 the station was well lit. Mr Cowper considered that these local enterprises constituted the first use of telephone and electricity in Cathcart.

Cathcart station was a friendly place, and, despite the fact that, as it was a terminus, all trains should be promptly despatched, it was a common event for Mr Cowper – and Mr Munro after him – to delay the departure of trains to allow the last stragglers to struggle up the cobbled incline and catch their trains.

By 31st July, 407,354 passengers, excluding season ticket holders, had been carried and a dividend for the six months to 31st July of one and a half per cent per annum was declared. Freight traffic

commenced in August, with goods and mineral stations at Mount Florida and Cathcart, the former at the foot of the Eildon Villas on the site of the 'buttercup park' and the latter, authorised in December 1886 at a cost of £290, adjacent to the passenger station. Nothing came of a proposal to provide a goods and mineral station at Crosshill, and there was insufficient room for such facilities at Pollokshields East and Queen's Park.

The reason for the relatively poor facilities provided at Cathcart was, of course, the imminent closure of the station when the line was extended. It will be recalled that the approach from the factor of the Pollok Estates to extend the line to Shawlands and west Pollokshields had been guardedly accepted in April 1885. Little had happened during the succeeding eighteen months, but on 2nd November 1886 an urgent meeting of the Cathcart Company's directors was called to decide whether the extension was to be promoted. At noon the directors met and decided to approach the Caledonian for its assent to the promotion of a Bill for the new 'loop line', as it was called, in the forthcoming Parliamentary session, with a working arrangement as if the new line formed part of the original scheme. The Caledonian approval was promptly obtained and the company's solicitors were asked to ascertain if any properties required for the new line other than those belonging to the Pollok Guardians could be obtained at advantageous terms before the Parliamentary notices were given. Within a week, on 11th November, the first property, Attyre Cottage at Shawlands, was purchased for £750.

It was of course the original intention that the line would be circular, proceeding beyond Cathcart through Shawlands and joining the GB&K line south of Strathbungo. This plan, together with the branch to Netherton, had been abandoned earlier, and the new proposal was for a much wider circle. Beyond Cathcart it was planned to pass Langside, Shawlands and, crossing the GB&K line, continue in a wide curve to rejoin the Central extension line at Strathbungo, this being the most economical point for the junction as pointwork already existed for a head-shunt.

Unlike the original line which served existing built-up areas, there was only one major area of settlement on the route of the extension, the village of Pollokshaws, which had grown up during the seventeenth and eighteenth centuries round the crossroads of the Glasgow/Irvine and Cathcart/Govan roads. Despite this apparent lack of potential passengers, four stations were planned in addition to the repositioned Cathcart: at Langside, near the bridge over the Cart at Millbrae, at Pollokshaws adjacent to the Macquisten Bridge over the Cart, at Maxwell Road, and near Strathbungo to serve the houses in the west of Pollokshields.

On 8th February 1887 a special general meeting of members sought approval for the extension Bill. Provost Browne, the Chairman, introduced the new project, emphasising the reasonable terms which had been obtained for the necessary land. He also explained that the Bill allowed the Company to abandon Railway Number 3, which was the connecting spur between the Cathcart Railway and the GB&K line to St Enoch near Queen's Park station. This provision was included in the original Act, since at the time of its passing the CDR had not formed an alliance with any of the major companies but, having since contracted with the Caledonian, there was no longer any necessity for a connection to the Glasgow & South Western St Enoch station. Mr Sommerville seconded Provost Browne's proposal, indicating that, without the extension, the present line was incomplete.

Mr Kerr, the shareholders' spokesman, stated that the members would be pleased to adopt the proposed line if they could be satisfied that the outlay would be profitable, and requested details of the construction costs.

Provost Browne stated that the 3-mile extension was estimated to cost £140,000 which favourably compared with the £230,000 cost of the existing 2½ miles and, in answer to Mr Kerr's comment that profitability depended on traffic, indicated that anyone who knew

Pollokshaws East station, the building sitting above the River Cart, on 18th May 1971.

J. KERNAHAN

Shawlands station on 19th October 1955. The Pollokshaws East Inner Circle distant signal can be seen above the roof of the building. W. A. C. Smith

the district knew very well that the traffic should be as large, if not larger, than on the present system.

This explanation would appear to be rather optimistic, as the new line was relying for its success on the fact that house building was likely to follow the railway, as it was already along the course of the existing line. This was doubtless the reason for the Pollok Trustees encouraging the railway by offering the land at agricultural rates, since with a railway in prospect they would be able to sell housing plots to future passengers at higher rates! The shareholders were, however, persuaded to embark on the scheme and the motion was adopted.

At the beginning of May 1887 the Bill came before a Select Committee of the House of Commons. The only opponent was the Glasgow & South Western Railway, three other petitioners, including the Coustonholm Paper Mills Company, having been placated. At the hearing it was argued on behalf of the promoters that the Glasgow & South Western was, out of sheer jealousy, merely fighting again the battle which it had lost six years previously when it had unsuccessfully opposed the working agreement between the CDR and the Caledonian.

The G&SWR opposition was based on the argument that the new railway crossed their line (although the line involved, the Glasgow Barrhead & Kilmarnock, was joint Caledonian and G&SWR) and that it destroyed the amenity of Strathbungo, which seems hardly credible as the line barely touched Strathbungo.

An alternative scheme involved the abandonment of the section of the new line which passed through the Pollok Estates which were not built-up, and the new line turning north after crossing the River Cart at Pollokshaws to join the GB&K joint line south of the proposed

Crossmyloof station, which in fact opened on 1st October 1888. This scheme would conveniently have allowed through running into the G&SWR St Enoch terminus and given that company a stake in what looked like becoming a profitable suburban route, but without the expense and risk of construction through the empty fields between Shawlands and Strathbungo.

Provost Browne stated in his evidence to the hearing that the existing railway had been a success, carrying 100,000 passengers per month, in addition to about 1,000 season ticket holders. The Bill for the extension had been promoted at the request of the people in the district, but it would not have been promoted if there had been no favourable agreement regarding the acquisition of land from the Pollok Trustees. To this, Mr Littler for the G&SWR asked whether the Cathcart Company would be prepared to join their new line to the Kilmarnock Joint Line if there had not been an arrangement with the Pollok Trustees. The Provost maintained that the proposed route was superior and would be pursued even in the absence of an agreement.

Witnesses were called to demonstrate the local support for the scheme from the Langside, Shawlands and Pollokshields districts and the Cathcart Company's engineer, Mr F. S. Colledge, stated that there would be four stations on the 3-mile line, at Langside, Kilmarnock Road, Pollokshaws and Haggs Bows. There would be need to remove only two small dwellings and that the Company would be very foolish if it missed the opportunity to obtain the required land at such reasonable prices.

Mr James Thompson, General Manager of the Caledonian, stated that the proposed line served a very beautiful district and 'railway facilities would be a great advantage, not merely to the working classes, who would certainly take advantage of these facilities, but to the middle classes, warehousemen, and others in similar positions, in order to get quickly away from the city into beautiful country'.

No adequate evidence against the scheme was led, and the Bill received the Royal Assent on 19th July 1887.

To finance the extension, the company was authorised to create new shares for £109,000 and circulars were sent out to existing shareholders requesting them to take part of the new stock. Only a small proportion were willing to increase their holding, which was hardly surprising in view of the promises of four and a half per cent dividends held out in the 1881 prospectus, and the one half per cent declared during the passing of the extension Bill through Parliament, where Provost Browne was asserting that the railway was a success. The relatively unpopulated area through which the new line was to pass was an additional factor inclined to dissuade potential investors.

The Caledonian agreed to subscribe sufficient to allow the land to be purchased so that no delays resulted due to lack of funds.

In October 1888 the Caledonian offered, subject to the approval of Parliament, to subscribe the whole Share Capital authorised by the Cathcart District Railway Act 1887, on condition that all shareholders in the company were given one vote for every £10 share, the intention being that the Caledonian should have equal powers of voting with the other shareholders of the company. In June 1889 the necessary Act was passed, authorising, in addition, the guarantee by the Caledonian of the Cathcart Company's debenture stock, no part of which had yet been raised, and powers for the Caledonian acquisition of the remaining Cathcart shares on terms to be approved by the two companies.

Some days after this Act received the Royal Assent, the company's treasurer and secretary since its incorporation, Mr J. M. Robertson, died, and was succeeded by Mr G. W. T. Robertson.

ABOVE: LMSR 0-4-4T No. 55268 passing Riverside Road on the approach to Pollokshaws East on 8th May 1954 with an Outer Circle train. This bridge was one of those built across the middle of open country, shortly to be filled by the suburban streets which followed the construction of the railway (see the map on page 37).   G. H. ROBIN

LEFT: CR '439' Class 0-4-4T No. 15170 passing over the houses for the Pollokshaws East and Shawlands stationmasters built in the viaduct just east of Shawlands station with an Inner Circle train on 16th April 1948.
G. H. ROBIN/BY COURTESY OF
THE MITCHELL LIBRARY, GLASGOW CITY COUNCIL

FACING PAGE: Maxwell Park station on Sunday 3rd June 1951, before Sunday services were introduced.
J. L. STEVENSON

By late 1889 the company was again facing financial problems, with mounting liabilities due to Morrison and Mason requiring settlement of the final retentions on the original line and a pending arbitration required to fix the price for the Pollok Estate lands despite the earlier agreement. The Caledonian was approached for assistance and, although it was unwilling to take over the CDR, it was prepared to make the company a loan sufficient to discharge its debts, thereby relieving the directors of the personal obligations which they had undertaken. A condition of the loan was that two existing directors would retire and be replaced by Caledonian directors. On 10th October 1889, accordingly, R. G. Sommerville and T. R. J. Logan resigned and were replaced by Hugh Brown and Joseph Cheney Bolton from the Caledonian. Five days later, at the first Board meeting to be held at the Caledonian offices at 302 Buchanan Street, Mr Bolton took over from Provost Browne as Chairman. Despite the Cathcart District Railway's nominal independence, effective control was passing to the Caledonian.

On 10th June 1890 a further Act was passed authorising a further £100,000 capital, with power to the Caledonian to subscribe for, or give guarantee for, the capital in whole or in part. The Caledonian was willing to advance sufficient to pay off the further debts which had accumulated in return for 'B' Debenture Stock for twelve months at 4 per cent. Despite the Caledonian domination of the Board, the secretary was asked to try to obtain more favourable terms elsewhere, but he was unsuccessful and the Caledonian offer was accepted.

Almost three years after the passing of the Act authorising the extension, the advertisement for tenders, excluding rails and signals, appeared, and on 9th October 1890 that of Messrs James Watson & Sons at £81,095:11/3 was accepted.

Things now appeared to be going more smoothly for the Cathcart Railway. It had the backing of the Caledonian as it required it, the contract for the extension had been let, and it was set to enjoy the hopefully lucrative suburban traffic. On 25th November 1890 the peace was shattered with the announcement of a new railway, the Glasgow South Suburban Railway, which threatened to destroy the CDR monopoly. This railway had no connection with the abortive 1879 scheme of the same name.

By the time the proposal came before the Select Committee on Railway Bills of the House of Commons on 12th March 1891 the line had the direct backing of both the Glasgow & South Western and a newcomer to suburban railways south of the Clyde, the North British, whose only other involvement in the area, also joint with the G&SWR, was the City of Glasgow Union.

This new line, nearly 9 miles in length, was to leave the North British north suburban line at Parkhead, at such a point to allow a direct route via Springburn to the NBR main line, run in a south eastern direction to Newton, crossing the Clyde at a point where the river was not navigable, on a viaduct 140 yards in length and 47 feet 3 inches above water level.

At Newton the line was planned to swing abruptly in a westerly direction, crossing the Cathcart District Line just south of Mount Florida station on an arch of 35-foot span and 14 feet high. It was then to follow the route suggested for its 1879 namesake, although the required tunnel under Queen's Park was only 145 yards in length compared with 310 yards required twelve years earlier, to join the GB&K joint line south of Strathbungo. The engineers for the line were Messrs Crouch and Hogg, and the Solicitors for the scheme were Messrs H. & R. Lamond and Lang. The aim of the line, which was to cost an estimated £306,030, was stated to be for the North British and the Glasgow & South Western working together to have a circular suburban route, 'just as the Cathcart District Railway', an interesting aim in view of the G&SWR's earlier prior opinion of the Cathcart scheme.

The scheme appeared to be more political than practical. The G&SWR contended that it should have had a share in the Cathcart traffic as a partner in the Kilmarnock Joint line, while the North British, riled by recent Caledonian penetration into its north bank territory, wanted access to the Lanarkshire coalfield, with the additional advantage of 'doing for the south side of the Clyde what the Caledonian Company has succeeded in forcing itself to obtain

Letter to Board of Trade intimating opening of the Cathcart Circle.

on the north side of the Clyde, namely parallel lines of railway as against the North British, giving the public on the north side of the Clyde the advantage of the two systems'. The principal objectors were the Caledonian and the Cathcart District. The Glasgow Barrhead & Kilmarnock Joint Committee were naturally split on whether to petition against the Bill but the arbiter decided against petitioning. After a week's hearing the committee found the preamble not proved in respect of the section between Newton and Strathbungo, and the scheme was abandoned.

During this anxious period, work on the extension was at last proceeding. The earthworks had been commenced without ceremony during October 1890, but as 1891 proceeded, the directors were becoming anxious about the slow progress, and their dissatisfaction was communicated to the contractors. This appeal had little effect and on 2nd February 1892 the company decided to apply to Parliament for an extension of time over the five years laid down in the 1887 Act. The necessary Act was obtained during May, although in the previous month the company had written to the contractors pointing out that the time for completion of the works had now expired and that the directors held them liable for all loss arising – this, despite the fact that three years delay had occurred between the Act being granted and the tenders let. Immediately on receipt of this communication, Messrs Watson replied, requesting permanent way material for a mile of line and undertaking to have it permanently laid at once and not to run trucks with earthwork or soil over it. The Caledonian was requested to supply the necessary materials.

By this time certain incidental claims and expenses arising from the construction of the new line had been met. Among these was a claim for £5, settled at £2, by Mr J. B. Dunlop as compensation in respect of interference with his right of grazing cattle at Newlandsfield, and an amount of £26:11/6 paid to the Joint Line Committee for alterations to telegraph wires between Crossmyloof and Pollokshaws due to the extension line operations. In reply to a claim by the Congregation of Hutchesontown Free Church that they had been obliged to deepen the foundation of the church presently being built owing to the contractors having encroached on their ground, the Engineer stated that the church builder had encroached on the Railway Company's land by one foot in deepening the foundations. The Railway would

Glasgow South Suburban Railway, 1890.

not insist on the foundations being taken back if the Congregation's claim was dispensed with.

On 20th March 1893 the contract for the six stations, including the repositioned Cathcart, was awarded to Messrs Alexander Eadie and Son of Cathcart Road, at £8,050. Further contracts awarded during 1893 were to Mr George W. Sellars for the painting of the woodwork of the new stations for £213:18/-, and to the Railway Signalling Company Limited of Fazakarley, Liverpool, for the signalling.

Although the arbiter had to be called in occasionally, the construction of the extension was not beset with the difficulties which had accompanied the original line, and it was hoped that the Circle might open on 1st February 1894. Major General Huchinson, however, did not make his inspection until 9th March, when a special engine and saloon were provided for him in Central station at 9am. The coach used for the inspection was one of the largest available at the time in order to check the width of bridges and abutments. Four heavy tender locomotives hired at a cost of £7:15/- from the Caledonian were also employed, coupled chimney to chimney, two on each circle, to run over the line to test the stability of the bridges, embankments and permanent way. The inspection was satisfactory and authority was given for immediate running into Cathcart new station on a single line to enable the contractors to obtain possession of the existing passenger station for the completion of the double set of rails at that point. Major Hutchinson approved a suggestion that the new lines be opened for goods traffic before the passenger opening, now scheduled for 2nd April, in order that the rails were well set for the passenger traffic', but the only formal opening prior to 2nd April, when the Cathcart Circle was fully opened, was the new station at Cathcart, which opened on 19th March 1894, the Sabbath peace of the area having been considerably disturbed on the day

before the opening by the workmen making the final preparations and track alterations.

The view from the new station at Cathcart was of a country aspect all round. Looking east there was not a house to be seen except the Wee Toll House at the corner of Carmunnock Road and the road leading to Crookston Coal Pit. To the north the nearest building was Keith's Church. Trains could be seen emerging from the cutting at Mount Florida, there being no buildings to obstruct the view. To the left there were no houses to be seen between the railway and the slopes of Langside Hill, only green fields and pasture land on the north side of the River Cart. Occasionally the scene did change when the river overflowed its banks and filled the whole expanse with water, sometimes necessitating rescue of the people at Aitkenlea by boat, with hens being drowned and pigs saved only with difficulty.

On the Wednesday before the Circle opened a reporter from the Southern Press had walked, in the company of a representative from Messrs James Watson & Son the contractors, the length of the new line. On arrival at the new station, they passed the ruins of the old station, where the site was being prepared for a new goods station. The new line required a total of nineteen bridges in its 3-mile distance, although the River Cart was only crossed twice. The first new bridge was over the Station Road and the river, and incorporated a footbridge leading to the eastern approach to the new station which lay immediately beyond the river, the platform actually being on the bridge. The booking office for the station was situated in a corridor between the western entrances. Leaving Cathcart, the line crossed Cathcart Road and turned sharply west passing Weirs' foundry and the photographic works on the right. Beyond Newlands Road, the open prospect was charmingly rustic, with the many acres of Messrs Austin and McAuslan's nurseries spreading out on the left.

LMSR 'Black 5' 4-6-0 No. 45367 crossing Titwood Road on 14th April 1962 with an Inner Circle football special. This bridge was originally built across open country, with sufficient span to anticipate the width of the street eventually built under it.
H. STEVENSON

Pollokshields West station in 1951.

J. L. STEVENSON

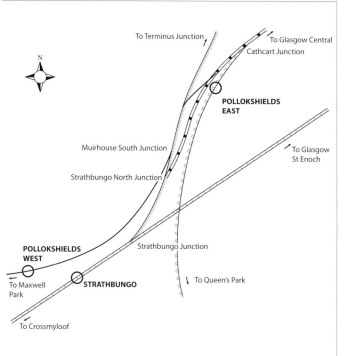

GB & K Joint Line

General Terminus branch

Central Station extension line

Original Cathcart District Railway

Extension Cathcart District Railway

Junction of extension line with existing lines.

Before reaching the next station, Langside, the track crossed a soft wide farm road on a bridge 60 feet wide, so constructed to allow a full street breadth at some future date. Several such bridges were built in open country to accommodate the streets of the future.

From Langside station a fine view of the surrounding countryside could be obtained, as the station was constructed on an embankment. To the north, beyond the River Cart, the Millbrae Road could be seen steeply ascending the hill, while between the station and the river lay the site of the mill from which the road took its name. This was where Nicholas Deschamp had set up his paper mill in the seventeenth century, the site now being occupied by Paper Mill Farm – famous, at the time of the coming of the railway, for its breed of Clydesdale horses. The accommodation for the passengers and station master was at platform level, while the booking office was at road level, at the only entrance to the station, from Millbrae Road.

Approaching Pollokshaws East station the line crossed the middle of a field on a large girder bridge, the space being eventually filled by Riverside Road, and ran beside the river supported by a large retaining wall. Between the river and the line lay the goods and mineral depot for the eastern area of Pollokshaws, access being by an inclined path from Kilmarnock Road. To the south lay fields and farmland, the Kilmarnock Road being used for cycle races between the new railway bridge and Mearns. Pollokshaws East station lay between Kilmarnock Road and Coustonholm Road, in the junction of which lay the Cartbridge Paper Mill. The station had entrances

ABOVE: Pickersgill '113' Class 4-4-0 No. 14462 entering Langside & Newlands with an Inner Circle train on 16th April 1948. The Cathcart West Junction distant signal, repositioned in 1936, can be seen behind the tree adjacent to the second coach. G. H. ROBIN/ BY COURTESY OF THE MITCHELL LIBRARY, GLASGOW CITY COUNCIL

LEFT: Fairburn 2-6-4T No. 42144 approaching Shawlands with the 6.13pm Inner Circle on 22nd June 1960. The signal is the Maxwell Park distant, later preserved for a few years in the former station master's room (page 74). W. A. C. SMITH/ TRANSPORT TREASURY

Fairburn 2-6-4T No. 42242 passing Muirhouse Junction on 8th September 1953 with an Outer Circle train. Pollokshields East station is on the left, still with LMSR station nameboard, while almost all signals are Caledonian lower quadrants. G. H. ROBIN/BY COURTESY OF THE MITCHELL LIBRARY, GLASGOW CITY COUNCIL

from both roads, with booking offices provided on landings on the approach stairways. The passengers' accommodation was provided in a neat wooden building, similar to all the others on the line, but built directly on top of the fine masonry bridge, a single span with a width of sixty feet between the parapets to accommodate the island platform, which carried the line over the River Cart.

The railway now faced a short climb at 1 in 65, the steepest on the Circle, through a 36-foot cutting through Shawhill, passing under the road which climbed the hill on a fine single-arched stone bridge. A rapid descent brought the line almost immediately to Shawlands station. The passengers on the trains were likely on this section to miss one of the principal features of the new line, namely the two four-apartment houses, provided for the station masters, which were built in the five arches of the viaduct carrying the line between the girder bridges at Rossendale and Pollokshaws Roads, the only evidence of the houses to the passenger being the chimneys growing from the parapets. Shawlands station, serving the northern area of Pollokshaws and western Shawlands, had only one entrance, on Pollokshaws Road, the booking office, as with the other stations, being at street level.

Immediately on leaving Shawlands the line crossed the Kilmarnock Joint Line on a very wide girder bridge, constructed in such a way as to allow the later quadrupling of that line. This was a provision required to satisfy the objections of the G&SWR, which was considering this expansion, as the station buildings at Strathbungo and Crossmyloof had been built at street level on the adjacent overbridges to facilitate this. Between Shawlands and Maxwell Park the line, which was now running on a high embankment, passed through fields on either side, crossed the Moss Road, and a further space provided for a future road, on girder bridges, before swinging sharply back towards the city centre. The second goods station on the extension was passed on the right before passing under a bridge supported by five iron pillars, and intended to carry a future roadway, although at that time it only provided access to the goods station. Maxwell Park station differed from the others in that, situated in a cutting rather than an embankment, it was approached by overhead gangways from both sides of the line terminating on a central landing containing the booking office and from which a wide flight of steps led down to the platform and the passengers' accommodation. From the booking office a good view could be obtained of the beautiful park given to the area by Sir John Stirling Maxwell, from which the station

took its name, while through the trees stood the fine Burgh Buildings.

A straight stretch, lying in a cutting, took the line to the last station on the Circle, Pollokshields West. On either side of this cutting new roads awaiting houses had been provided, as well as a connecting footbridge outside Maxwell Park station and a road bridge midway between the two stations. Pollokshields West station was similar in design to Maxwell Park, the building being of two storeys approached by overhead gangways.

Immediately beyond Pollokshields West, the line, now adjacent to Strathbungo station, passed under Nithsdale Road by means of a 'covered way' built on the 'cut and cover' principle. It was now heading straight for the Joint Line into St Enoch station, but instead of joining it, the new railway swung to the left to join the former General Terminus branch at Muirhouse Junction. It had originally been intended that the Circle would join the Central extension line at Strathbungo Junction, south of the divergence of the Terminus branch, but this would have required substantial track alterations to that junction. Details of the proposed alterations to the layout and the development of Muirhouse Junction are given in Appendix 15. A short connection, built across two existing headshunts which were abolished, between the Terminus and the Central Station extension line permitted trains to run back to the Central station, completing the Circle.

No part of the new extension line was on the original surface of the land, being either in cutting or on embankment, 300,000 cubic yards of earth having been moved in the construction. Due to the frequency of the service to be provided, the permanent way was of especially heavy construction, the 32-foot steel rails weighing 80lbs per yard. The 3-mile extension cost £140,000 compared with £300,000 for the original 2½ miles to Cathcart.

Unlike the original line, which had opened quietly with no ceremony and in atrocious weather conditions, the opening of the extension was celebrated on a day of perfect weather. On Saturday 31st March 1894 a special train carried the Chairman and Secretary of the Cathcart District Railway, the officials of the Caledonian Railway, and the press on a tour of inspection. At each station the party disembarked to examine and admire the sparkling new stations, and at Langside a longer halt was made to permit the guests to enjoy a luncheon served at tables set up along the Outer Circle platform.

On Monday 2nd April 1894 the Cathcart Circle was at last open for business.

CHAPTER 3

THE LINE IN THE NINETEENTH CENTURY

When the railway first opened in 1886 a publication, printed for private circulation, was produced to introduce and promote the new line. This consisted of a historical note and description of the district, extracted from Hugh MacDonald's *Rambles Round Glasgow* and, before listing the frequent service of trains provided, stated that 'in connection with the above [the district of Cathcart] a first-class double line of railway has recently been constructed at an enormous cost between Glasgow and Cathcart, whereby visitors can leave the Central Station, Glasgow and be set down in the heart of this beautiful and romantic district in about quarter of an hour, while the trains are run very frequently and are thoroughly well appointed.'

An excellent service was indeed provided, with thirty-two trains operating in each direction between 7.25am and 11.10pm. The fares between Glasgow and the new stations were:

	Single		Return	
	1st	*3rd*	*1st*	*3rd*
Pollokshields East	2d	1d	4d	2d
Queen's Park	3d	1½d	5d	3d
Crosshill	3d	2d	5d	3d
Mount Florida	4d	2½d	6d	4d
Cathcart (when opened)	5d	3d	8d	5d

The line opened to goods traffic on Monday 2nd August 1886, the traffic being worked from and to Polmadie yard by train 24, which passed on to the new line at Cathcart Junction at 9.25am and ran direct to Cathcart. It was scheduled to shunt Cathcart yard until 10.05am and leave at 10.10am following the 10.07am passenger train, to Mount Florida, the only intermediate goods station, where only about ten minutes were allowed for shunting, as the train had to leave Mount Florida at 10.25am and be clear of Cathcart Junction by 10.30am despite the fact that the next passenger train did not leave the Cathcart terminus until 10.47am.

During its entire life, the Cathcart line has seen much football traffic. It was not only the huge crowds attracted to international matches at Hampden Park who required special trains, but also the smaller contingent attracted to Cathkin Park, the home of Third Lanark FC, adjacent to Crosshill station. From the beginning of November 1886, the timetable showed two additional trains on Saturdays only from Glasgow to Cathcart, calling at all stations, leaving the city at 2.35pm and 2.55pm, returning from Cathcart at 4.25pm and 4.37pm with the proviso that, if these trains were run in conjunction with football matches at Hampden Park, they were not to leave Cathcart until the Station Master at Crosshill had wired for them to be sent on.

In January 1887 a new rake of coaches was provided for use on the Cathcart line. Designed by the Caledonian Locomotive

Mount Florida goods yard, taken from the additional platform for football specials built in 1938. The signalbox, closed when the platform was constructed, stood close to the point where the photographer is standing.

G. H. ROBIN

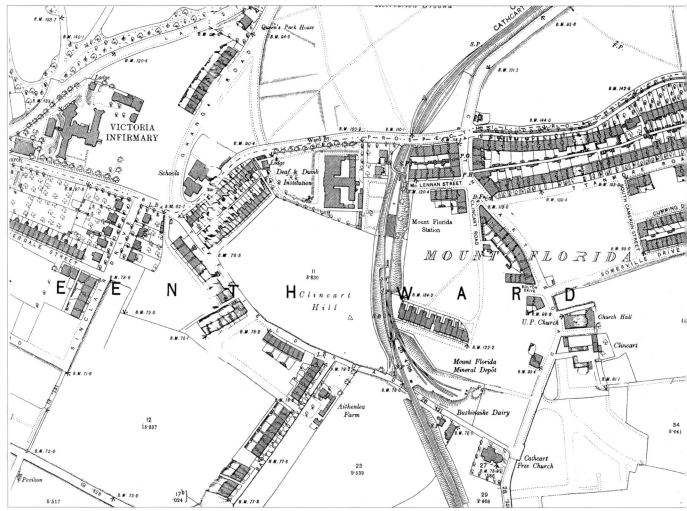

The maps on the following eight pages show the house building which followed the construction of the railway. Mount Florida in 1895.

Superintendent, Dugald Drummond, and built at that company's St Rollox Works, the set of eight close-coupled vehicles had central buffers, and were claimed to be fitted with all the latest improvements. The set was heated throughout 'by the exhaust steam from the engine' and had been fitted with gas by the Patent Lighting Company Limited. Three such sets were provided to work the original line, each one consisting of three first class, three third class and three brake third class carriages, additional carriages being attached to some of the morning, mid-day and evening trains during the week, and on afternoon trains on Saturdays, as traffic required. The regular coach sets were washed at Glasgow, the spare carriages being kept and washed at Cathcart. The detailed carriage diagram for January 1893 is set out in Appendix 11.

By the time of the opening of the extension line, these carriages were past their prime, especially with regard to lighting. Contemporary reports indicate that trains were very poorly lit, and that a shilling's worth of gas kept a Circle train lighted about an hour, although new patent lights were being tried in a first class carriage at the beginning of 1896. In January 1902 a set of new four-wheeled carriages, consisting of three first class (numbers 6, 92 and 189), three third class (numbers 283, 636 and 651) and two brake thirds (numbers 451 and 513) appeared on the line. This set was fitted with a new chain communication and was not suitable for running in conjunction with stock fitted only with cord communication. Rakes of coaches of this type often crammed to capacity were the mainstay of services on the line for over twenty years.

It did not take much time after the opening of the line for the passengers to start demanding additional facilities. In December 1886 two petitions were received by the CDR urging the construction of an entrance to Pollokshields East station at its south end by means of a gangway across the parallel Central Station extension line to Darnley Street. The request was rejected by the Caledonian. Passengers at Mount Florida asked for an entrance at the south end of their station and were given a footbridge which provided access to the platform from both sides of the line.

Additional facilities for passengers were provided, firstly by the Automatic Machines Company which provided one of its confectionery vending machines at each station in 1887, and in 1891 by the Scottish Automatic Supply Company Limited, which was granted a similar privilege at a like payment of £3 per annum per machine. More personal service to the customer was provided from Mr F. W. Wilson's bookstalls, constructed first at Cathcart, followed by Mount Florida in 1891, and Pollokshields East and Queen's Park in 1892. In 1893 the Pollokshields East passengers were once again refused their request that the stairway to the station be covered in. The new extension line stations had this luxury, but none of the original stations ever boasted a covered stairway, despite the Caledonian's suggestion that this be provided at Queen's Park. The first station to suffer fire damage, which eventually hit several stations, was Queen's Park which was partially destroyed in 1893. Even before the extension was opened, Mr Wilson, obviously cheered by the success of his venture at the original stations, was granted

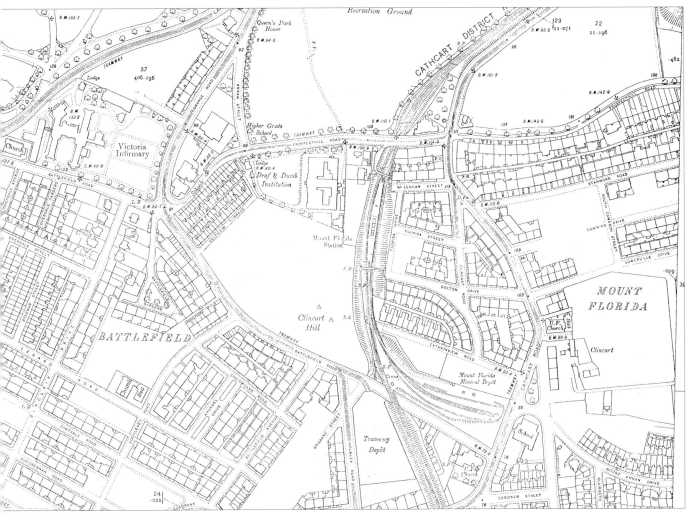

Mount Florida, 1912.

permission, at a rent of 5s. per month per bookstall, to erect his stalls at Pollokshields West, Shawlands and Pollokshaws East. He was not interested in Langside or Maxwell Park, where there was no obvious population to give him custom.

A feature of the extension line, which was absent from the original line, was the provision of houses for the station masters. As mentioned earlier, the stationmasters at Pollokshaws East and Shawlands lived underneath the railway in two four-apartment houses built in the arches of the viaduct east of Shawlands station. There were some initial complaints of dampness in these houses, but, more probably in view of the overhead noise despite special insulation materials being used in the roof spaces, the rents charged for these houses, at £10 per annum, were cheaper than other station masters' houses by around a third. Those at Langside and Maxwell Park were given slightly quieter accommodation in neat, but fairly narrow, two-storey houses built by Messrs Eadie, the contractor who constructed the station buildings and the viaduct houses, in 1894, just after the extension opened. The position of the house at Langside, at a short distance away from the line, as compared with the house at Maxwell Park which is adjacent to the line, was decided by the fact that, at the time of its construction, consideration was being given to the provision of a goods station. It never was constructed, and the space left for it is now occupied by housing.

The Cathcart Railway was a regular target for ridicule and a constant cause of complaint during the last decade of the nineteenth century. The old 'temporary' Cathcart station had few facilities for

passengers, and the lack of fires in the waiting room was a regular cause of complaint. Even before the Circle line opened one newspaper contributor was mystified, as indeed many have been after him, that a passenger could travel to Pollokshaws East from Glasgow for twopence halfpenny, but was allowed to travel via Cathcart, where the Glasgow fare was threepence. On 3rd May 1894, a month after the Circle had opened, the directors decided that tickets between Maxwell Park and Glasgow would be available for travel via Queen's Park, and vice versa, leaving only Pollokshields East and West as stations to and from which travelling in either direction from and to Glasgow was not permitted.

The lack of dividend was a constant embarrassment to the CDR Board, Provost Browne at the shareholders' meeting just after the opening of the extension line being 'still hopeful, and believing that the line has a great future'. The Cathcart shareholders were dubious of their 3-mile stretch through fields on the outskirts of Glasgow ever rewarding their investment. In fact a fairly insignificant dividend, never above one per cent, had been paid from the date of the opening in 1886 until January 1889, but this was followed by a particularly lean period until July 1897 when a staggering one and three quarter per cent was paid for the preceding half year. The company's worst position was reached in January 1892 when the accumulated deficit being carried forward had reached £11,022, a daunting position for the board when the annual receipts at that time had not reached £9,000 with the line running through a relatively densely populated area and the prospect of the imminent opening of the extension

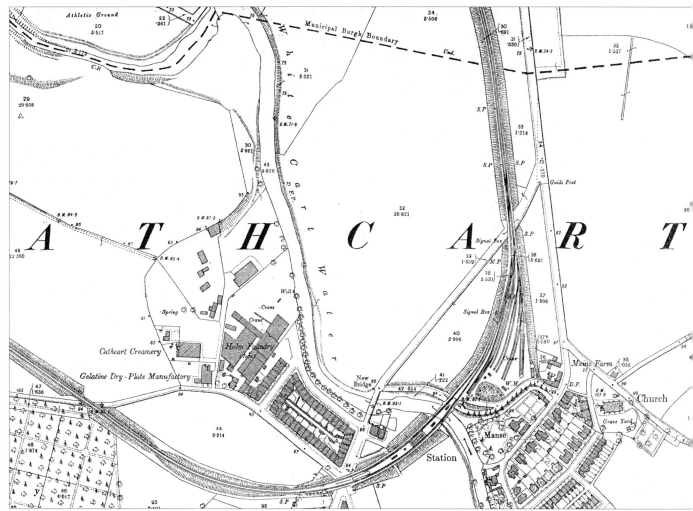

Cathcart in 1895, just after the opening of the extension.

running through open fields. The payment of a dividend for the first time in eight years was duly noted by commentators. A cartoon appeared in an evening newspaper showing shareholders fainting at the news, while a pantomime joke was: 'Have you heard of the terrible accident on the Cathcart Railway? They have paid a dividend!'

To diverge for a moment from the story of the Cathcart District Railway, it is of interest to record a railway invention patented by two local men, John Collins of 1 Holmhead Terrace, Cathcart and Archibald Brown of Thornbank House, in 1895. This was a simple but ingenious fog signal device, a forerunner of the automatic warning system installed during the 1960s on many British lines, including the Cathcart Circle, although the Great Western Railway had adopted a satisfactory system prior to the Second World War. The system devised by the two Cathcart gentlemen consisted of a mechanical device attached to the sleepers in such a way that it could be pulled aside by means of a connection with the signal post. When the signal was at danger the mechanism rested in the four foot way between the running lines and came in contact with a trigger fixed below the engine which thereupon activated a cord attached to the engine's whistle. The whistle would then blow continuously until stopped by the driver. If there was no requirement to stop the train the mechanism in the four foot was not activated. The inventors claimed that in addition to its main use as a fog signalling device it could also be used on underground railways, and for protection of platelayers working on the line, especially at curves, and for protection at level crossings. The device found little favour with the

railway companies, and there is no evidence of its use by any of the Scottish companies.

The opening of the extension line resulted in an increase in income and it is interesting to compare the takings in April 1894, the first month of operation of the Circle, with those of the original line in the previous April:

	April 1893	April 1894
	£	£
Passengers	734	1,318
Parcels	22	32
Goods	29	27
Minerals	77	103
Mails	3	3
	865	1,483

Word of the Cathcart Circle appears to have spread overseas instantly. On 5th April 1894, three days after the opening, a letter seeking employment was received from James Logan of Londonderry! It was referred to the Caledonian as the operating company.

Efforts were made to encourage traffic on the extension line by the publication in June 1894 of a sixteen page pamphlet called *Cathcart and District*, describing the area and containing a map and timetable of the new line. The pamphlet consisted entirely of cuttings from the by then out-of-print book by Hugh MacDonald entitled *Rambles Round Glasgow* which had already been used in 1886, but a contemporary

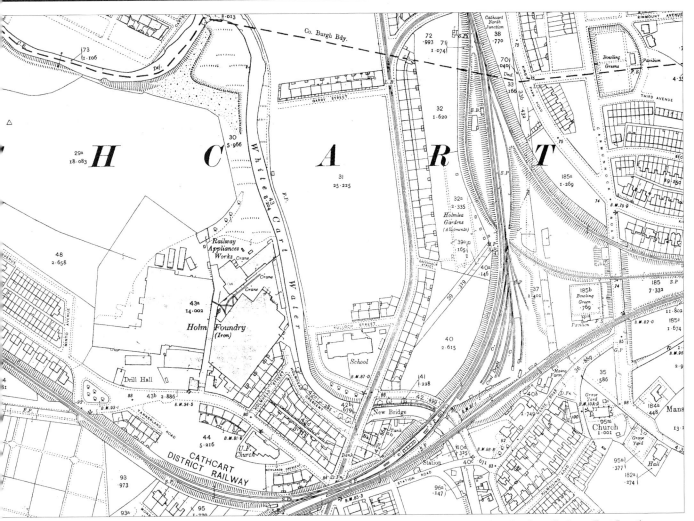

ABOVE: Cathcart in 1912, after the opening of the Lanarkshire & Ayrshire Railway. Note that the burrowing junction from Cathcart East Junction uses a roadbridge constructed when the original line to Cathcart opened.

BR 2-6-4T No. 80027 arriving at Mount Florida with the 3.30pm Outer Circle on 26th October 1955.   W. A. C. SMITH/ TRANSPORT TREASURY

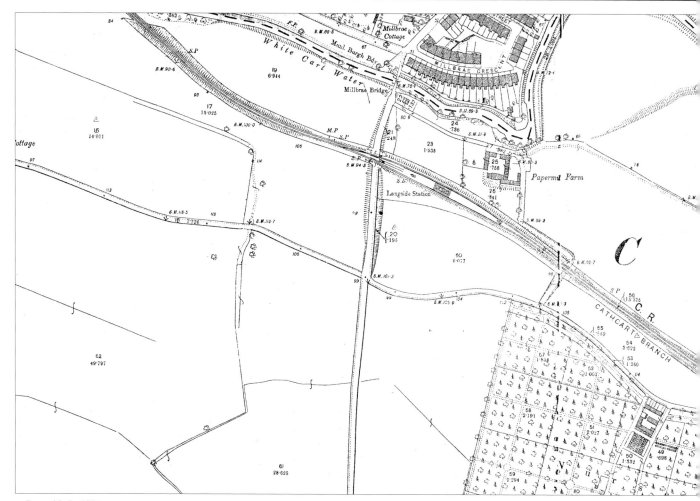

Langside in 1895.

newspaper report stressed that the descriptions were now 'grievously inappropriate', as the 'circular railway itself blotted the landscape all along its route'. It was not, however, on the 'tourist' coming from the city to enjoy the country air of Langside and Shawlands that the Cathcart Railway was pinning its hopes for the success of the new venture, but on the eventual extension of suburban building round the route of the line. It was not long until these hopes were being fulfilled, and within a year of the opening of the Circle, an unprecedented boom in building had commenced, with tenements and villas springing up at Cathcart, Langside, Shawlands upper and lower, and Pollokshields. The winter of 1894/5 saw a great number of skaters attracted to Maxwell Park pond, which was described as the 'rendezvous of all the youth and beauty of Pollokshields'. The same winter brought to an end the short life of the bookstall on the new Cathcart station when it was blown off the platform during a gale on the night of Friday 28th December 1894.

The new building on which the railway was to depend for its living did not appear overnight, however, and in the short term the Company was faced with yet another problem – that of severe competition from the Glasgow Corporation Tramways for the passengers who were available. The problem of the Cathcart Bus, whose proprietor had sought amalgamation with the railway in 1886, was overcome by its being withdrawn on 11th October 1894 after having plied between Cathcart and the City for more than twenty years. There was a tendency to wax lyrical about such events and the following lament for the bus, written by local poet James Donaldson, commemorated the event:

Oh, my sun has sunk at midday,
And my sky is blotted out,
For a cloud of hopeless sorrow
Has encompassed me about
And the birds have got the hiccough
All along Cart's flowery shore,
And they try to sing, but cannot,
For the 'bus is now no more.

Oh, it was n't 'natural causes'
Was the cause of its demise,
'Twas of hunger and starvation,
Thro' a few monopolies
It had nothing in its stomach
Save but wind, which pained it sore,
And in hopeless necessity
It died and is no more.

Nevermore upon the dickey
Will the poet now be seen,
He has gone to live at Windsor,
And be Laureate to the Queen,
He'll have time to poetise, now,
As he never had before;
But we'll miss him, ah! we'll miss him,
Since the 'bus is now no more.

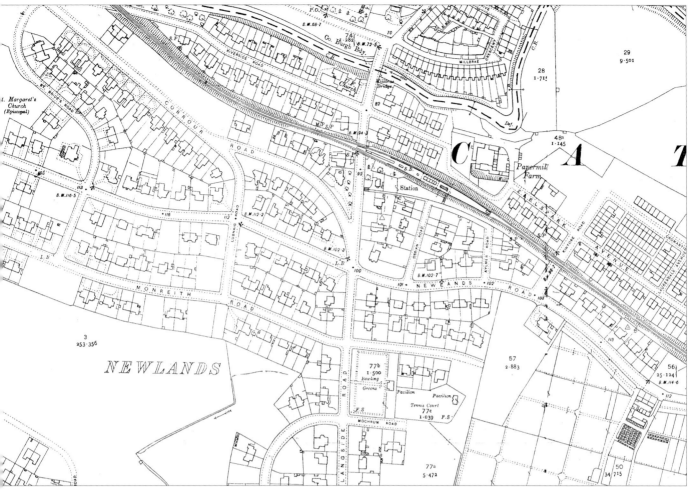

Langside & Newlands in 1912.

I will dye my yellow whiskers
To a sombre shade of brown
And join the host respectable
That train it to the town.
Hang the everlasting talkee
Of each dull suburban bore –
Drat the fate that slew the old 'bus –
Slew the 'bus we'll see no more.

The tramways were another matter. Lines were now in operation linking the city with Queen's Park (opened 1875), Mount Florida (1876), Shawlands (1880), and Pollokshaws (1882). Although these routes had been in operation from before the opening of the original railway line to Cathcart, it was only with the introduction of the halfpenny per stage fare by the Corporation in 1894 that the competition began to be felt. This meant a fare of twopence from Shawlands to Argyle Street, which was further reduced on 31st August 1894 to three halfpence, compared with the fare by train of two pence halfpenny. The half-yearly meeting of shareholders on 2nd November was told that the tramway competition had caused the results from the new stations to be less good than anticipated, but dividends were promised. Six months later the shareholders were informed that the results were 'poor', and the tramway competition 'severe'. The board kept assuring shareholders that the low fares charged on the trams would bankrupt the Transport Department. Instead, the trams continued to make increasing profits.

At the half-yearly meeting of shareholders on 30th October

1895 Mr J. C. Bolton, a Caledonian representative on the Cathcart Board, reported a decrease in traffic receipts as a result of tramway competition, but expressed the hope that by-and-bye the phenomenally low fares lately introduced would enable the company to show better returns. The *Glasgow Evening News* carried the following poetic commentary, entitled 'In the Sweet By-and-Bye':

We'll be happy by-and-bye
So, shareholders, do not sigh,
But join with me in choruses of Hope,
If it seems quite necessary
That our plans we still should wary
With the Tramway competition for to cope.

To each traveller we'll give free
At each station, buns and tea,
And encouragement in every other way,
We'll have Pullman cars to sleep in,
And buffet cars to steep in
And facilities for those at cards who play.

I would also further mention
That it is our firm intention,
By a plan that is still secret, and unique,
The eleven-twenty out
To keep hanging round about
For the man who's late – no matter though a week.

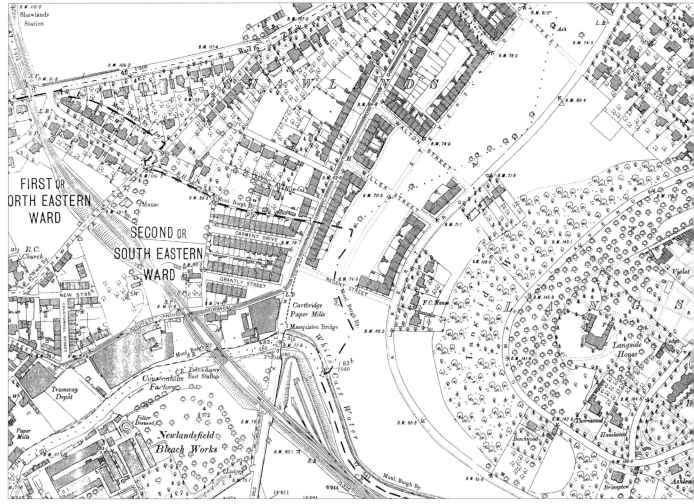

Pollokshaws East in 1895, showing that there was already a settlement in this area.

By enterprise like this,
You'll agree we scarce can miss
Scooping in the suburb traffic, now so shy;
We'll give Young and Duncan spasms,
In their dividends cut chasms,
When we have pulled our sox up – by and bye.

John Duncan and his successor John Young were the managers of the tramway system.

Throughout the summer of 1895 the company was encouraged to reduce the fares, especially since the quality of the service did not appear to justify a higher fare than the tram. The coaches were filthy – one newspaper suggested that 'an enterprising passenger would not take long to gather from the cushions enough dust to fill an ordinary-sized flower pot, and yet the company made no extra charge'. Timekeeping was also poor, one commentator indicating that he had seen rhubarb growing faster than some of the Cathcart trains travel.

The fares reduction came on 8th August when, for example, the Pollokshaws East to Glasgow third class return was reduced from fourpence to threepence. The new fares were considered to be the lowest in the United Kingdom, and the passengers flocked to the trains, resulting in overcrowding and more complaints, which were partially satisfied by the provision of additional morning trains.

It was not merely the condition and timekeeping of the trains which gave cause for concern, but also the behaviour of some of the passengers apparently left much to be desired. It was suggested in March 1896 that it was high time that special compartments were provided on late trains for drunks, while similar separate accommodation was desirable for workmen, a number of whom were said to disgrace themselves by their dirty habits and manners. Worse offenders, apparently, were schoolboys whose conduct in the Central Station was described as scandalous and uproarious. On the trains they 'shouted, screamed, whistled, groaned, shoved, and smashed – not in one compartment, but all over the train wherever an empty compartment was to be found'. It was also not unknown for schoolboys to travel between stations outside the trains on the running boards, actually passing trains in the other direction *en route*!

In February 1899 a 'bogus inspector' was imprisoned for 60 days for blackmailing passengers between Maxwell Park and Pollokshaws East by threatening to report indecent conduct. An equally mysterious event was the discovery in January 1894 in a train of this communication in a lady's handwriting – 'There is no need for you to hide from me. I know all. The sooner we meet the better – J-B.'

The Company attempted to make improvements, notably by planting trees at Cathcart and Langside stations. In response to a request by the Caledonian that 'automatic locks be put on the station water closets (except at Pollokshaws East)', the Cathcart Board authorised locks for *all* the stations at a cost of £60:1/3d: one wonders what the Caledonian had against Pollokshaws East and its passengers! There was some trouble at the opening of the Circle over the meaning

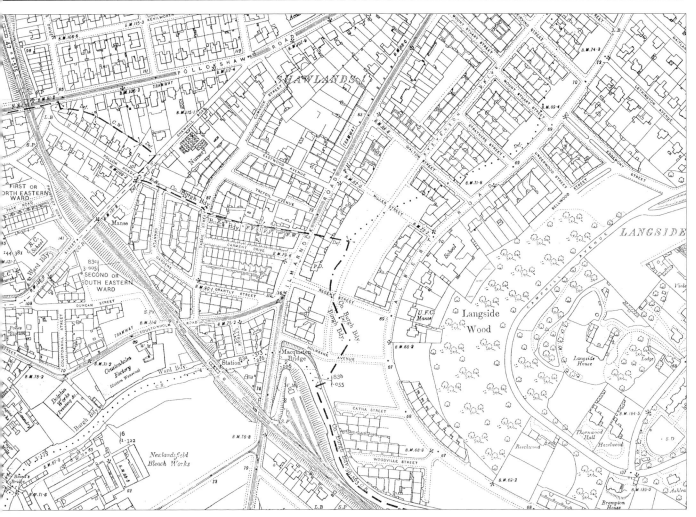

Pollokshaws East in 1912.

of the terms 'inner circle' and 'outer circle' and apparently the signposting at Glasgow Central left something to be desired. Many passengers, particularly on the last trains, had rather longer journeys than they bargained for! There was also some difficulty in discovering the names of the stations from passing trains both by day and night. A complaint was received in 1895 regarding the adequacy of the nameboards, but no changes were made. All the stations were gas-lit, and this also led to problems of identification, especially as the stations were so close to each other and looked identical.

At the close of the nineteenth century the Circle was at last achieving success. Building work was in progress along the length of the extension, the tramway competition had been met, as far as possible, by the reduction in fares, the trains were well-filled, and the company was again paying a dividend.

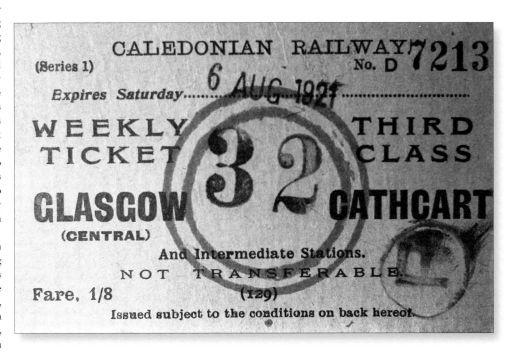

LEFT: BR 2-6-4T No. 80026 on an Outer Circle train, taken from Pollokshaws East signalbox on 5th September 1957.   G. H. ROBIN/BY COURTESY OF THE MITCHELL LIBRARY, GLASGOW CITY COUNCIL

RIGHT: Eglinton Street on 17th April 1957, taken from the headshunt for the goods yard and engine shed. The shed had become disused around the time of the First World War although it was not demolished until April 1957. The yard continued in occasional use until 1959. G. H. ROBIN/BY COURTESY OF THE MITCHELL LIBRARY, GLASGOW CITY COUNCIL

BELOW: Shawlands station shortly after electrification.

CHAPTER 4

THE LANARKSHIRE & AYRSHIRE RAILWAY

The Cathcart Circle was built as a suburban passenger railway with freight and mineral traffic a secondary consideration. The Lanarkshire & Ayrshire was the opposite. It was built as a freight line, with passenger services provided, at least at the outset, as an incidental extra. The two counties first appeared in a railway title in 1865, although the line in question, the Lanarkshire & Ayrshire Junction, lay only in Renfrewshire and Lanarkshire. The title indicated the reason for the line's promotion rather than its geographical location, as it was mooted by the Glasgow & South Western in connection with its Kilmarnock Direct line. It was intended to leave this line by a triangular junction near the village of Waterfoot and head east for about 18 miles, directly through 'enemy' Caledonian territory to connect with the line of its ally, the North British, from Shotts and the coalfields of Linlithgowshire. Connecting spurs were also planned with the Caledonian's lines at East Kilbride, Hamilton and Law, allowing the line to be used for Lanarkshire as well as Linlithgowshire coal. The purpose of the line was thus to capture the profitable trade in transporting coal to the port of Ardrossan, where the G&SWR had been established since its earliest days, and to which the coal would be conveyed via the new Kilmarnock Direct line. At that time the Caledonian was also promoting a line to Kilmarnock, and a joint line was eventually built, but this incorporated no provision for a connection to the coalfields to the east. The only junction which the G&SWR ever had with the North British, apart from at Canal Junction in Carlisle, was via the City of Glasgow Union.

The Caledonian was thus able to ward off this attack by the G&SWR directly into its Lanarkshire territory, and the coal traffic was taken by the CR to Glasgow where the G&SWR took over for the remainder of the journey. By 1880 this traffic had greatly increased and the Caledonian, anxious to secure a greater mileage for itself, promoted the 6½-mile Barrmill & Kilwinning Railway between Barrmill on the Glasgow Barrhead & Kilmarnock Joint Line Beith branch and the G&SWR Ardrossan line at Kilwinning roughly over the same route as the intended Ardrossan branch of the 1845 Glasgow Kilmarnock & Ardrossan Railway. The Caledonian, by using this new and comparatively inexpensive line, could, via the Larkfield Junction–Langside Junction spur and the joint line through Barrhead, carry the coal to within 6 miles of Ardrossan. The Barrmill & Kilwinning was authorised on 20th August 1883, but almost immediately there were developments which caused the G&SWR to worry about more than just a mere reduction in their coal mileage. Almost a year after the Barrmill & Kilwinning obtained its Act, a further Act was passed authorising its continuation from Kilwinning by a new line, parallel with the G&SWR line, to Ardrossan Harbour. The Act also authorised branches from Giffen to Kilbirnie and from Kilwinning to Irvine, the latter branch facing ominously south towards the G&SWR stronghold at Ayr. The crunch came, however, in section 40 of the 1884 Act which left no doubt about the reason for the railway. Despite the fact that the new construction lay entirely in Ayrshire, the now enlarged Barrmill & Kilwinning was to be known as the Lanarkshire & Ayrshire Railway. Although worked by the Caledonian for 50 per cent of the gross receipts, almost all the capital was raised locally.

Cathcart West Junction taken from the Lanarkshire & Ayrshire line leading to Muirend. The lines to the right are to Cathcart East Junction, avoiding Cathcart station which can be seen in the centre at the top of the photograph.

BR 2-6-4T No. 80027 passing Cathcart West Junction with a train from the Lanarkshire & Ayrshire line. The bridge to the left which carried the line to/from Cathcart East Junction was removed when the junction was remodelled in 1961 for electrification, allowing through running from the West side of the Circle to the Kirkhill line.

J. R. HUME

The double line between Barrmill and Ardrossan opened on 4th September 1888, although it was nearly two further years until the new Montgomerie Pier at Ardrossan opened. The branch from Giffen to Kilbirnie, bringing the Caledonian almost into the heart of the great Glengarnock steelworks, opened at the close of 1889, and on 2nd June 1890 the short single-line branch to Irvine was opened. Despite petitions from many prospective customers tired of the G&SWR monopoly, nothing came of an extension to Ayr.

Although built with freight traffic in mind, the new line proved to be extremely convenient for an entirely new venture in passenger traffic to which the Caledonian was pledged at the close of the 1880s. This was steamer traffic on the Firth of Clyde. Of the twelve stations opened on the new Lanarkshire & Ayrshire Railway, nine duplicated existing G&SWR stations, and the remaining three, Giffen and Auchenmade on the main line and Brackenhills on the Kilbirnie branch, served very sparse populations. Giffen, a neat station with a through platform in the southbound direction and an island platform in the northbound direction giving a cross platform connection for the Kilbirnie branch, was little more than an exchange platform. No real attempt was made to cater for local passenger traffic, but the fact that the Caledonian route from Glasgow to Ardrossan was 3 miles shorter than its competitor was a substantial benefit in vying for the Arran traffic. To coincide with the opening of the new pier at Ardrossan a new steamer, the pride of the Caledonian Steam Packet Company, the 553 ton *Duchess of Hamilton* was built by Wm Denny & Bros of Dumbarton for the new route. The service provided by the Caledonian was of such high quality that it was immediately successful, and most of the former G&SWR passengers

transferred their allegiance to the new service. There is little wonder at this, with a service comprising a fast comfortable train, the Arran Express, of newly designed and built coaches hauled by a modern 4-4-0 locomotive connecting with a magnificent new steamer taking only ninety minutes for the journey from Glasgow to Brodick. The G&SWR soon fought back, and 1892 saw the commission of the beautiful twin-funnelled paddle steamer *Glen Sannox* plying in connection with their trains also giving a ninety-minute timing. As well as the Arran service, the Lanarkshire & Ayrshire provided a connection into G. & J. Burns' paddle steamer *Adder* to Belfast.

All this activity relating to coal and steamer traffic was of course of no interest to the directors or shareholders of the Cathcart District Railway, who during this period were involved in troubles with contractors and struggles to build a 3-mile extension. But by the end of the nineteenth century the Caledonian, objecting to paying the tolls required on the joint line and thus parting with some of its profits to the G&SWR, sought its own independent route to Barrmill direct from Glasgow and this brought the village of Cathcart and its railway into involvement with the Lanarkshire & Ayrshire.

Three things were disturbing the inhabitants of Cathcart in the spring of 1897. The first was the state of pollution of the river – despite all the Circle's shortcomings 'the Cathcart trains were easier to catch than the Cathcart fish'! The second was a proposal to introduce three new licences into the parish and the third was the Lanarkshire & Ayrshire Railway. Public meetings were held about the licences and the railway, that concerning the latter being in a crowded Couper Institute on 9th March 1897. At the meeting Mr Forman, the engineer, explained the advantages to Cathcart of he new line which was to start at a junction with the Caledonian at Newton, south of Cambuslang, and run due west to Cathcart where where would be connections to the Cathcart Circle. At Cathcart the line was to turn south towards Mearns and then veer west again through Neilston and Uplawmoor to join the existing Lanarkshire & Ayrshire line at Barrmill, providing a through route to Ardrossan without utilising the joint line at any point. Where the line crossed the East Kilbride line spurs would be provided to allow through running to Busby and East Kilbride. Stations in the Cathcart area were planned at Bogton and Merrylea as well as at Cathcart and a branch from the line to Barrhead and Paisley was planned. In answer to questions, Mr Forman stated that it had not yet been decided where the new Cathcart station would be situated, but it would be near the present one. A large petition had, however, been raised in Cathcart against the new line and one of the objectors who had seen the plans was at pains to point out to the meeting that the line was not being constructed for the benefit of Cathcart, but for the transit of the Lanarkshire minerals to the Ayrshire coast.

No mention appears to have been made at the meeting of the distinct possibility of the new line south of Cathcart being used in conjunction with the Circle for the express boat trains and that the timekeeping of the suburban services would be further upset by the intrusion of the expresses. Mr Forman is unlikely to have mentioned this and the point seems to have been missed by the objectors. No motions were allowed at the meeting and no vote was taken.

The board of the Cathcart District Railway had originally intended to object to the new line, but as the board was virtually under Caledonian control it is unlikely that the objection would have got very far. The principal objector was, of course, the G&SWR, but at a meeting held between the Caledonian and the G&SWR on 28th May 1897 it was agreed that the Caledonian would not oppose the G&SWR's Kilbirnie loop line and the G&SWR would not oppose the Lanarkshire & Ayrshire extension. The Caledonian would appear to have achieved the best of this bargain. For the small price of allowing the G&SWR to construct a line through Kilbirnie, where it had the terminus of a small country branch line, the Caledonian was allowed freedom to build an important cross-country mineral line. This now left the new railway unopposed and the Lanarkshire & Ayrshire Railway Act received the Royal Assent on 23rd July 1897.

The ceremony of cutting the first sod of the Lanarkshire & Ayrshire extension held at Lugton on Monday 6th June 1898 had unfortunately to be cut short due to a rainstorm. The Hon. Mrs Grenville Vernon, wife of the chairman of the company, performed the ceremony and was presented with a suitably inscribed full-size silver spade and polished oak barrow by Mr McAlpine the contactor. Lunch was

served in a tent in a neighbouring field and after the normal toasts to the success of the line and 'The Ladies', proceedings closed with the National Anthem.

Construction of the line proceeded and the upheaval in the Cathcart area was of advantage to one section of the community, albeit a minority. The geologists found an interesting field of study in the new cuttings which were excavated for the line. Reports of the many interesting fossils discovered, particularly where the East Kilbride line crossed the new line, were sent to the Glasgow Geological Society.

An accident which could have had disastrous effects occurred during the final phase of construction. On the evening of Monday 23rd March 1903 an engine and nine wagons of slag were standing at Whitecraigs when the engine coupling broke and the wagons ran back to Cathcart where they collided with a light engine. No one was seriously injured but both the engine and the wagons were severely damaged.

On 1st April 1903 the first portion of the line was opened to goods and mineral traffic. This was the stretch from Clarkston East Junction on the East Kilbride line to the existing line at Giffen. All freight traffic for Ardrossan now travelled via the newly opened line instead of via Barrhead. Trains from the Polmadie marshalling yard travelled via Langside Junction, Busby Junction and Clarkston East Junction, being rounded at this latter junction. The timetable provided for four trains daily using this route with the locomotive being required to run tender first between Polmadie and Clarkston East Junction. Trains to the new line from the Motherwell and Hamilton area were able to run direct using the line from Hunthill Junction at Hamilton via East Kilbride.

One month later, on 1st May 1903, the section between Cathcart and Clarkston West Junction opened and passenger traffic between Glasgow and Ardrossan was transferred to the new line. Passenger stations were opened at Whitecraigs (for Rouken Glen), Patterton (for Darnley), Neilston, Uplawmoor and Lugton, with Muirend following on 1st July 1903. A connecting link with the joint line at Lugton was opened on 20th September 1903. The Ardrossan boat trains now flew round the eastern section of the Cathcart Circle through the walled cuttings at Queen's Park and Crosshill, allowed eight minutes for the section between Glasgow and Cathcart in a forty-five-minute timing for the complete journey. The 9.5am from Glasgow ran non-stop to connect with the Belfast steamer and was followed by the 9.10am which called at Cathcart to pick up at 9.18am and arrived at Ardrossan at 9.57am for the Arran steamer. A similar return service operated in the evening.

The Caledonian promptly withdrew its through service to Ardrossan via the joint line, although additional local services from Glasgow Central to Beith were introduced. The G&SWR, hopeful of capturing some traffic from the Caledonian, considered operating a service from St Enoch to Barrhead and thence to Ardrossan via its newly opened link to Paisley via Potterhill. Such a service, which would have required a reversal at Barrhead, would have been most unlikely to attract through passengers and there was little chance of sufficient local traffic being forthcoming to make the venture a success. It was never attempted, although the journey was possible by changing at Barrhead and Paisley.

Freight services continued to use the joint line until the following year when the final section of the Lanarkshire & Ayrshire, between Newton and Cathcart, was opened. Goods and mineral trains started to use the new line between Newton and Cathcart West Junction on 6th January 1904. Connecting lines at both ends, between Kirkhill Junction and Westburn Junction at Newton and a spur between North and East Junctions at Cathcart, were opened for freight traffic on 20th June 1904, while passenger services were introduced to all these lines on 1st August with the exception of the section between East and West Junctions at Cathcart. New passenger stations were provided at Kirkhill and Burnside. A notable exception was Cathcart.

CR '812' Class 0-6-0 No. 57564 passes Cathcart North Junction on 30th August 1957 with an Inner Circle train. To the right can be seen the single-line connection from Cathcart East Junction (see page 74).

(see page 74)

G. H. ROBIN/BY COURTESY OF THE MITCHELL LIBRARY, GLASGOW CITY COUNCIL

Despite the mention of a repositioned station when the line was being promoted, and suggestions of a direct service between Cathcart and Edinburgh, the Lanarkshire & Ayrshire passed through the middle of Cathcart and no passenger station was built. The reason for this was probably the fact that it was impossible to reposition the station to allow the line from Cathcart East to make a junction with the Circle line north of the station, and also that no regular passenger services were planned over the East to West spur.

An agreement was signed between the Cathcart District and the Lanarkshire & Ayrshire whereby, if the L&A opened a goods or mineral station within half a mile of the existing station at Cathcart, the L&A would account to the Cathcart District for any traffic originating which would otherwise have been carried by the Cathcart District, although this would not apply to traffic to or from Lanarkshire & Ayrshire stations. Muirend goods station was 1100 yards from Cathcart!

In order to avoid delays arising through conflicting movements the junction at Cathcart North was not of the conventional double track design but employed a 'flyunder' device. The line leading towards Glasgow from Cathcart East burrowed under the Cathcart Circle, using an existing road bridge, and then swung sharply north to join the Inner Circle from the west. This allowed trains from the Kirkhill direction to join the Inner Circle without delaying trains on the Outer Circle. It is more than possible that the Lanarkshire & Ayrshire employed this useful layout more to avoid delay to its expresses than out of consideration for the Cathcart Circle commuters! The G&SWR used the same layout at Elderslie where speedy operation of the Greenock boat trains was equally important.

Local passenger services over the Lanarkshire & Ayrshire were still considered incidental to the mineral traffic and the boat trains, and most stopping trains to Ardrossan called at no Circle stations except Cathcart, although circular services over the Kirkhill line were provided, returning to Glasgow Central Low Level and continuing to Possil.

This completed the network around Cathcart, but there is one other line which is worth noting in passing, as a reminder of this less successful venture is to be seen on the line between Patterton and Neilston. Authorised one month after the Lanarkshire & Ayrshire extension, the Paisley & Barrhead District Railway was to connect the two towns in its title with the new line at Lyoncross, near the Balgray Reservoir, two separate lines running to Paisley from Blackbyres Junction outside Barrhead, a single line with passing loops at stations via Stanely and Glenfield to Paisley St James, and a double line via Dykebar to Paisley East, where an intended junction

with the main line at Arkleston was never completed although the earthworks were built.

The line through Barrhead was double track and was particularly expensive to construct, requiring both a lengthy viaduct through the town and a substantial cutting, reputedly the deepest in Scotland on the approach to Lyoncross. The ill-fated little line has itself a fascinating history, remaining always a freight-only backwater. Despite the fact that fine stations, principally island platforms with buildings of Caledonian twentieth-century design, were constructed, the company never applied for Board of Trade permission to operate a passenger service. At the Barrhead end the South station buildings remained unfinished, but, other than that, the railway was completed, fully signalled with signal boxes and, so it is said, even down to tickets in the booking offices. It was probably the electric tram, coupled with the recently introduced but short lived G&SWR service between Paisley and Barrhead which killed the line, but it remained in use for freight until 1963, although the section to Paisley East from Blackbyres Junction had been closed some three years earlier and the line between Barrhead South and Lyoncross Junction had been abandoned in the early 1950s.

At Lyoncross, however, the double track still slews to permit the construction of an island platform at the junction. The line was built that way and the station would probably have resembled Muirend in appearance. It was never constructed, and the stations on the Paisley & Barrhead District Railway were converted into comfortable, if unusual, dwelling houses for railwaymen. The mileposts on the Paisley & Barrhead, as on the Lanarkshire & Ayrshire between Newton and Giffen Junction, were measured on the Caledonian basis from Carlisle as zero, but the original Lanarkshire & Ayrshire was not altered on the opening of the new line and continued to be measured from zero at Barrmill Junction.

The Lanarkshire & Ayrshire enjoyed only a few years as an important freight route, since after the opening of Rothesay Dock on the north bank of the Clyde in 1908 much of the mineral traffic was shipped through the new dock rather than Ardrossan. After the grouping of the railways in 1923 the former rivals for the traffic to Ardrossan came under common ownership of the LMSR, and the inevitable elimination of duplicate routes resulted in local passenger services beyond Uplawmoor being withdrawn from 4th July 1932. By that time the Lanarkshire & Ayrshire was beginning to develop its new role as an outer suburban passenger route as housing expanded, with new stations opening at King's Park, Croftfoot and Williamwood. The section between Neilston and Uplawmoor closed for passengers on 2nd April 1962.

CR '439' Class 0-4-4T No. 55189 between Crosshill and Mount Florida with the 12.30pm Outer Circle train on 25th October 1958.　J. L. STEVENSON

CHAPTER 5

TWENTIETH-CENTURY DEVELOPMENTS

At the close of the nineteenth century there was a train every ten minutes for most of the day on the Cathcart Circle, a frequency unequalled outside London. This despite the tremendous competition from the Corporation Tramways. The Circle fares were probably the cheapest in the country. The building boom along the line of the 1894 extension through Langside, Shawlands and Pollokshields was now in full swing, new passengers were being attracted to the line weekly, and there was constant pressure to increase the service further. There was spare line capacity on the Circle, but Glasgow Central posed a problem. In 1899, 17 million passengers passed through the cramped nine-platform terminus, and a further 6 million used the Low Level station. The lines from Lanarkshire, Renfrewshire and Ayrshire were also clamouring for extra accommodation at the terminus. In 1899 authority was obtained for the much needed Central extension. The new works involved the closure of Bridge Street station and the extension of the tracks to the enlarged Central station on a new viaduct parallel to the existing four-track viaduct. It was also necessary to build a further bridge over Argyle Street.

The new thirteen-platform station was completed in 1905, Bridge Street station closing on 1st March of that year, and the accommodation for trains was almost doubled due to the lengthening of existing platforms, in addition to the four new ones. Platforms 7 and 8 were allocated to Cathcart Circle trains. Platform 7 was designated for the Outer Circle and Platform 8 for the Inner. Crucial to the operation was the Cathcart engine siding which lay between the lines approaching these platforms. Immediately on arrival the engine would take water from the water crane provided at the end of the platform. On the departure of the train the engine ran into the engine siding. On arrival of the next Circle train the engine came onto the head of that train from the siding and so the operation continued. Thus, for example, the 10am Outer Circle would arrive at Platform 7 at 10.33 and the

Glasgow Corporation 'Red' Standard tramcar 308 approaching Pollokshaws East along Kilmarnock Road. The original bookstall can be seen on the station platform, while in front of the tram is the tall chimney from the booking office which can still be seen today. The posts for the gas lamps at the station entrances and the small hut just beyond the entrance are also still extant. The boarded-up window of the booking office can also be seen behind the city-bound tram stop. The photograph was taken after 1912, as the barometer has been fitted to the station building.

BY COURTESY OF THE MITCHELL LIBRARY, GLASGOW CITY COUNCIL

76—77

GLASGOW (Central Station) AND CIRCLE LINE.

CENTRAL .... leave
Eglinton Street ....
Pollokshields (East) .....
Queen's Park ....
Crosshill ....
Mount Florida ....
Cathcart ....
Langside & Newlands ...
Pollokshaws (East) ......
Shawlands ....
Maxwell Park ....
Pollokshields (West) ....
Pollokshields (West) ....
Maxwell Park ....
Shawlands ....
Pollokshaws (East) ......
Langside & Newlands ...
Cathcart ....
Mount Florida ....
Crosshill ....
Queen's Park ....
Eglinton Street ....
CENTRAL .... arrive

74—75

TRAIN SERVICE FROM AND TO CATHCART

CENTRAL .... leave
Eglinton Street ....
Pollokshields (East) .....
Queen's Park ....
Crosshill ....
Mount Florida ....
Cathcart ....
Langside & Newlands ...
Pollokshaws (East) ......
Shawlands ....
Maxwell Park ....
Pollokshields (West) ....
Pollokshields (West) ....
Maxwell Park ....
Shawlands ....
Pollokshaws (East) ......
Langside & Newlands ...
Cathcart ....
Mount Florida ....
Crosshill ....
Queen's Park ....
Eglinton Street ....
CENTRAL .... arrive

CR '439' Class 0-4-4T No. 429 at Glasgow Central. Built in 1907, it was withdrawn in 1950, by that time numbered 55191 by British Railways. The fully panelled six-wheel coach has four compartments with a brake compartment in the centre. The white upper panels were reintroduced to the Caledonian livery from around 1890, but much of the Cathcart Circle stock retained all-over brown until the grouping in 1923. J. MacIntosh collection

ngine would immediately fill its tank in the time available until the departure of the coaches which formed the 10.40 Outer Circle. After he 10.40 departed the engine was released into the engine siding. At 10.45 the 10.10 Inner Circle would arrive at Platform 8, its engine mmediately taking water. The engine in the siding came on to the coaches in Platform 8 to form the 10.50 Inner Circle, the engine which had brought in the train being released to the siding to run on o the coaches which would arrive at Platform 7 at 10.53 to form the 11am Outer Circle and so on. Thus the operation of the ten-minute Circle service required only four sets of coaches and five engines.

An event which affected both the Cathcart Circle and the new Central station was the electrification of the Glasgow tramway system. This had the effect of taking a proportion of the railway's customers to the ramways, 3 million fewer passengers passing through Central station n 1904. South of the Clyde, Battlefield Electric Tram depot near Mount Florida, accommodating 200 trams, was opened on 25th April 1901 to service routes covering Shawlands, Pollokshaws, Langside, Queen's Park, Mount Florida and Cathcart. With the modern electric tram providing a cheap attractive alternative mode of transport at so many points on the Circle, it was inevitable that passengers would be lost, especially in view of the conditions under which the railway was operating at the time. In addition to the cramped accommodation at the Central station, the problems involved in completing the enlarged terminal gave rise to innumerable delays. In an attempt to regain lost traffic, on 1st October 1902 the return fare to the city from Cathcart, Langside, Pollokshaws East and Shawlands was reduced from fourpence to twopence halfpenny, while from the other stations the fare became a penny halfpenny, with corresponding reductions in season ticket rates. The passenger revenue dropped from £19,000 in 1900 to around £15,000 in 1903. After the new Central station was completed traffic recovered gradually, the previous level being regained in 1907.

RIGHT: CR '92' Class 0-4-4T No. 100 at Glasgow Central station. The engine is in the Cathcart engine siding referred to above, and displays the route indicator for the Inner Circle. It was built in 1897, originally for use on the Glasgow Central Low Level lines for which it was fitted with condensing apparatus. K. NUNN

FACING PAGE: Cathcart Circle timetable for October 1905.

The possibility of operating the Cathcart Circle by electric traction was first considered in 1899. It was decided on Caledonian advice to await the results of electrification experiments being made in England, notably on the underground Mersey Railway and the circular suburban routes out of Newcastle where the electric tramway was also affecting traffic. Nothing came of the scheme and Cathcart had to wait a further sixty years before it saw electric trains.

Another 1899 proposal which came to nothing was that for a branch from Cathcart to the village of Carmunnock, some 2 miles to the south-west. No doubt it was considered that with the alterations being made at Cathcart for the junction with the Lanarkshire & Ayrshire there would be no difficulty in making an additional junction for the branch.

A contemporary report in 1900 described Cathcart as 'an old place which is renewing its youth', and the building boom following the railway certainly bore this out. The mineral stations at Cathcart, Pollokshaws East and Maxwell Park, which had rarely seen much more than a couple of wagons of coal at a time, were now full of the wagons bringing the masonry blocks for tenements and villas. An unfortunate accident occurred at Pollokshaws East in September 1907 during the unloading of masonry blocks when a crane cord snapped, causing serious injuries to one of the workmen. At this time the south entrances to Maxwell Park and Pollokshields West stations, which had been provided at the opening of the line in 1894 but had remained boarded up, were opened. This probably explains why until recent years at both stations there were internal wooden doorways to the station buildings only on the south side, which appeared to the modern traveller to be rather pointless from the security point of view.

By 1908 there was a noticeable reduction in the mineral traffic as much of the area had become built up. During this period the small mining village of Pottersfield, on both sides of Haggs Road near Pollokshaws, which had prospered until the earlier closure of Lochinch Coal Pit, was finally demolished and replaced by modern terraced houses. By 1922 the last of the bridges which had been built in anticipation of the housing developments was utilised by the construction of Titwood Road, and the green fields through which the railway originally passed had all but disappeared.

It was inevitable that requests would be received from the new passengers for more convenient access points to certain stations. In 1896 the Cathcart Board approved a proposal for an entrance, by way of a footbridge, to the northern end of Shawlands station but it was not until 1902 that tenders for the work were invited, and 1904 that the bridge, with entrances to the east and west of the line, was constructed. The question of an entrance to Langside station at the Cathcart end was first raised by the Newlands District Committee in 1898, but the request was turned down as 'premature'. As there was no competition from the tram at this station there was no need to provide an added inducement to the passengers to use the trains. The CDR Board did, however, approve on 11th October 1899 the Caledonian proposal that the station be renamed Langside and Newlands. That, at least, did not cost as much as a new entrance! Newlands was the name of a farm approximately a third of a mile south west of the station, and had given its name to the area now developing for the construction of villas. The new name came into effect on 1st August 1901.

One of the problems associated with providing additional entrances was the fact that the booking offices on the extension line stations were at street level and that if additional entrances were provided an additional booking office, and a consequent increase in staff would be required. A cheaper solution suggested by the Caledonian was found by closing the existing booking offices and providing one central office in the building on the platform, usually at the expense of the station master who was deprived of his separate accommodation. The original booking offices, one each at Cathcart, Langside and Shawlands, and two at Pollokshaws East, must have been particularly miserable places in which to spend a working day, especially so for the young clerkesses who were a novel and welcome feature of the extension when it opened. These offices still remain, now bricked-up although the ticket windows remain inside. One small barred window was all that provided light, and the clerkesses probably had to work by gaslight all day. The fireplaces still remain, and the discerning eye will notice the otherwise unexplainable tall chimneys which still remain at all the stations except Cathcart. No changes were required at Maxwell Park and Pollokshields West, and fine spacious offices were already provided in the top storey of the station buildings, but between 1905 and 1907 the offices at Langside and Shawlands were moved following the construction of the new entrances and, although

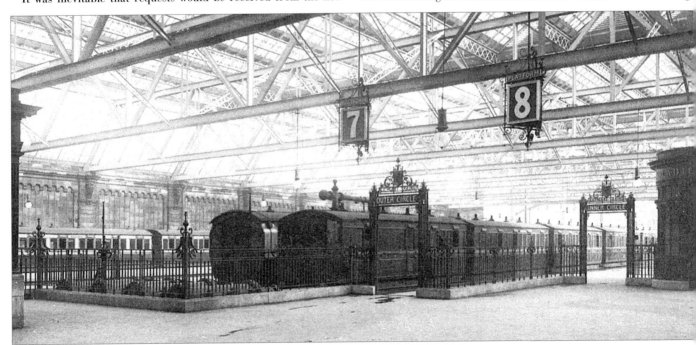

Platforms 7 and 8 at Glasgow Central, the platforms used for the intense ten-minute service round the Circle. Note the water tower used to replenish the engine tank immediately on arrival – trains were only at the platform for seven minutes. The absence of both an engine at the buffers and passengers suggests that the photograph was taken on a Sunday.

was not necessary as it had offices at both entrances, a similar change was made at Pollokshaws East, presumably to reduce staffing costs, the alterations costing only about £30 per station. The new eastern entrance at Langside was provided during 1907 by means of a subway at a cost of £1,702, which compared rather unfavourably with the figure of under £100 for the new footbridge at Shawlands. The additional entrance at Cathcart was not opened until after 1912, following a period of experimental opening at peak periods, although it had been built when the line opened in 1894. In 1897 a fire at Mount Florida resulted in certain adjustments being required to fireplaces at all the stations. The opportunity was taken at Mount Florida to construct an enlarged booking office with separate accommodation for the station master, in conjunction with the new entrance. Another fire started around 4am on 29th December 1903 which caused extensive damage to Shawlands station. Starting in the porters' room it spread to the station master's room and the gents' lavatory which was completely burned out. The cost of the damage was estimated at £250, and the reconstructed building included the new booking office and a slightly altered design at the northern end.

Despite the fact that they were now receiving a dividend, the shareholders were still dissatisfied at the traffic being lost to tramway competition especially as it was considered that the railway had created the market for the tramways. It was several times suggested by shareholders that the Caledonian might take over the Cathcart District, but the Caledonian always replied that it was 'not yet ready'

to take over the company. Improvements in the frequency of services were also called for. One shareholder hoped that there would be a five-minute service when the extension to Central station was completed, and it was regularly pointed out that while the tramcars groaned under their loads of passengers, in particular to Rouken Glen, on Sundays, the railway lay unused. A Sunday service for churchgoers had been suggested when the Circle opened in 1894, but no Sunday trains were introduced until electrification in 1962. The shareholders were certainly full of suggestions for the improvement of their railway. It was explained at the half-yearly meeting on 30th October 1908 that electrification would be a very expensive business, and that it was still a long way off. A shareholder suggested that an alternative might be to operate more, but shorter, trains enabling the same class of locomotive to get up to the maximum speed quicker. This seemed to ignore the fact that the number of locomotives would have to be increased, at a cost which was unlikely to be recovered by increased traffic receipts, although the shareholders were told by the chairman that 'they must bear in mind that some of the suggestions, if carried out, would have the effect at future meetings of making the dividend much smaller than two and a half per cent'.

Not all passengers paid the due fare for the journey, despite the fact that the fares were so cheap, A Mount Florida correspondent to the *Pollokshaws News* in 1909 commented that a great many wicked people whose 'morals were utterly deformed and lacking' travelled on the Cathcart Circle. He believed that about 40 per cent of those

LEFT: The chimney from the fireplace in the former street-level booking office at Langside can still be seen, as can those at Pollokshaws East and Shawlands.   J. KERNAHAN

BELOW: CR '439' Class 0-4-4T No. 15219 on an Outer Circle train at Cathcart on 12th May 1948, a few months after the formation of British Railways.   G. H. ROBIN

An Outer Circle train has just left Mount Florida. The signal in the foreground was installed after the opening in 1903 of the Lanarkshire & Ayrshire line to Kirkhill (diagram on page 73). Note also the fine lattice ironwork of the footbridge provided very soon after the opening of the station following requests by passengers.

who occupied first class carriages held only third class tickets and were enabled to commit this fraud due to the poor standard of ticket collection. Most of the off-peak trains called at Eglinton Street for two minutes on the journey into Glasgow for ticket collection purposes, an extra platform having been provided in the Glasgow-bound direction at the time of the enlargement of Central station, but at peak hours to save journey time and also to increase line capacity, calls at Eglinton Street were omitted and tickets were collected at Central station where it was impossible at the barrier to tell a first from a third class passenger. In the event of a surprise check by the 'Flying Squad', as the itinerant ticket inspectors were affectionately known, the offending passenger either calmly handed over an excess fare of a penny or produced a first class ticket which he had ready for such an emergency. This ability to produce a valid first class ticket was facilitated by the use of 'bulk tickets', whereby passengers could buy twelve undated tickets, valid in either direction and at any time, for the cost of six return tickets. This scheme was discontinued due to such abuse in favour of weekly zone tickets on 1st April 1908 but was re-introduced on 20th September 1909 and continued intermittently until the 1940s.

The antics of schoolboys who travelled to the City Centre schools were notorious. In 1901 matters had become so serious with boys writing offensive matter in the first class carriages that detectives were engaged to travel on the trains in an effort to discover the offenders. In June 1907 a man was fined £10 after having been arrested in Cathcart Goods station, accused of betting, contrary to the Betting Act 1906. An almost unbelievable activity practised during the period of poor timekeeping while the Central station extension was being completed was for passengers on trains coming from Maxwell Park direction and held at the signals at Muirhouse Junction to jump down onto the track and run across the ballast to Pollokshields East, jumping over the wall and joining an Inner Circle train from the 'non-platform' side in the hope that they would arrive in the city a few minutes sooner!

It was also not unknown for locomotives to part company with their trains while on a trip round the Circle. On one occasion a driver, having mistaken a guard's signal to back up and recouple the train for a 'right away' signal, set off from Cathcart with one coach in the direction of Langside, hotly pursued by the guard! It was also not unknown for trains to travel between stations with compartment doors swinging open. Despite these irregularities most accidents resulting in injury were normally the result of some stupidity by the person concerned. Almost as soon as the line opened in 1886 a youth was killed while trying to board an already moving train in Central station, while on 30th December 1899 a girl suffered severe head injuries after falling out of a train in the cutting near Cathcart. A woman was injured in a similar incident at Shawlands in March 1901, and it was also at this station, on the evening of Saturday 15th June 1907, that an unfortunate accident happened to Alex McIntosh, the sixteen-year-old porter at the station. He was standing near the track at the south-west end of the station watching a brass band which had arrived from Glasgow, when he was knocked down by an Outer Circle train. The engine passed over his right foot which was afterwards amputated at the Victoria Infirmary.

Despite the railway's many shortcomings its staff and even its buildings were quick in finding a place in the affections of the passengers. Particularly in the areas where there were few shops, such as Langside and Maxwell Park, the stations became the focal point of the community, the bookstall being the sole shop in the area. All the staff were characters, from the station master who ruled the small world of the station to the ticket girls and boy porters, as the Circle seemed to be the training ground for staff for the whole Caledonian system. This contrasted with the drivers, most of whom were 'pensioned off' from the main line, and whose twelve-hour day involved as many as fourteen trips round the Circle, requiring the locomotives to be stopped and started 210 times in the course of a day, prior to the closure of Bridge Street station in 1905.

James R. Smith, who retired in 1967 as an inspector at Glasgow

Central, recalled his first days in railway employment when he commenced duty as a boy porter at Pollokshields West in 1916 at a wage of 12/6d (62.5p) per week. The station master at that time was Allen Mason, a brother-in-law of John Maclean the famous socialist. John Hannah was also employed there as boy porter and Jean Brand was forewoman porter. Sir Robert Bruce, former editor of *The Glasgow Herald* used the station and called daily at the booking office for his *Herald*, left there for collection by the girl in the bookstall. Mr Smith transferred to Langside and Newlands in 1917 before promotion to ticket collector at Glasgow Central in 1920. He had many happy memories of his days as a boy on the Circle, in particular of the fine people he met and their kindness and generosity to him.

The stationmasters in particular were much respected members of the community. It was almost their duty to know all the passengers, and passengers felt honoured if the stationmaster had a few words with them each day. Presentations on retirements were not unknown. On 1st June 1911 a number of gentlemen residing in the neighbourhood gathered on the platform of Langside and Newlands station to present Duncan McLachlan the stationmaster with a testimonial on the occasion of his retirement, which took the form of a purse of 60 sovereigns. Mr M. F. Findlay, who made the presentation, expressed the regret felt in the district on Mr McLachlan's retiral from active duties through ill health. A similar presentation took place in November 1916 in the Unionist Rooms at Cathcart to Mr W. J. Munro on his retiral after more than forty years service with the Caledonian Railway, twenty-eight years of which had been spent as stationmaster at Cathcart. Mr Alex Gartshore presided over the meeting, where many compliments were paid to Mr Munro's friendly and efficient manner as well as to the many services he had rendered to the community. Mr James Houston made the presentation, which consisted of a cheque for £36 and a pair of field glasses for Mr Munro

and a gold bracelet for his wife, subscribed by daily passengers at the station, the various businesses in the vicinity, notably Messrs Weir Ltd and the Wallace Scott Tailoring Institute, as well as other stationmasters and staff on the Circle.

The stationmasters were not the only donees on the railway. The station building at Pollokshaws East boasted a barometer, probably the only station barometer in the country, matching and adjacent to the clock, which bore the simple inscription 'Presented by a number of subscribers – 1st May 1912'.

No work on the Cathcart Circle would be complete without a mention of the famous story centred on the line, *Snooker Tam of the Cathcart Railway*, written by Captain R. W. Campbell in 1919. It tells the rather incredible tale of Snooker Tam, a boy porter so called because of the length of his nose, Maggie McCheery, the ticket girl, and Maister McMuckle, the station-master, at a fictional station on the line called 'Kirkbride'. Set during the First World War it gives a fair idea of the operation of the Circle during this time, when the railway had to be run by 'bits o' lassies and deevils o' boys', in the absence of the men away at the war, although contemporary indications were that the Circle had always been run by rather young staff. Nonetheless, if one disregards the rather incredible tales of the capture of Italian spies and the letters received by the railway claims department, such events as the daily delivery of parcels to the houses, the perpetual war waged between the station boys and the schoolboys and the life of relief staff at Pollokshields are all indicative of fact rather than fiction. Maister McMuckle had his presentation on the occasion of his jubilee in railway service, while the rivalry between stations in the annual gardens competition reflects a state of affairs which continued well into the 1960s. Even the chapter on Railway Nationalisation was strangely prophetic.

The First World War brought inevitable economies on the line to save resources and release manpower. The services were reduced

Passengers joining an Outer Circle train at Pollokshaws East in 1912. Almost everyone wears a hat! Note the signal, where the Shawlands distant can be seen under the Pollokshaws East starter. As Shawlands signalbox was closed between 1900 and 1927 the distant signal always moved in conjunction with the starter during these years.
BY COURTESY OF THE MITCHELL LIBRARY, GLASGOW CITY COUNCIL

and, in common with many stations in Britain, Pollokshields East and Crosshill were closed on 1st January 1917, to be reopened after cessation of hostilities – Pollokshields East on 1st March 1919 and Crosshill on 1st June 1919. During the war women were encouraged to take the jobs of men enlisted in the services, and Miss Elizabeth Crighton, then aged 20, became the first female guard on the Caledonian Railway in 1915, working on the Circle, where it appears she endeared herself to several of the gentleman passengers who would present her with flowers! She did not continue with this employment after the war, believing that it was unfair for a single woman to be taking a man's job while so many were unemployed. Despite the problems of the War the Cathcart Circle prospered during this difficult period. Following the Government control of the railways, shareholders of a company which owned lines worked upon terms based on traffic receipts (and the CDR still received 55 per cent of the receipts as arranged in the original agreement) were guaranteed a minimum dividend equivalent to that received for the year 1913, although if receipts were sufficient a greater dividend would be paid. In 1913 the Cathcart District paid £3:12/6d per cent, and this dividend was exceeded in every year except 1914 until 1920. At the Annual General Meeting in 1921 the Chairman of the CDR, in addition to reporting an increase in traffic, particularly on the freight side which had required the expenditure of £2,054 on a new siding and sheds at Cathcart, gave the shareholders his thoughts on the future of their company. He explained that, unless there was some form of Government intervention, the CDR would find itself in a very favourable position following the end of Government control. He also brought to their attention the white paper published the previous summer on the future of the railways. This had proposed six groups, including one group for the whole of Scotland, but the railway companies had commenced negotiations to procure a more financially stable amalgamation in the form of four groups. It had also been suggested that the minor companies, such as the Cathcart District, should in the first place amalgamate with their working company.

The end of the independent Cathcart District Railway Company came with the passing of the Railways Act 1921. The CDR Chairman, addressing the 1922 annual meeting, denounced the grouping as an 'arbitrary interference with existing contract rights', going on to explain that no final arrangements about the amalgamation were known, but until that date 1913 net receipts would be guaranteed and the valuation of the company on amalgamation would also be based on the 1913 revenue, ensuring that shareholders would not suffer any capital loss and, although dividends might not increase, there would be an advantage in the greater marketability of the stock. After a life of 43 years, remarkably still independent, even if that independence was possibly merely a technicality in view of the Caledonian shareholding in the Company and its dominance of the Board of Directors, the Cathcart District Railway was one of the fourteen Scottish Companies, which also included the Lanarkshire & Ayrshire, which became part of the London Midland & Scottish Railway from 1st January 1923. The shareholders met for the last time on Friday 16th March 1923 to approve the Absorption Scheme which provided for the holders of the 4 per cent debentures to receive a similar amount of 4 per cent LMSR debentures. Ordinary shareholders, however, received only £51 Ordinary LMSR stock (market value £57) for every £100 CDR stock. This was not quite the settlement which had been hoped for, but was probably better than would have been granted if the matter had gone to arbitration. One shareholder, ever hopeful, expressed the view that the line would develop more rapidly than any main line, and that probably in ten years the dividend would be doubled. No allowance had been made for this in the settlement. The chairman tactfully replied that he was afraid they could not successfully argue along these lines before the tribunal. By the time of this final meeting of shareholders the directors had already met for the last time. On 21st February 1923 they had transacted their final business by awarding the following payments for loss of office:

Secretary	£804
Solicitors	£321
Engineers	£100
Directors	£150 each
Auditors	£50 each

The Secretary was also to receive £50 in addition to his salary

ABOVE: CR '812' Class 0-6-0 No. 57555 takes the line to Kirkhill at Cathcart North Junction on 28th August 1958.   G. H. ROBIN/BY COURTESY OF THE MITCHELL LIBRARY, GLASGOW CITY COUNCIL

LEFT: Miss Elizabeth Anderson Crighton, the first female guard on the Caledonian Railway, taking the place of a man who had enlisted in the First World War.   (C) CULTURE AND SPORT GLASGOW (MUSEUMS)

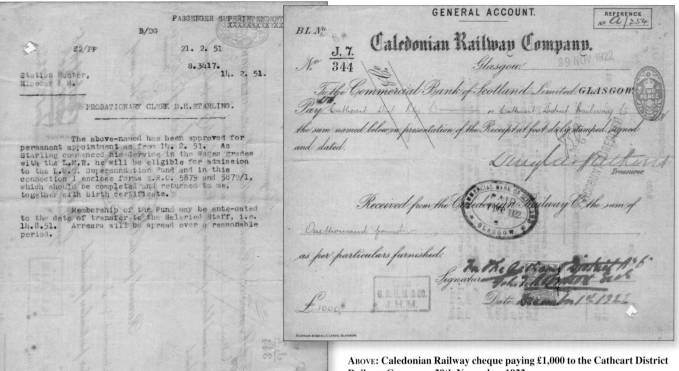

ABOVE: Caledonian Railway cheque paying £1,000 to the Cathcart District Railway Company, 29th November 1922.
RIGHT: The reverse of the above cheque, showing it was used for an internal letter in 1951.

to cover extra work involved in the winding up. He was asked to retain all the secretarial books until such time as the LMSR could find accommodation for them. He also ensured that his own pass be immediately validated for travel south of Greenhill. On 27th June 1923 the remaining sum in the Cathcart District Railway's bank account, £922:17/5d, was transferred to the LMSR. Thus the little local railway, official mileage 5 miles, 2 furlongs, 2 chains, 10 yards, which had played a small but not insignificant part in the development of the southern suburbs of Glasgow, disappeared into the great national railway which stretched from London to Thurso.

Between the Wars the Cathcart Circle prospered, services being improved from the half-hour service to which the line had been reduced through tramway competition in the early Twenties, to a fifteen-minute service by the outbreak of the Second World War. Among improvements made to the stations the wooden edgings of the platforms were replaced by coping stones. In 1931 an additional approach to Shawlands station from a new housing development was provided. In addition to a new pathway, this involved the construction of a footbridge alongside the existing girder bridge which carried the Circle over the GB&K line, built by Lambhill Ironworks at a cost of £124:8/3d. A later development was the provision of an additional platform at Mount Florida, authorised by the LMSR on 13th July 1937. This was a wooden platform on the Inner Circle line 450 feet in length constructed over the site of the signalbox, closure of which was authorised at the same time, with access to Battlefield Road. It was for use only on the occasion of important football matches, as considerable overcrowding and congestion occurred at these times due to the large crowds having to leave and arrive at the station by means of the two narrow stairways. The cost of the platform, together with the necessary signalling alterations, was £2,328 and annual savings were estimated at £186.

The economies of the Second World War caused a great reduction in the timetable, an hourly service with up to ninety-minute gaps at morning and afternoon off-peak times being introduced, and indeed it was not until well into British Railways days that a regular interval service was reintroduced.

Although deaths on the Circle, particularly suicides, are not unknown, apart from the three railway operating accidents which are described in Chapter 7, there has been only one murder on the line. This was the bizarre affair at Pollokshields East in 1945.

Shortly after 7.30pm on Monday 10th December 1945, as the three members of staff were sitting talking in the stationmaster's room at Pollokshields East, the door burst open and a man, revolver in hand, sprang in and without saying a word shot all three. Almost immediately he made off into the darkness carrying with him two tin boxes snatched from the adjoining booking office. Of the three on duty, Miss Annie Withers, a 35-year-old clerkess who lived as a boarder in Grantley Gardens near Pollokshaws East station, died in an ambulance while on the way to Victoria Infirmary; Robert Gough, a fifteen-year-old junior porter was shot through the right wrist and stomach and was taken, in a critical condition, to the Infirmary; while William Wright, porter-clerk, escaped serious injury by ducking. Wright was able to telephone an alarm to nearby Pollokshields East Junction signal box, but an immediate search of the area by police discovered no clues. Miss Withers, described as being of a quiet home-loving disposition, was a native of Galston in Ayrshire, having been in domestic service at Whitecraigs before joining the railway in 1940. Robert Gough, the boy porter, died two days after the shooting after managing to give a brief description of the assailant.

The search for the murderer was by this time well underway, led by Chief Superintendent William Ewing of the CID, who described the murder as one of the most callous and cold-blooded ever perpetrated in Glasgow. Information was limited to a brief description of the man – that he was about 33 years of age, 5 feet 9 inches in height, and wearing a light coloured 'demobilisation' raincoat and a felt hat – and the fact that the gun used was apparently a German Luger 9mm automatic revolver with a magazine of ten bullets, six shots having been fired in the station.

On 17th December, in an attempt to accelerate matters, Glasgow Magistrates offered a reward of £1,000 for information leading to an arrest, but the Lord Advocate disapproved of this reward and ruled that, if paid, it would have to be met out of local funds. As it was, there was no need to worry about who was to pay the reward, as no-one came forward with the necessary information. Apart from the discovery on the last day of 1945 in Shuttle Street of a revolver similar to that which had apparently been used, nothing happened for a further nine months.

On 9th October 1946 PC John Byrne was on points duty at the junction of Newlands Road and Clarkston Road when he was approached by a man who handed him a cardboard box containing a Luger pistol and confessed 'I did a murder.' The man was Charles Templeton Brown, a twenty-year-old railway fireman, and when searched a book of railway rules was found in his pocket with, inside it, a note: 'I am not sorry for anything I did, only for the things I did not do. Goodbye and good luck to Bilt McKay and you.' Apparently Brown had attempted to commit suicide earlier that morning, but the gun failed. The pistol, bullets and Brown's fingerprints all tallied and Wright, the porter-clerk, identified Brown in an identification parade. On 13th December Brown was sentenced to death, the sentence to be carried out at Barlinnie on 3rd January 1947. Apparently, however, he was suffering from schizophrenia and following a successful appeal a reprieve was granted on 30th December, the sentence being reduced to penal servitude for life.

The motive for the crime was robbery, a wage packet containing £4:3/8d being stolen. Thirty years after the murder the mark of one of the stray bullets could still be seen on the skirting board of the old stationmaster's room opposite the door, although the building was demolished after being badly damaged by a fire in April 1976.

The first stations to be modernised with the installation of electricity were Queen's Park and Crosshill in January 1958. With electrification the other stations were similarly brought up to date, although Shawlands, Pollokshields West and Pollokshields East were still lit by gas when the first electric trains started running. Patterton on the Neilston branch, continued to be lit by oil Tilley lamps at this time. The stations were all repainted but the atmospheric gas lamps and coal fires in the waiting rooms disappeared. Station masters continued to preside over station staffs comprising porters and clerks, the stations being fully staffed while traffic ran, and securely locked at other times. This could cause problems for potential passengers if the staff failed to put in an appearance for the first train!

The author of *Snooker Tam* indicated that 'everybody on the Cathcart Circle was a personality' and that 'next to the married men and the typist passengers, the staff was the most interesting gathering outside of Pickard's Waxworks.' Each station tended to have a senior porter in charge, such as Peter McGinley at Langside and Gregor McGregor at Pollokshaws East, whose stentorian tones were heard as late as the 1960s announcing the station name with equal accents on all four syllables as the Blue Trains entered the station. This contrasted with the melodic tones of the porter at Crosshill in 1895 who shouted 'Ker-oss-ell' in the key of F with the centre syllable three and a half tones up and strongly accented.

Often more associated with country lines, gardens were a feature at several stations, and competition was sometimes strong between Langside, Pollokshaws East and Maxwell Park. The remnants of once fine displays on the embankments at Pollokshields East and West are now almost impossible to discern. At Pollokshields East the display was latterly of an engine, at Pollokshields West it was the station name while at Mount Florida, appropriately, a football scene was depicted.

The stationmasters, who were possibly feared more by some

Fairburn 2-6-4T No. 42055 shortly after leaving Maxwell Park with an Outer Circle train. This engine hauled the last regular steam-hauled train on the Inner Circle, the 1pm on Saturday 26th May 1962.

W. S. SELLAR

CR '439' Class 0-4-4T No. 55189 at Pollokshields East with the 4.30pm Outer Circle train on 14th March 1956. A regular engine on the Cathcart Circle in the 1950s, 55189, restored as CR No. 419, is preserved by the Scottish Railway Preservation Society. W. A. C. Smith

passengers than by the station staff, were replaced by an area manager from 28th March 1966. The area covered the Cathcart Circle and the lines to Kirkhill, Neilston, East Kilbride, and the Glasgow Barrhead & Kilmarnock line as far as Lugton, together with the freight branch to Giffen. The area manager's office was at Mount Florida and the accounts and administration offices were established at Queen's Park, where the booking office was reconstructed in the corridor of the existing building.

Fire took its toll on station buildings, Langside being badly damaged on 13th August 1966 and Pollokshields East almost ten years later on 21st April 1976. The booking office remained intact at Langside and a waiting shelter was provided for passengers, but eventually a new station building was provided, at one point having high railings between it and the entrances to ensure revenue protection. Pollokshields East was provided with a new building at the foot of the entrance stairway. The remaining bookstalls at Mount Florida, Langside and Maxwell Park were closed and demolished.

In 1983 Strathclyde Regional Council proposed the closure of the Neilston branch beyond Whitecraigs, which would have resulted in the closure of Patterton and Neilston stations. This never reached any formal stage and it is fortunate that the closure did not take place as new housing development around Patterton has resulted in it now being the fourth busiest in the Cathcart Circle/Newton/Neilston area, the second busiest being Neilston!

From 13th April 1987 the stations between Langside and Pollokshields West became unstaffed, and the other stations on the Circle are staffed only in the mornings. Tickets are issued and checked by travelling ticket collectors on the trains, but in recent years ticket issuing machines have been installed at the stations. After the unstaffing the buildings at Langside, Pollokshaws East and Shawlands were demolished and shelters provided for the passengers. The story of the fate of Maxwell Park and Pollokshields West is told in Chapter 9. Stations are now covered by closed circuit television and many have electronic train information systems. Mount Florida, the busiest on the line, has benefitted from the installation of new toilet facilities and is the only station which has a lift.

There are occasional suggestions for major alterations, such as that in 1987 by the City of Glasgow District Council Town Planning Department that a new interchange station be constructed near Pollokshields East and lines constructed and electrified to permit all South Side lines to be linked to the North Side electrified system through the line past the former St Enoch station, with new stations at Trongate and Hutchesontown. Cathcart was to be provided with platforms on the line from Kirkhill, but trains from the eastern side of the Circle and Neilston would have been unable to access the new interchange. In 1992 the Integrated Transport Strategy for Strathclyde Region suggested the conversion of the Cathcart Circle, including the lines to Newton and Neilston and with new branches to Castlemilk and Newton Mearns, to the light rapid transit system, effectively making it a tramway system, but this did not, of course, come to fruition.

Queen's Park station in 1956. J. F. McEwan

CR '812' Class 0-6-0 No. 57562 passing Glasgow Central signalbox on 9th July 1957. This box controlled the station area from 5th April 1908 to 2nd January 1961.

G. H. ROBIN

CHAPTER 6

ELECTRIFICATION

Nationalisation on 1st January 1948 had little immediate effect on the Cathcart Circle, but the services gradually deteriorated and by the early 1950s off-peak services were very sparse. On 21st September 1953 a regular service was reintroduced with trains every hour on each line, leaving Glasgow Central on the hour for the Inner Circle and on the half hour for the Outer Circle, operating throughout the day until 11pm. The line continued to handle substantial commuter traffic, witnessed by the fact that Circle stations accounted for five of the nine stations where 'Ultimate' ticket issuing machines were first introduced in Scotland on 16th April 1956.

A diesel multiple unit first appeared on the Circle on 7th July 1958. This was a Gloucester RC&W Co. unit from the Edinburgh–Glasgow via Shotts service which was given a filling-in turn round the Circle, contemporary newspapers explaining that this gave the unit a chance to 'cool down' after its long journey from Edinburgh! The first services to be dieselised were the 7.30am and 3.30pm Outer Circle services, together with the 1.25pm Glasgow Central to Whitecraigs and 2.27pm return. The public announcement of the dieselisation included the 9.30pm and 10.30pm services, but the necessity for urgent economies announced on 30th June – only one week before dieselisation – meant that the two trains not only were not dieselised but never ran again as the Circle, along with several other local lines, was closed after 7pm on weekdays and 2pm on

Saturdays. Complaints of rough riding by the twin sets on the route from Edinburgh led to the introduction in December 1958 of a three-car inter-city set on certain services, including the 3.30pm Outer Circle. This set usually included a buffet car, but its services were not available to the Cathcart commuters. The delivery of further twin diesel sets, built by Cravens and Metropolitan Cammell, led to the dieselisation of most off-peak services from 6th July 1959.

Electrification, first considered by the board of the Cathcart District Railway in 1899, was again under discussion following the 1923 grouping. In June 1924 proposals for the electrification of Glasgow's suburban railways were submitted to the Minister of Transport, Mr Harry Gosling, by the Scottish Socialist Group. Neither the Minister nor his department were empowered to impose such a scheme on a railway company, but they could make representations and, it was suggested, make Government financial assistance available under the Trade Facilities Act. The scheme had a two-fold purpose – to bring relief to the overcrowded streets and give work to the unemployed, particularly in the engineering industry.

On 29th November 1924, Dr S. Parker-Smith, Professor of Electrical Engineering at the Royal Technical College, Glasgow, delivered a lecture to the College Scientific Society in which he called for suburban electrification, instancing the Cathcart Circle at an estimated cost of £40,000 per mile. He also suggested that the

A 'Gondola', used for measuring the overhead electric wiring, is propelled through Maxwell Park on 24th July 1963 by English Electric Type 1 (later Class 20) No. D8085. Two of these diesel engines, D8085 and D8086, were fitted with air brakes to move electric multiple units between the North and South Glasgow systems as at that time there was no electrified connection between the two systems.

H. STEVENSON

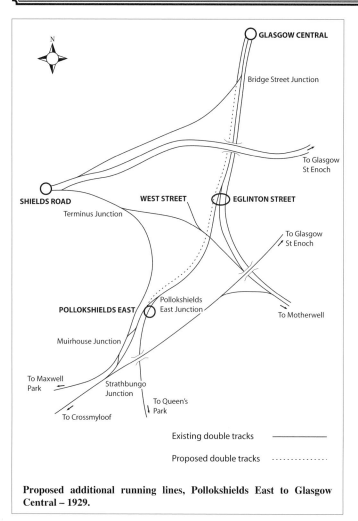

Proposed additional running lines, Pollokshields East to Glasgow Central – 1929.

Existing double tracks ————————

Proposed double tracks ················

City Council should petition Parliament for a law making it illegal to bring steam engines into the city, as in New York.

A similar meeting of the Royal Philosophical Society held on 11th March 1925 heard of a proposal by Mr F. F. P. Bisacre who advocated the electrification of 326 track miles on the 1,500 volts DC system, his plans including the Cathcart Circle, Barrhead and Busby routes, but excluding the lines to Kirkhill and Uplawmoor, as at this time the suburban house building had not spread to the areas served by these lines. The first major proposal to electrify the Cathcart Circle came in 1929, and included the Lanarkshire & Ayrshire lines to Kirkhill and Neilston, reflecting by this time the new use of these routes for suburban commuter traffic. It was, indeed, the outer suburban housing developments which prompted the proposed modernisation. The recently opened King's Park station was proving popular, and a further station between King's Park and Burnside was soon opened at Croftfoot. On the Neilston line housing developments at Williamwood, between Muirend and Whitecraigs, were projected and a further new station was obviously required.

In 1929 the line between Mount Florida and Glasgow was being fully utilised at peak hours and it was impossible to provide additional trains to handle the increased traffic offered, particularly at the morning and evening rush hours, from the new housing estates. This operating problem resulted in poor time-keeping and, despite the railway's attractions – steam heated and electrically lit coaches – over its rivals on the roads, its share of the traffic was not increasing in proportion to the increase in population in the districts served. It was argued that if the lines were not modernised, with the bus and tramway competition becoming more intense, the railway would soon be unable to retain its traffic. A comparison of rail, bus and tram journey times is given in Appendix 12. During the morning

rush hour, trains passed Pollokshields East Junction going into Glasgow Central at an average of three-minute intervals for about one and a half hours. Electrification of existing tracks, incorporating improved signalling, would increase the capacity of this section by only 20–25 per cent, but the provision of an additional pair of running lines between Pollokshields East Junction and Bridge Street Junction would, coupled with electrification, increase capacity by 200 per cent.

The only other track alteration envisaged was the connection between the Lanarkshire & Ayrshire line from King's Park to Muirend and the western half of the Cathcart Circle at Cathcart West Junction to permit through running from Glasgow to Kirkhill via Langside and release more paths on the Mount Florida route for traffic from the Neilston line.

The electric trains to be used were to be in units of three carriages which was sufficient for off-peak services, but could be coupled to provide six-coach trains during the peak hours. Ordinary compartment stock with side doors was chosen in preference to central vestibule stock as this maximised carrying capacity and facilitated quicker loading and unloading. An interesting point which was stressed was the requirement that, for safety reasons, it was essential that the doors opened in the opposite way from the standard practice as the platforms were islands and the inner rather than the outer side of the coach would be at the platform. The three-car sets were designed so that the train was the same from either end and passengers would become familiar with the situation of their accommodation, thus increasing the speed of handling passengers at stations. The middle coach thus contained eight first class compartments providing eighty seats, 30.7 per cent of the three-car unit's accommodation, while the first and third coaches had respectively seven and eight third class compartments providing 180 seats.

Thirty-six of these three-car units were required plus two spare motor vehicles and six spare trailers to cover for repairs and overhaul. Substantial carriage sheds and repair shops were planned for the area between the tracks at Cathcart North Junction. Ten storage roads, each holding six coaches, five of these roads having inspection pits, were envisaged, as well as a repair shop capable of holding two units of three carriages, alongside the existing goods shed.

A complete replacement of the existing signalling equipment to provide shorter sections and complement the increased acceleration of the electric trains was essential. At Cathcart a new power box near the existing Cathcart North Box was to replace the three manual junction signal boxes, while at Muirhouse a similar replacement of Pollokshields East Junction, Strathbungo Junction and Muirhouse Junction was planned. Automatic colour light signals, about a quarter of a mile apart, were to be installed on the section between Pollokshields East and Cathcart via Queen's Park, while the western side of the Circle, where there was to be a less intense service, was to have slightly longer sections. Over the lines from Cathcart to Kirkhill and Neilston the signals were to be as much as a mile apart. All the manual signal boxes were to cease to be block posts, but at all stations where goods yards were retained, including Lyoncross for the connection to the Paisley and Barrhead District line, all the equipment was to be retained for operating the yards, released by electric 'key levers'. The heavy occupancy planned for the eastern half of the Circle and at Cathcart West Junction meant that certain trains serving the Maxwell Park side would require to be turned at Langside by means of an additional crossover, ironically only recently removed with the permanent closure of the signal box after many years of disuse, and a 'key lever' to be operated by the guard.

The major engineering feature of the proposed modernisation was, of course, the quadrupling of the track north of Pollokshields East Junction. The new lines were to leave the line from Pollokshields West, just north of the Albert Road bridge, parallel to the end of Pollokshields East station and run to the west of the existing running lines through Muirhouse sidings and under the reconstructed

Driver	Electrical Equipment	Guard and Luggage	3rd	3rd	3rd	3rd	3rd	3rd	3rd
3' 6"	7' 6"	4' 11"	5' 10"						

Motor Driver Car (58 feet)   84 Third Class Seats

1st	1st	1st	1st	1st	1st	1st	1st
7'							

Trailer (57 feet)   80 First Class Seats

3rd	3rd	3rd	3rd	3rd	3rd	3rd	3rd	Guard and Luggage	Driver
							5' 10"	5' 7"	3' 6"

Driver Trailer (58 feet)   96 Third Class Seats

Proposed three-car electric units, Cathcart electrification scheme – 1929.

Maxwell Road bridge to Eglinton Street station. There was now very little traffic handled at the 'High Level' Circle line platforms and partly for this reason and partly to further speed the services it was intended to close the station. The platform would then be demolished and the new line utilise the area occupied by the old platform and the existing loop line. Closure was also proposed for the small engine shed at Eglinton Street, access to which would become very difficult if the new running lines were built. Fairly substantial arches were required to carry the new lines through Salkeld Street, which was to be reduced in width, to Bridge Street Junction.

The existing engine loop and No. 6 siding between Bridge Street and Central station were to be converted to complete the through running lines, the only major problem being Bridge Street Junction signal box which stood directly in the path of the new lines. The alternatives were to dispense with the box or rebuild it in an adjacent position. The latter exercise was estimated to cost between £50,000 and £60,000 and in view of the simplification of the layout at this point and the resignalling of Central station it was proposed that the signal box be dispensed with. At Glasgow Central five platforms, numbers 6 to 10, were to be equipped for electric trains and the 1908 pneumatic signalling installation, which was already old fashioned, was to be replaced by a colour light system controlled from a new signal box to be constructed between the Clyde Bridges adjacent to the existing box.

The stations were to receive facelifts for the new trains. Some platforms required slight alterations in alignment to take the electric trains and it was also the intention to asphalt all the platforms. All the stations, with the exception of the recently opened King's Park, were lit by gas and the modernisation proposals included the replacement of this outdated system by electric illumination. Stairway improvements were required at Mount Florida, Langside and Pollokshaws East, while a thoughtful consideration for intending passengers was the suggested construction of covered ways along the centres of the platforms to the verandahs so that the passengers would be under cover from the time they arrived at the stations. Automatic ticket issuing machines for booking to Glasgow Central were planned, but normal booking office facilities for other destinations were to be retained. Indeed, additions to station staff were envisaged, possibly by redeploying the men made redundant from the signal boxes to be closed.

While the tank locomotives working the Cathcart Circle trains were between twenty and thirty years old, the vintage coaches had only recently been replaced by nine rakes of five-coach vacuum braked compartment stock at a cost of £141,000. This stock was to be transferred to the Central underground lines – although steam would not disappear from the Queen's Park section of the line as Lanarkshire & Ayrshire trains to Ardrossan were still to be steam hauled, but were to run as expresses between Glasgow and Neilston. Five electric power sub-stations were needed to feed the new overhead wires, at Kirkhill, Lyoncross, Cathcart North Junction, Muirhouse Junction and Glasgow Central.

The estimated cost of the scheme totalled £1,470,600, made up:

	£	£
Rolling stock, electrical plant and sub-stations		1,000,000
Signalling:		
120 Automatic colour light signals	72,000	
Glasgow Central – new signal box	4,000	
150 track circuits	15,000	
new locking frame	90,000	
Eglinton Street Junction – 50 lever power frame	15,000	
Muirhouse Junction – 100 lever power frame	30,000	
Cathcart – 100 lever power frame	30,000	
Ten stations to be equipped with master levers	10,000	
Four illuminated diagrams	4,600	
Automatic magazine train describers:		
Glasgow Central, Eglinton Street (2), Muirhouse (2), Cathcart	10,000	
Alterations to telegraph lines	7,000	
		287,600
Engineering works between Central, Bridge Street and Smithy Lye		28,000
Widening of line between Bridge Street and Pollokshields East Junction		72,000
Other land works and alterations		35,000
Carriage sheds and sidings at Cathcart		45,000
Alterations in carriage gas supply at Dawsholm		3,000
		1,470,600

The increase in traffic envisaged is best seen from the statistics for weekly train mileage:

	To be withdrawn Present steam mileage	To commence with Proposed electric mileage	Possible maximum Electric mileage
Cathcart Circle trains	4,424	9,480	12,204
Glasgow – Kirkhill	1,330	2,320	7,641
Glasgow – Neilston	1,296	2,300	5,417
	7,050	14,100	25,262

An increase in revenue of £30,000, or 40 per cent of the present earnings, was estimated for the first year of electric traction, and it was anticipated that the increased housing should lead to an additional revenue of 10 per cent per annum for the next ten years. Application was made for Government assistance, but nothing came of this ambitious project as it could not be commercially justified and it was not until after Nationalisation in 1948 that proposals were once again made for electrification.

Following the change from cable to electric traction on the Glasgow Subway in 1935 an extension was planned in 1937 between Robroyston and King's Park, utilising the existing route between Buchanan Street and Bridge Street stations. The Second World War intervened to prevent the construction of this line and in 1948 Mr E. R. L. Fitzpayne submitted to the Corporation Transport Committee his 'Report on the Future Development of Passenger Transport in Glasgow'. The original remit had been to consider an extension of the subway to serve the housing estates in the east of the city, but the eventual proposal was for a new electric railway from Tollcross to Barrhead running underground between Castle Street and Pollokshields, parallel to the existing subway between Buchanan Street and Bridge Street.

Also proposed was the merging of Glasgow's four main-line terminal stations into two – a 'North' and a 'South' station, with the new line passing under both stations. The new line was to be of standard four feet eight and a half inches gauge rather than the four feet gauge of the existing subway and a connection with the Cathcart Circle at Pollokshields East was proposed to allow through running from the existing south suburban routes to the north. The stations on the new line were to have no platforms, access to the trains being direct from subways between the tracks. The relevant access doors would be under the control of the train drivers.

The Fitzpayne proposals were overtaken by the Inglis Report in 1951. This report recommended the electrification of the Cathcart Circle, the extension of the station at Cathcart to include platforms on the adjacent Lanarkshire & Ayrshire line, and the provision of a new connection at Cathcart to permit through running from Kirkhill to the western side of the Circle, at an estimated cost of £25,000 for engineering works and £7,000 for signalling. New halts, costing an estimated £7,000 each, were to be provided to serve the housing areas between Croftfoot and Burnside, and between Burnside and Kirkhill. It was anticipated that King's Park would be a railhead for connecting bus services to the neighbouring housing schemes. The proposed electrification was to be in three stages, the Cathcart Circle being included in the first stage and the Uplawmoor and Kirkhill routes, together with the circular line from Kirkhill to Motherwell and Hamilton, in the second. The trains were to be three-car units with one power car, using the 1,500 volts DC overhead

A steam hauled excursion calls at Shawlands after electrification. The new lighting had only recently been installed, gas lighting still being in use when electric services started.

H. STEVENSON

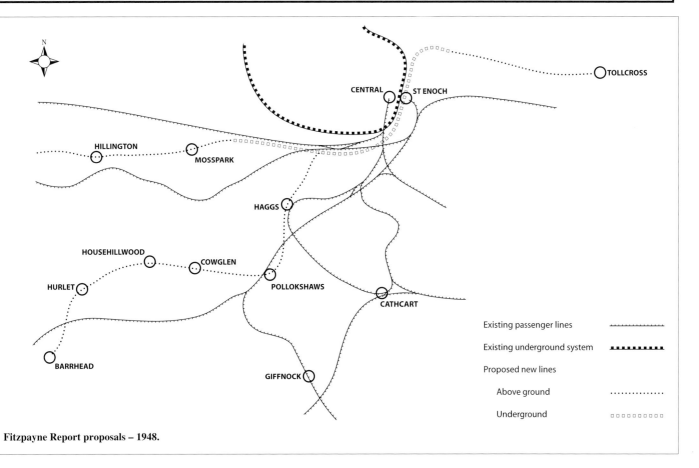

Fitzpayne Report proposals – 1948.

Legend:

Existing passenger lines

Existing underground system

Proposed new lines

    Above ground

    Underground

Pollokshaws East after the construction of the high-rise flats which now dominate the scene. The clock on the left and the barometer on the right (presented by a number of subscribers on 1st May 1912) can be clearly seen at the booking office end of the station building.

YOUR Blue Trains to Glasgow
from Langside and Newlands

Via Queen's Park		Via Maxwell Park
2 TRAINS AN HOUR USUALLY AT 2 & 32	**WEEKDAYS**	**4 TRAINS AN HOUR USUALLY AT** 15 & 45 29 & 59
Minutes past the hour from 6.32 a.m. to 11.32 p.m.		Minutes past the hour from 6.15 a.m. to 11.29 p.m. NOTE:—5.59 p.m. train runs on Saturdays only
HOURLY AT 38	**SUNDAYS**	**2 TRAINS AN HOUR AT** 12 & 43
Minutes past the hour from 9.38 a.m. to 10.38 p.m.		Minutes past the hour from 9.12 a.m. to 10.43 p.m.
13 MINUTES	**JOURNEY TIME**	12 MINUTES

YOUR FARES

CHEAP SINGLE - - - - - 7d.
CHEAP DAY RETURN - - - - 11d.

SEASON TICKETS

WEEKLY - - - - - 7/6
MONTHLY - - - - - 28/-
THREE MONTHLY - - - - 76/-

Special Season Ticket Rates for young people under 18 years

REMEMBER YOUR SEASON TICKET INCLUDES WEEKEND TRAVEL AT NO EXTRA COST

Ask at your Station for the new Glasgow Electric Timetable for full train service details and particulars of additional weekday trains at the morning and evening peaks

B.R. 35001—B 33554—YC—May, 1962.   McCorquodale, Glasgow

system, the existing motive power depots being adapted for the new sets.

The announcement that electrification was at last to become a reality came on 27th April 1956. Seventy-one route miles were to be electrified, covering the lines through Queen Street Low Level to Helensburgh, Balloch, Milngavie, Airdrie and Bridgeton Central and from Glasgow to Kirkhill, Neilston High and the Cathcart Circle. The lines north of the Clyde were to be ready for traffic before those south of the river due to the substantial engineering work required in re-signalling Central station. The system to be used departed quite dramatically from the previous proposals in that the 25Kv overhead method, pioneered by French National Railways and already used successfully in a British Railways experiment between Lancaster and Morecambe in 1952, was to be used. Clearance problems meant that voltage reduction to 6.25Kv was required within the Glasgow City boundary.

Much of the work involved in the modernisation concerned the complete re-signalling of the area and this is dealt with in the next chapter. The electric service on the network north of the Clyde commenced on 7th November 1960 and it was only after that date that efforts were concentrated on the south lines. By this time the route to be electrified had been extended to include the section of the Lanarkshire & Ayrshire between Kirkhill and Newton and the main line from there to Motherwell via Uddingston.

It was no easy task to rebuild a railway and endeavour at the same time to maintain a regular service. During off-peak times one of the 'circles' was closed, the services being diverted to the other rail; thus engineers could enjoy a lengthy occupation of the Inner Circle while

LEFT: Handbill for the opening of the electric services in 1962.

BELOW: An electric multiple unit approaching Maxwell Park on the Inner Circle on the first day of electric operation, Sunday 27th May 1962.   J. L. STEVENSON

ABOVE: The first electric multiple unit to appear in Glasgow Central. Unit 004 on display in September 1959 as part of the Scottish Industries Exhibition.

J. L. STEVENSON

BELOW: In 'Strathclyde red' livery of the 1990s, unit 303043 leaves Shawlands on the Outer Circle.

J. KERNAHAN

ABOVE: Since the withdrawal of the Class 303 units, Circle services have been operated almost exclusively by Class 314 units, built in 1979 for the reopening of the Central Low Level lines. Unit 314213 awaits departure from the refurbished Maxwell Park. J. KERNAHAN

LEFT: AM3 (later Class 303) electric unit 036 enters Maxwell Park on New Year's Day 1965 with the 15.02 Glasgow to Motherwell. One train per hour operated on the Western side of the Circle on this day – the day, incidentally, on which British Railways became British Rail. H. STEVENSON

Queen's Park by night in January 1958. Queen's Park and Crosshill stations were given electric lighting and heating at that time, prior to the other Circle stations. The booking office now occupies this end of the station building. Note the well-lit signalbox on the platform.   BRITISH RAILWAYS

...ll trains ran on the Outer Circle and vice versa. From 6th March ...961 the opening of the new connection at Cathcart permitted the ...1.10am and 3.21pm trains from Glasgow to Kirkhill to run via ...axwell Park, further facilitating the electrification work.

Delays were nonetheless inevitable during this period, particularly ...ollowing the opening of the new power signal box at Glasgow Central on ...nd January 1961. For the first three days Gourock and Wemyss Bay ...ervices were diverted to St Enoch, but thereafter chaos reigned, and ...he passengers soon deserted the trains for more reliable transport. ...lasgow Corporation was not slow to take advantage of the situation ...nd notices appeared in their buses apologising for the overcrowding ...due to the present rail irregularities'. The major disruption occurred ...t the end of April 1961 when the work on replacing the girder bridge ...arrying the Circle over the Glasgow Barrhead & Kilmarnock line at ...hawlands station was not completed during the weekend as intended. ...s explained earlier, historical agreements had resulted in the bridge ...eing much larger than originally intended, provision being made ...or the quadrupling of the GB&K line, an event which, of course, ...ad never taken place. On Monday 1st May 1961 the new bridge ...vas not in position and Cathcart and Maxwell Park became termini ...or the day, with diesel multiple units providing shuttle services with ...lasgow Central and buses providing a connecting service between ...he two Circle stations.

On Sunday 10th December 1961 electric power was switched on ...hroughout the Cathcart Circle, the Neilston branch, Platforms 6–11 ...t Glasgow Central and the section from Bridge Street to Smithy Lye ...arriage sidings. Trials with the electric multiple units commenced on ...8th December when units 015 and 075 ran from Glasgow to Neilston ...nd back, and after that the new 'blue trains' became a regular ...ight on the Cathcart Circle during the mornings and afternoons. ...ull trials on Sundays commenced on 25th February 1962 and on ...th May it was announced that public services would commence on ...unday 27th May. On 9th May a special electric train, conveying the

Lord Provost of Motherwell and several British Railways officials, ran from Glasgow to Motherwell and back.

The Lanarkshire & Ayrshire line had only been electrified as far as Neilston – the line beyond, and the station at Uplawmoor, closing to passengers with effect from 2nd April 1962, from which date the station on the nearby Glasgow Barrhead & Kilmarnock line which was previously known as Caldwell was renamed Uplawmoor for Caldwell. Another station which closed following electrification was Strathbungo on the GB&K line adjacent to Pollokshields West, although it survived until Saturday 26th May, the day before the new trains commenced.

As with the routes north of the river, regular Sunday services had never been provided on the Cathcart Circle, but Sunday 27th May 1962 saw this dramatically altered as a full weekday service was operated. The new service, offering a fifteen-minute service over the Circle and Kirkhill lines and a thirty-minute service to Motherwell and Neilston, was an outstanding success. During the first week 150,000 passengers were carried, compared with 53,000 prior to electrification. Revenue increased by 175 per cent, and numbers of passengers trebled at Muirend and Whitecraigs.

British Railways were not entirely confident about the reliability of the new units, as steam engines were strategically placed in the goods yards to rescue failed trains. Their services were required, as on Wednesday 30th May a failure caused the first major disruption, and Standard 4-6-0 No. 73063 was to be seen hauling an electric set ignominiously through Queen's Park station.

The modernisation of the railways encompassed the stations as well as the trains. Electric lighting replaced the old gas installations, except at King's Park and Croftfoot where the original LMSR lighting was retained, and at Patterton where the retention of the paraffin lamps contrasted strongly with the 25Kv running through the wires above the tracks. The old brown and cream colours of the 1950s gave way to new shades of light and dark grey and the glass canopies of the original Circle stations were given a thorough clean. New hoardings for posters, of a much lighter construction than the originals they replaced, were put up, but unfortunately the poles on which those at Pollokshaws East and Cathcart were erected were not strong enough for the exposed position of these platforms, and one morning after gale-force winds the station staff arrived to find the boards bent parallel to the platforms. This rather embarrassing matter was rectified as quickly as possible.

One original plan for the stations included in the electrification proposals was that they should be extended to take nine-coach electric trains. This would have involved substantial engineering operations at most stations due to their island construction and was never carried out. The only major alteration which was made was at Cathcart, where the track alterations necessary to allow through running from the western half of the Circle to the Kirkhill line caused the southern end of the platform to be cut away. A permanent extension was constructed at the northern end, but as this gave only a platform accommodating a six-coach electric train, a temporary wooden-sleeper extension was provided during the remaining period of steam operation. At Crosshill the track was lowered under the adjacent road bridge to give the required clearance for the wires and consequently the platform was also lowered. The station building is thus now surrounded by concrete round its exposed foundations. This narrow building by this time incorporated the booking office which had been housed in a small building at street level until the late 1950s. Langside and Newlands station reverted to its original name of Langside when electric services commenced.

Another interesting feature in connection with stations was the retention at Lyoncross on the former Lanarkshire & Ayrshire between Patterton and Neilston of the slewed track provided in connection with the Paisley & Barrhead District Railway. At the time of the electrification of the Neilston line the suburb of Auchenback was developing to the south-east of Barrhead, and it was intended that a station be built at last at Lyoncross to serve this new community. No platform was built at this time and although the track remains slewed it is unlikely that it will ever be constructed.

ABOVE: Queen's Park station shortly after electrification.

RIGHT: Fairburn 2-6-4T No. 42276 on a Neilston train after the remodelling of Cathcart West junction and the replacement of the junction signal seen in the photograph on page 42 with two separate signals.   J. R. HUME

CHAPTER 7

SIGNALLING AND ACCIDENTS

A traveller on the Cathcart Circle a century ago would pass the almost incredible number of seventeen signalboxes on the 8-mile round trip from Glasgow Central back to Glasgow Central, thirteen of them on the 5¼ miles of the Circle itself.

The first signalbox to come into use was Cathcart Junction, where the new line to Cathcart left the 1879 Central Station extension line from Strathbungo to Eglinton Street, which was provisionally sanctioned for use on 21st December 1885 to allow access for construction materials. The box had a 15-lever frame, eleven of the levers being working, with four spare. When the Cathcart line was opened to traffic on 1st March 1886, in addition to Cathcart Junction, signalboxes were provided at Queen's Park, Crosshill and Mount Florida. The box at Queen's Park was not a yet block post, having only four of its eight levers in use, a home and a distant on each line used solely for the protection of trains standing at the platform. At Crosshill all eight levers were in use as there was a crossover, necessary because there was only a single line in operation from there to Mount Florida due to the failure of a retaining wall. Mount Florida had a 13-lever frame, all but two of which were in use. Signals were also provided at Pollokshields East, operated from Muirhouse box, which did not

lie on the line but which was perfectly sited to give the signalman a clear view of passing trains. Muirhouse, which had opened on 1st July 1879 when the Central station extension line opened, took its name from the small hamlet called Muir Houses which had been built during the eighteenth century along Pollokshaws Road close to what is now known as Eglinton Toll, but was originally called Muirhouse Toll. The signalbox when opened had a 40-lever frame. At the time of the opening of the Cathcart branch thirty-seven levers were in use.

The single line between Crosshill and Mount Florida was worked by train staff and tickets, the staff and tickets being coloured red. This lasted until the line's opening to Cathcart, the section from Crosshill to Mount Florida being doubled from that date. The new box at Cathcart had a 20-lever frame, of which three were spare.

The line between Strathbungo Junction and Terminus had opened as a single line through countryside and orchards on 30th March 1849. Within ten years it had been doubled, but it was not until 20th October 1892 that it was approved for use by passenger traffic. By this time all forty levers in Muirhouse Junction signalbox were in use. When the Cathcart Circle extension line was authorised, it was intended that it would join the Central Station extension line at Strathbungo Junction, where a new signalbox had been opened on

CR '782' Class 0-6-0 No. 56305 passing through Cathcart station on the Outer Circle with a short freight on 28th October 1955. The section of platform beyond the station entrance seen in the photograph, on which the photographer is standing, was removed when Cathcart West Junction was remodelled in 1961.

W. A. C. SMITH

Bridge Street Junction signalbox, which closed on 2nd January 1961.

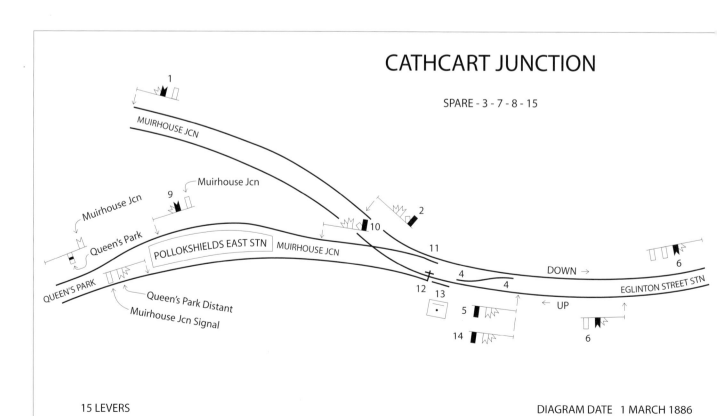

CATHCART JUNCTION

SPARE - 3 - 7 - 8 - 15

15 LEVERS

DIAGRAM DATE 1 MARCH 1886

POLLOKSHIELDS EAST JUNCTION

SPACE - 7

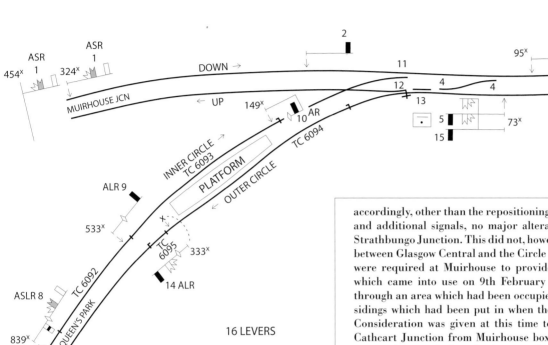

16 LEVERS

DIAGRAM DATE 1929

1st July 1879 replacing an earlier small box adjacent to the junction points on the northern side of the line on the Glasgow side of the Nithsdale Road bridge. The proposed new junction at Strathbungo would have required the reconstruction of the junction between the Central Station extension line and the Terminus line 112 feet nearer Glasgow. However, it was decided in 1893 that the Cathcart Circle should join the Terminus line at Muirhouse Junction and that,

accordingly, other than the repositioning of a siding and some altered and additional signals, no major alterations would be required at Strathbungo Junction. This did not, however, permit through running between Glasgow Central and the Circle extension and further works were required at Muirhouse to provide the necessary connection, which came into use on 9th February 1894, and was constructed through an area which had been occupied by two headshunts for the sidings which had been put in when the signalbox opened in 1879. Consideration was given at this time to the possibility of working Cathcart Junction from Muirhouse box, but it was to be a further sixty-eight years before this happened.

An enlarged signalbox was constructed at Muirhouse which came into use in December 1893. A 72-lever frame was provided, fifty-three of which were in use. The substantial additional traffic to be handled by the signalman at Muirhouse meant that it would have been difficult for him to continue to oversee movements through Pollokshields East station, and accordingly a 9-lever signalbox was provided at the Queen's Park end of the platform, brought into use on 20th December 1893, although formal inspection was not until February 1894. The Cathcart District Railway received a bill from

POLLOKSHIELDS EAST STATION

SPARE - 3 - 5

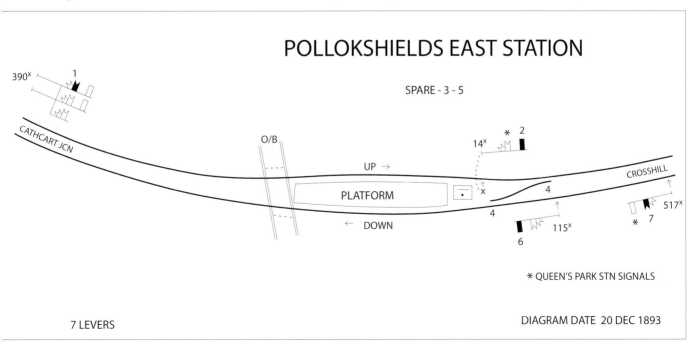

* QUEEN'S PARK STN SIGNALS

7 LEVERS

DIAGRAM DATE 20 DEC 1893

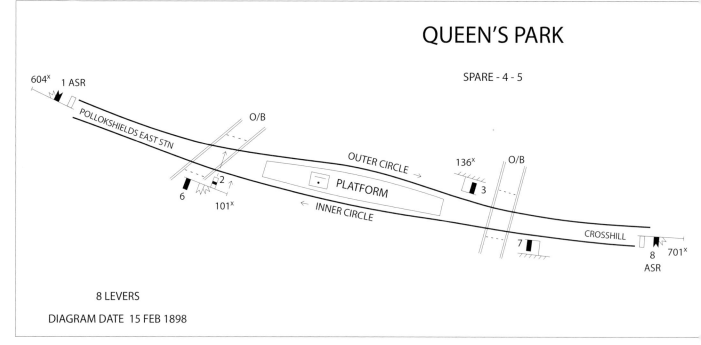

QUEEN'S PARK

SPARE - 4 - 5

604ˣ   1 ASR

POLLOKSHIELDS EAST STN

O/B

OUTER CIRCLE →

136ˣ   O/B

PLATFORM

2

6

101ˣ

← INNER CIRCLE

3

CROSSHILL

7

8   701ˣ
ASR

8 LEVERS

DIAGRAM DATE 15 FEB 1898

Queen's Park signalbox. Behind the box is the 3.30pm Outer Circle, formed of an InterCity diesel multiple unit, which went round the Circle between Edinburgh Princes Street–Glasgow Central duties.

J. R. Hume

he Caledonian for £3:3/- for the clock in the new signalbox. Only seven levers were in use, three for home, starting and distant signals on each line and one for the new crossover provided just beyond the box in the direction of Queen's Park. The Board of Trade inspector, Major General Hutchinson, initially required runaway points on the line from Queen's Park, a full train's length from the home signal, but when it was pointed out that before reaching Queen's Park the gradient rose, the Board accepted that there was no danger of a runaway vehicle reaching the next block post and did not insist on the runaway points. Queen's Park was not at this time a block post. It did not achieve this status, with the necessary additional signalling, until 15th February 1898.

In June 1892 a temporary siding was laid at Cathcart, behind the single line platform, to the masonry pier being constructed for the bridge over the river Cart, to provide access for the contractors to bring materials to the site. This siding was fully interlocked in the signalbox and utilised two of the three spare levers available.

The Circle extension line was ready for inspection at the end of February 1894 and Major General Hutchinson reported on 10th March that he had 'inspected the extension of the Cathcart District Railway from Cathcart station to its junction with the Caledonian Railway at Muirhouse Junction, near Strathbungo Junction, a length of 3 miles 15.23 chains.' He explained in his report that 'by means of this extension line trains will be able to run from the Central Station by the old line and back to the Central Station by the new line and vice versa without the engine having to leave the head of its train.' He reported that before the new line could be opened a considerable amount of work was required in connecting the new line with the old line at Cathcart station. For this purpose it was necessary to temporarily use the new station at Cathcart as a terminal. He had no objection to this, subject to proper signal arrangements being temporarily made in the old cabin at Cathcart. The new station at Cathcart accordingly opened on 19th March 1894, when the new Cathcart signalbox replaced the 1886 box. The full Circle opened on 2nd April 1894. A further inspection, reported on 21st April, confirmed that, apart from a small adjustment required at the goods yard connection at Cathcart, the remedial works required by the previous inspection had been carried out. These were principally the installation of runaway points at Shawlands and Langside, fencing at the top of the bank at Pollokshaws East and the fitting of handrails on two bridges.

Signalboxes were provided at all stations, including a new box at Cathcart, approximately 70 yards south of the original box. The boxes at Cathcart, Pollokshaws East and Maxwell Park, which controlled access to goods yards, had 17-lever frames, while the boxes at the other three stations had 10-lever frames. The boxes at these three stations had seven working levers, three for the signals on each line plus a crossover. The number of working levers at the other boxes were twelve at Cathcart, fifteen at Pollokshaws East and fourteen at Maxwell Park – which also had a 2-lever dwarf frame controlled from the box to permit exit from the goods yard, due to the distance of the exit from the box and the lack of visibility because of the intervening road bridge. This frame was governed by a series of rather complex regulations. It could only be unlocked by the Staff Key which was kept by the signalman. To unlock the frame the key had to be inserted in the Staff Box beside the frame and given a half turn to the right. This released the levers which had to be placed in their normal positions before the key could be withdrawn. No. 1 lever worked the points and No. 2 the ground signal controlling the exit from the yard. The station porter operated the frame as required during the day, but at night, or when the station staff were off duty, it was worked by the guard or, in the case of a light engine, the fireman. The release of the key from the signalbox locked the Inner Circle home signals, so that if any trains were to remain in the sidings for a considerable time the frame had to be locked and the key returned to the signalman.

The contract for the signalling of the extension had been awarded to the Railway Signal Company of Fazakerley, Liverpool and accordingly the signalboxes were not of standard Caledonian design. All were substantial boxes, the only anomaly being Langside which, despite the availability of plenty of land as the company had acquired sufficient to construct a goods yard, was placed on the station platform between the entrance and the platform building. It was a much larger box than Crosshill and Queen's Park and was accessed by a short flight of steps.

In connection with the opening of the Cathcart Circle an additional loop line and island platform were constructed at Eglinton Street early in 1894, so that two Glasgow-bound trains could be at the station at the same time for ticket collection purposes. The existing down platform was widened to form the new island platform, a passenger shelter provided and a new subway constructed to connect the platform with the rest of the station.

At Pollokshaws East and Maxwell Park distant signals were provided in respect of the access to the loops. These were removed in January 1905.

At the beginning of the twentieth century there was a pattern service operating with an interval between trains on each circle of twenty minutes, the trains leaving Glasgow for the Inner Circle on the hour and at 20 and 40 minutes past the hour, and for the

Queen's Park Outer Circle starting signal, seen from the front of a diesel multiple unit. In the walled cuttings, some signals had to be mounted on the walls, and the anchor points for this signal are still visible today.

J. R. HUME

The Crosshill Outer Circle home signal. Work has started on installing the posts for the electric catenary.

J. R. HUME

Outer Circle at 10, 30 and 50 minutes past the hour from 6am until 11.25pm. Although additional trains were operated at peak periods such a service did not require as many signal boxes as then existed on the line, and those on the extension at Langside and Newlands, Shawlands and Pollokshields West were closed from 5th November 1900. Crosshill was opened only at peak periods and Queen's Park was opened only when required. The closure of the extension line signal boxes resulted in some alterations to peak hour services. The 8.15am and 8.32am Inner Circle trains from Shawlands and the 8.55am Inner Circle train from Langside and Newlands now started from Pollokshaws East.

The next major signalling alterations came with the opening of the Lanarkshire & Ayrshire Railway. During the construction a temporary signal box, opened only when required for construction trains, was provided from March 1902 at the site of what was to become Cathcart North Junction, although it was actually eight chains on the Mount Florida side of Cathcart North Junction box and on the other side of the track, the key being kept under the control of the signalman at Cathcart. A similar box was in use on the Busby Junction to East Kilbride line at Clarkston, admitting trains for the construction of the L&AR between that point and Lugton.

The permanent alterations took place as far as the Cathcart Circle was concerned on 1st May 1903 when the 1894 box at Cathcart was closed and replaced by new boxes at Cathcart North Junction and Cathcart West Junction. To avoid confusion Cathcart Junction was renamed Pollokshields East Junction on 1st July 1903. A list of signal boxes on the Lanarkshire & Ayrshire Railway is contained in Appendix 6, but it is worth mentioning at this point the closure of the 31.5-chain connecting spur between Clarkston East and West Junctions. This spur was used only by the freight traffic from Lanarkshire to Ardrossan prior to the opening of the line through Burnside and thus became redundant a mere nine months after its opening when the Burnside line opened on 6th January 1904. The two junction signal boxes were officially closed on 29th October 1907. Clarkston East Junction signal box was not, however, removed until 1930, by which time Williamwood station had been built on the site of the West Junction thus precluding the reopening of the spur.

Similarly, although closed in 1900, the boxes at Langside and Newlands, Shawlands and Pollokshields West remained fully equipped, and by 1905 Langside and Newlands had been reopened, even if for only thirty minutes during the morning peak traffic. Queen's Park and Crosshill boxes were similarly opened only at peak hours, although their facilities were required in the morning and evening. Station staff at these five stations were exempted from the normal regulations requiring the signals to be put at danger behind trains stopping at platforms for a normal period while the signal boxes were switched out, although, if trains were likely to be delayed at the station, the signal had to be replaced to protect the train. Similarly the home and distant signal lamps were kept lit although the starters were not.

With the increase in passenger traffic over the eastern half of the Circle caused by the opening of the Lanarkshire & Ayrshire, Crosshill and Queen's Park were soon opened all day, but no such increase was forthcoming on the western half. The three boxes lay unused, with their signals permanently lowered, for nearly twenty-seven years.

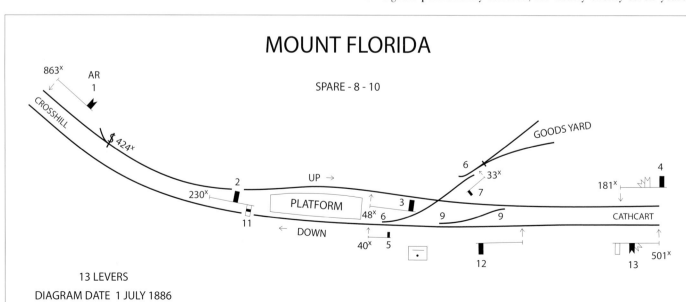

MOUNT FLORIDA

SPARE - 8 - 10

13 LEVERS

DIAGRAM DATE 1 JULY 1886

except for the occasional use of Langside and Newlands during the first decade of the twentieth century. The Caledonian and Cathcart District Railways must have been over-optimistic that a five-minute interval service would eventually be needed, although how Glasgow Central could have accommodated the trains is difficult to imagine. The local station staff did not, however, share their employers' optimism, and by the 1920s Langside and Newlands signal box had been converted by the stationmaster into a very pleasant greenhouse. The LMSR equally did not share their predecessors' hopes for expansion and the equipment was finally removed with the official closure of the boxes on 23rd August 1927.

On the original line to Cathcart the signalboxes were of standard wooden construction, with the exception of Crosshill and Queen's Park which were small wood-and-brick buildings situated on the platforms. The boxes opened in 1903 at Cathcart in connection with the Lanarkshire & Ayrshire Railway were of current Caledonian design in common with the others on that railway and were much more commodious. Cathcart North Junction was of wooden construction and had a 32-lever frame of which only one was spare, twenty-three levers being required for the Cathcart circle and eight for the L&AR. It controlled Cathcart goods yard, access to which was off a loop line built from the single line leading to Burnside constructed in September 1907, as well as the burrowing single line from Cathcart East Junction. Cathcart West Junction was built of brick and had a 34-lever frame of which twenty-eight were in use, one was spare and there were five spaces. Six of the working levers were used for the Cathcart Circle, fourteen solely for the Lanarkshire & Ayrshire line and the remaining eight controlled the junction.

In December 1906 Muirhouse Junction was remodelled by a general slewing of the lines to improve the curves with a rearrangement of the junctions and siding connections. The layout now made the route between Pollokshields West and Pollokshields East Junction the principal route with no difficult curves, resulting in easier running through the junction for Cathcart Circle trains. It became less obvious that the original line at this point, built nearly sixty years earlier, had been the single line connection from Strathbungo to Terminus. Part of the works at this time involved the construction of a signal gantry just to the Glasgow side of Strathbungo Junction signalbox. The gantry was removed in 1961, but the brick supporting piers are still extant. After the remodelling the number of levers in use at Muirhouse increased by one to fifty-four. Despite the remodelling, old names were still in use until 1960 in Strathbungo Junction box where the brass plates on the block instruments for the two double tracks to Muirhouse Junction read 'Central Extension Line' and

The Crosshill Inner Circle starting signal, with the Queen's Park distant mounted below. Only five distant signals on the Circle had their own posts when the line was originally signalled. G. H. ROBIN/
BY COURTESY OF THE MITCHELL LIBRARY, GLASGOW CITY COUNCIL

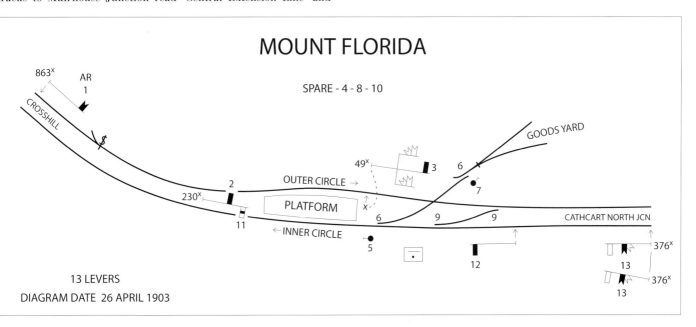

MOUNT FLORIDA

SPARE - 4 - 8 - 10

863ˣ AR
1

CROSSHILL

GOODS YARD

49ˣ 3 6

OUTER CIRCLE →

2 7

230ˣ PLATFORM

11 x

6 9 9 CATHCART NORTH JCN

← INNER CIRCLE

5

12 376ˣ

13

13 LEVERS

DIAGRAM DATE 26 APRIL 1903

376ˣ

CATHCART NORTH JUNCTION

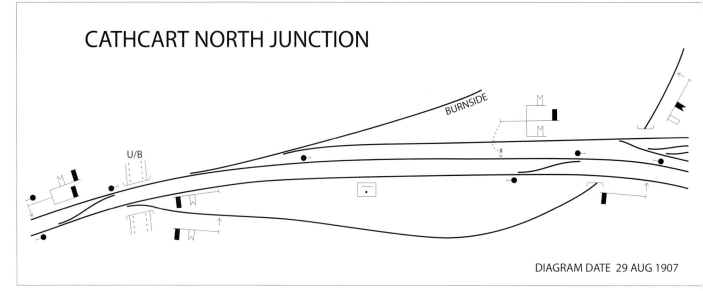

DIAGRAM DATE 29 AUG 1907

'Terminus Line'. The large box at Muirhouse contrasted strongly with the adjacent box at Cathcart Junction (later Pollokshields East Junction) which had only a 15-lever frame, two of which were spare, making it a smaller installation than Pollokshaws East.

For many years the intensity of the passenger traffic made it necessary for the bulk of the freight traffic to be worked at night. The train left Polmadie every night, except Saturdays and Sundays, at 11pm and on Sunday nights at 11.55pm. It ran via West Street and Terminus Junction where it ran round and proceeded to Muirhouse Junction. To avoid all the signal boxes on the Cathcart Circle remaining open the signalman from Cathcart North Junction met the train at Muirhouse Junction and worked the signal boxes at Maxwell Park, Pollokshaws East and Mount Florida. Cathcart West Junction remained open all night and worked to Bridge Street Junction, all other boxes being closed and the points at Eglinton Street and Pollokshields East Junction set in favour of the line via Queen's Park. This was principally for the operating of night traffic, particularly boat trains, to Ardrossan and it was necessary that the nightly freight trip round the Circle did not interfere with any of these trains. If the freight did require to go forward to Cathcart or Mount Florida it was necessary for the travelling signalman to telephone the signalman at Cathcart West Junction and switch in the boxes at Cathcart North Junction and Mount Florida for the duration of the time when the freight was shunting the yard. The freight was specifically prohibited from returning to Polmadie via Bridge Street and had to go via Maxwell Park.

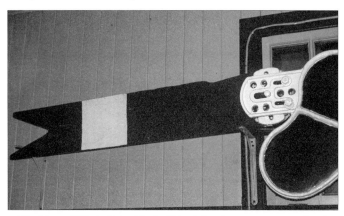

The Maxwell Park Outer Circle distant signal arm, as preserved and restored to its original red colour, mounted inside the former station master's room in the late 1960s. A photograph of it in its original position appears on page 29.   J. KERNAHAN

The first signal box to close officially, other than the two boxes at Cathcart which had been replaced in 1894 and 1903, was Pollokshields East on 7th August 1921, its function and several of its signals being transferred to Pollokshields East Junction. This economy was possible due to the installation of track circuiting permitting the Pollokshields East Junction signalman to have an electrical indication in his signal box of the presence of trains in the station as well as a safety lock on the relevant protecting signals. The Caledonian suggested this economy to the Cathcart District Board in 1919, and on 10th November of that year the Chairman of the CDR wrote to the Caledonian approving the closure. Strangely it took nearly two years before the work was carried out.

Prior to the closure in 1927 of Langside and Newlands, Shawlands and Pollokshields West signal boxes, the Cathcart Circle was so closely signalled that only five distant signals required individual posts, all others being mounted beneath the starting signal of the box in rear. The distants which had their own posts were, on the Inner Circle, those for Shawlands and Crosshill and, on the Outer Circle, those for Crosshill, Mount Florida and Maxwell Park. The removal of the redundant signals in 1927 was very neatly and thoroughly done, with the distants where mounted below the starters being heightened to the position of the starters at all stations except at Pollokshields West station, where the Muirhouse Junction Outer Circle and Maxwell Park Inner Circle distants were replaced by LMSR 'corrugated' type upper quadrants in the same position as the Caledonian ones they replaced.

The next LMSR 'corrugated' type upper quadrant signals on the Cathcart Circle were installed in 1936. This followed provision, after approval of the proposal by the relevant Scottish local committee on 15th September of that year, of an outer home signal from the Pollokshaws East direction at Cathcart West Junction with the distant signal being moved out to the required braking distance, resulting in the distant signal being sited immediately opposite the Langside and Newlands station building. This additional signal was required to permit the free acceptance of a train from the Lanarkshire & Ayrshire line. In addition to improving the timekeeping of existing services the alteration allowed additional services – which were now required due to the building developments around Williamwood and Whitecraigs – to be introduced.

The next signal box closure occurred on 6th March 1938 when Mount Florida was closed partly as an economy and partly to allow the construction of the additional platform for football special traffic. The starting signals were retained, the arms being replaced by the only LMSR 'corrugated' arms on the line other than those mentioned earlier and became intermediate block signals controlled

CATHCART

17 LEVERS (12 WORKING, 5 SPACES)

DIAGRAM DATE 26 MARCH 1894

632ˣ   228ˣ   60ˣ   GOODS YARD

MOUNT FLORIDA

312ˣ   109ˣ

OUTER CIRCLE
INNER CIRCLE

PLATFORM

333ˣ

351ˣ   LANGSIDE

1146ˣ

Cathcart West Junction, with a 2-6-4T approaching the station with a train from Neilston.   H. C. CASSERLEY

by Crosshill and Cathcart North Junction signal boxes. Cathcart North also assumed control of Mount Florida goods yard which was now controlled by a ground frame released by Annetts Key. Despite the fact that Arthur F. Bound, the LMSR Signal and Telegraph Engineer from 1929 to 1944, had required all signals to be placed on the left of the running line, banner repeaters being provided in cases of poor visibility, the intermediate block signals at Mount Florida were situated at either end of the island platform on the right hand side of the running line. Due to the circular nature of the line,

several signals were similarly placed between the Inner and Outer Circles, but probably the worst sited signal was the Queen's Park Outer Circle home which was suspended under the Inner Circle starter underneath a bridge and on the Inner Circle embankment, which could not have been a further contravention of Mr Bound's decree. The signal had been moved to this position from its original location on the high wall adjacent to the Outer Circle at the time when Queen's Park became a block post in 1898, as the curve of the line made visibility extremely difficult.

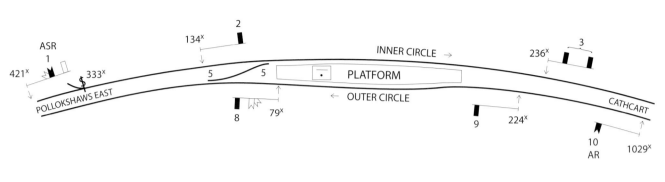

LANGSIDE

SPARE - 4 - 6 - 7

10 LEVERS   DIAGRAM DATE 2 APRIL 1894

No further major signalling alterations took place until electrification, which required the complete resignalling of the area and the replacement of the old original signal boxes with modern power installations controlling multiple aspect colour light signals. The major electro-pneumatic installation at Glasgow Central which, with 374 levers, was at the time of its opening in 1908 the largest of its type in the country was replaced by a new power box which opened at 6am on 2nd January 1961. This new box also took over control of the area formerly controlled by Bridge Street Junction, Eglinton Street Junction and Eglinton Street station boxes and worked, for a short time at least, to Pollokshields East Junction by train describer.

The Cathcart Circle itself was to be controlled by two boxes and the first of these, the new Muirhouse Junction, opened on 7th August 1961, on which date the old Muirhouse Junction and Pollokshields East Junction boxes closed, the latter exactly forty years to the day after the closure of Pollokshields East station box. The new signal box at Muirhouse, a neat modern brick building, contained a 40-lever Stevens frame, thirty-four of which were working, operating the points immediately outside the box, access to the workshop sidings and Tradeston gasworks and the relative ground signals. The only electrically controlled points were those at Pollokshields East Junction – reputedly, after electrification, the most frequently operated points in Glasgow. All colour light signals worked from the box were controlled by thumb switches mounted beneath the illuminated diagram, tiny bulbs illuminating red or green to remind the signalman of the aspect showing. The Pollokshields East Junction points were also controlled by thumb switches, with indicators showing whether the points were lying in normal or reverse position and whether the interlocking freed the point to be moved. A similar thumb switch released a small ground frame controlling a seldom-used crossover opposite the site of Pollokshields East Junction signal box while a further thumb switch controlled the illumination of the ground disc shunting signals. The new box worked to the new Cathcart box via the Inner and Outer Circles and to Glasgow Central by the track circuit block system, and to Strathbungo Junction and Terminus Junction by the absolute block system, the bells and block instruments being mounted in the panel alongside the thumb switches. White, green and red lights were used in the block instruments to indicate line blocked, line clear and train on line. The illuminated panel above the lever frame, in addition to showing the position of trains, showed their description using a four-letter code. The first letter indicated the type of train using the system current at the time of the design of the box, namely A – Express Passenger, B – Ordinary Passenger, C – Empty Coaching Stock, etc.

The second letter was used only for electric trains, when E was used otherwise it was blank. The last two letters indicated the destination of trains leaving Glasgow, or the originating station of trains going to Glasgow; for example EK for East Kilbride, BK for Barrhead and Kilmarnock line and CO for Cathcart Outer Circle. Thus BEKI was an electric ordinary passenger train to Kirkhill via the Inner Circle and A–BK an express train to or from the Barrhead and Kilmarnock line. For many years a particular anomaly was the code for Neilston trains, LN, which stood for Lugton and Neilston, although the line between them had long since been lifted! The code SN for Strathaven was also available, but was probably never used. Motherwell trains always used KI or KO in preference to ML so that an indication of the route to be taken round the Circle was given. No descriptions were required for trains passing between Strathbungo Junction and Terminus Junction as these boxes did not have describer equipment although routing bells were provided.

The Cathcart Circle was controlled by two new power boxes Muirhouse Junction and Cathcart, each box controlling its own immediate area together with the lines approaching it, the latter usually by automatic signals which could, if necessary in cases of emergency, be reset to danger in blocks by the signalman. Thus Muirhouse Junction controlled the Outer Circle from Langside station and the Inner Circle from Mount Florida, while Cathcart controlled the Outer Circle from Pollokshields East and the Inner Circle from Pollokshields West.

It was thus necessary, before any of the signal boxes on the circle could be closed, that Cathcart box should be opened, as the lines at each end of the old boxes were to be controlled by different power boxes. For some two months, therefore, Muirhouse Junction power box worked to Queen's Park and Maxwell Park, Caledonian two-position block instruments being installed in the modern box for this purpose. On 2nd October 1961 the new box was opened and on that date all the manual boxes in the Cathcart area, together with Crosshill and Queen's Park, were closed, automatic signalling and track circuit block coming into operation between Cathcart and Muirhouse Junction via Crosshill. The extension line hung on for another fortnight and Maxwell Park and Pollokshaws East boxes closed on 16th October 1961.

Cathcart new power box was, like Muirhouse, built of brick, but there the resemblance ended. It had no lever frame and the signalman sat at a console. The control panel was the first in Scotland to be equipped with a Westinghouse miniaturised push-button OCS (One Control Switch) combined control desk and diagram and was the first in Britain to utilise miniature plug-in relays throughout – both inside

ABOVE: Corkerhill based 0-6-0 No. 44001 at Langside and Newlands on the 8.30pm Outer Circle on 5th July 1957. Evening services such as this were withdrawn a year later, but were reinstated on electrification in 1962. The photographer is standing on the site of the signalbox which closed in 1900, but was not demolished until 1927.   W. A. C. SMITH

BELOW: Langside station after partial destruction by fire on 13th August 1966.   J. KERNAHAN

POLLOKSHAWS EAST

SPACES - 8–14
SPARE - 5

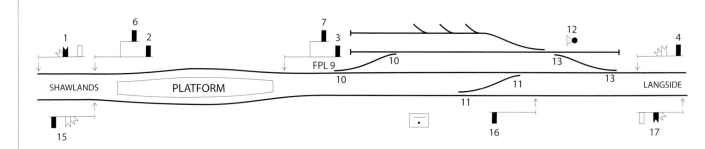

SHAWLANDS   PLATFORM   LANGSIDE

FPL 9

DIAGRAM DATE JAN 1905

and outside the signalbox. Route buttons were spring controlled to a centre position, pushed to clear and pulled to restore. For controlled signals the push-button was illuminated white when pressed and the illumination extinguished when restored. Signal indications (red/ green for main and white for subsidiary and shunt signals) were provided adjacent to each push-button.

The setting of a route was indicated on the diagram by a series of white lights over the route signalled which changed to red with the occupation of track circuits as the train progressed. Automatic signals were provided with restoration buttons on the console, arranged with groups of three or four signals on one switch. The illumination of the push-buttons for automatic signals differed from those of controlled signals, as with the switch normally depressed the signals worked automatically with no illumination of the push-button, but the pulling of the switch restored all signals in that group to danger together with the push-buttons illuminating red. Point

Fairburn 2-6-4T No. 42128 passing Pollokshaws East signalbox with the 5.30pm Outer Circle on 21st April 1960.   W. A. C. SMITH

SHAWLANDS

SPARE - 4 - 5 - 7

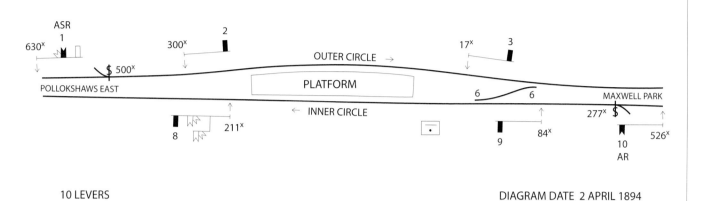

10 LEVERS

DIAGRAM DATE 2 APRIL 1894

ndications of 'normal', 'reverse' or 'free' were given, similar to those previously described at Muirhouse Junction for the power-operated points at Pollokshields East Junction. Train descriptions as at Muirhouse were employed. The box controlled both tracks between Cathcart and Newton and worked the Kirkhill Junction to Westburn Junction section by absolute block – the block instrument, like those at Muirhouse, being mounted on the console. The crossovers at Kirkhill and Kirkhill Junction were remotely controlled from the box by high frequency transmission over a single pair of wires, the first installation of its type in Scotland. On the Lanarkshire & Ayrshire line the box worked to Neilston High where the existing box was modernised, power operation having commenced on 24th July 1961 – although Muirend box was retained and modernised, but only opened very occasionally in cases of emergency and during engineering operations.

Special regulations applied in the new Cathcart box for the

BR Standard Class 5 4-6-0 No. 73064 approaches Shawlands with a football special. The engine is about to pass the site of Shawlands signalbox on the right.

H. Stevenson

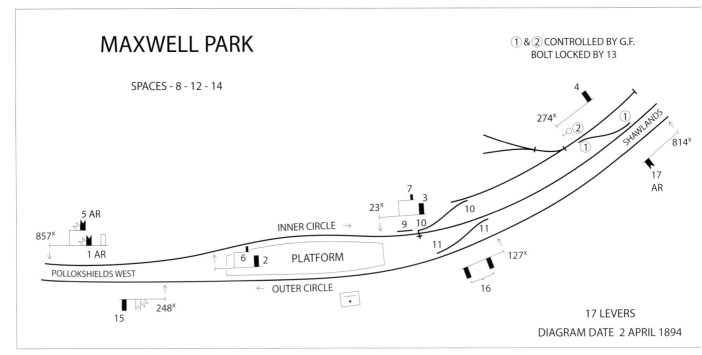

MAXWELL PARK

① & ② CONTROLLED BY G.F.
BOLT LOCKED BY 13

SPACES - 8 - 12 - 14

17 LEVERS

DIAGRAM DATE 2 APRIL 1894

operation of return football traffic from Mount Florida, incorporating permissive working of empty trains. The normal service on the Inner Circle was suspended and prior to the termination of the football match empty trains were placed one behind the other, just as in the days of manual signalling, under permissive conditions commencing with signal 51 and extending back to signal 55. Special calling on and delayed yellow aspect signals without advance overlap proving were provided to facilitate this working which were normally out of use, but which were brought into use by the operation of a special sealed

switch in the relay room by the lineman on a written request from the traffic department.

As in the nineteenth century, Ministry of Transport inspection of the new installations was required, but the inspecting officer, Colonel D. McMullen, had the comfort of the cab of a diesel locomotive for his inspection on 7th February 1962. All that was required from his trip round the Circle was slight adjustment to the focussing of a few signals. His report confirmed that the works were complete and in exceptionally good order with only minor adjustments on the

Maxwell Park signalbox.

approach locking of a few signals being required after his visits to the signalboxes.

Timekeeping improved tremendously with the opening of the new boxes, although occasional errors in routing at Pollokshields East Junction took place, as on 4th December 1961 when the 12.27pm from Glasgow to Kirkhill went round the Inner Circle by mistake and took the irate commuters, who presumably missed their lunch break at home that day, back to Central station!

Part of the original Central station extension line of 1879, that between Strathbungo North Junction and Muirhouse North Junction, latterly known as the East Kilbride Loop, was removed on 18th September 1960, while the goods loop at Maxwell Park was converted to a siding by the disconnection of the facing point from the Inner Circle on 11th June 1961. A similar operation had been carried out at Pollokshaws East during the early 1940s when, in addition, the Inner Circle outer home signal had been removed. This signal, like its counterpart at Maxwell Park, had been unusual in that it carried a full size signal for the loop, repeating the actual loop signal mounted with the inner home (see diagram on page 78). Pollokshaws East goods yard had closed on 1st June 1959, followed by Mount Florida on 23rd January 1961, leaving only Maxwell Park and Cathcart to be included in the resignalling scheme. Cathcart was under the direct control of the new power box, but Maxwell Park lay on a section of automatic signalling, and a ground frame was provided, released from Cathcart box, the two colour light signals in the rear being semi-automatic, so that the signalman could operate them if required.

Certain track alterations and rationalisation were made in connection with the resignalling. The major alteration was, as mentioned earlier, at Cathcart West Junction, where through running between the western side of the Circle and the Kirkhill line became possible from 6th March 1961. No platforms were provided at Cathcart, however, and passengers for Kirkhill line stations had to travel via Mount Florida where a very poor connection was normally offered.

The next major alteration took place on 17th September 1973 when the power box at Muirhouse Junction was closed and control of the area which it formerly signalled passed to Glasgow Central. Although there was an intention in March 1967 to close Muirend and Neilston High boxes, their closure did not take place until 16th November 1980 and 31st October 1982 respectively, control of the Neilston branch passing to Cathcart, where an additional panel was installed. The Neilston branch signalling operates automatically, including the changing of the points after the train has entered the headshunt beyond the station, although switches are available to allow the Cathcart signalman to manually operate the points at both Neilston and at Muirend, the latter retained for emergency and engineering use.

The original alphabetic system of describing the trains has been replaced with the conventional alpha numeric system. The first numeral describes the type of train, all passenger services being '2' for stopping trains, except for the one morning peak hour train from the Neilston branch and the evening return which run nonstop between Muirend and Glasgow Central which are class '1' as expresses. The next letter describes the route: O for Outer Circle, I for Inner Circle, N for Neilston, P for Newton via Queen's Park and M for Newton via Maxwell Park. The final two numbers are unique to the individual service.

In Cathcart signalbox many of the original controls went out of use within a few years of the box opening. Of the twenty-three point switches, only ten remain in use and the three ground frames controlling Maxwell Park, Burnside and Kirkhill goods yards closed on 6th January 1964, 28th October 1963 and 4th April 1966 respectively. Cathcart goods yard closed on 5th April 1965 although the loop was retained for several years. The line from Kirkhill Junction to Westburn Junction closed on 1st August 1966, but the block instrument built into the panel of Cathcart box remains,

Maxwell Park Inner Circle home signal. This signal was unusual in that it had an arm for the goods loop, but another similar signal, also with an arm for the goods loop, lay before the points for the loop.
W. A. C. SMITH

having been out of use for over forty years. All catch points have been removed, rendered unnecessary as all trains are fully braked, and no special regulations are now needed for football traffic. Newton power signalbox, opened on 5th September 1960, closed on 26th August 1973, when its area of control passed to Motherwell signalling centre. Cathcart box accordingly now controls the Kirkhill line as far as Burnside, from where the signalling is controlled by Motherwell. The train descriptions mentioned in the previous paragraph no longer appear on the signalling panel itself, but are displayed on two large modern monitors positioned above the panel.

Glasgow Central signalbox closed on 24th December 2008, when its area of control was passed to the new West of Scotland Signalling Centre at Cowlairs. Cathcart box still remains, and it is intended that West of Scotland Signalling Centre will take over its function in 2012. By that time it will have been in use for fifty-one years, nearly as long as many of the boxes which it replaced around Cathcart and on the Lanarkshire & Ayrshire lines.

Considering the volume of passengers carried and the number of trains operated, the Cathcart Circle's safety record is remarkable, with only three major accidents in its history, all of these within yards of one another.

Probably the first fatality occurred on 12th June 1886, only a few months after the line opened, when William Dunn, a telegraph boy, attempted for some reason to leap onto the 7.27am from Cathcart as it was drawing into Central station. He fell between the train and the platform and was dragged a short distance, the coaches passing over both his legs. He died several hours after being admitted to the Royal Infirmary.

The first major operating accident occurred on Friday 20th

POLLOKSHIELDS WEST

SPARE - 4 - 6 - 7

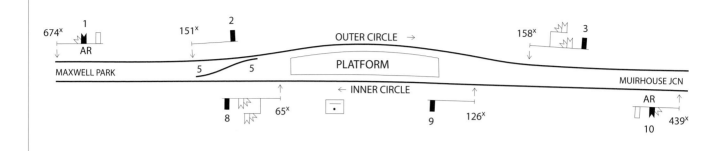

MAXWELL PARK

OUTER CIRCLE →

PLATFORM

← INNER CIRCLE

MUIRHOUSE JCN

10 LEVERS

DIAGRAM DATE 2 APRIL 1894

September 1940 when the 12.35pm Glasgow Central to Uplawmoor ran into the rear of the 12.32pm Cathcart Inner Circle which had stopped at Pollokshields East Junction. The rear coach of the Inner Circle train was badly smashed and thrown on its side on the embankment. The passengers were thrown almost to the roofs and several were injured by broken glass. Sixteen were taken to the Victoria Infirmary, nine being allowed home after treatment. The guard of the Inner Circle train, realising that the Uplawmoor train was immediately behind his train ran back waving his red flag, but he was too late to prevent the collision as the driver of the Uplawmoor train did not see him in time to make anything other than a last-minute emergency brake application. The accident was caused very simply by the signalman at Pollokshields East Junction accepting from Eglinton Street the Uplawmoor train while the intervening section between the two signal boxes was still occupied by the Inner Circle train which was standing at the home signal.

Fairburn 2-6-4T No. 42275 approaches Pollokshields West with an Inner Circle train. Strathbungo Junction signalbox, on the right, did not control any signalling on the Cathcart Circle.

W. S. SELLAR

The principal interest of the accident was legal rather than operational. A case for compensation brought against the LMSR by a Miss Anne Gray as a result of the accident was simply settled at £100 plus £12:12/- for expenses. Another case, however, was not so simple and eventually landed, on appeal on a point of law, in the House of Lords. Miss Margaret Stewart brought an action against the LMSR on two counts: firstly, as an individual, for damages which she had suffered personally and which were settled at £250 plus expenses; and secondly as executrix of her deceased sister, Miss Mary Stewart, who had been the only fatality of the accident, to recover damages in respect of the injuries received by her sister. The court decided that as an executrix she had no title to sue an action for injuries to her deceased sister and gave an award, with costs, in favour of the railway company.

The second accident occurred on Saturday 21st April 1951 on one of the Circle's busiest days of the year – Scottish Cup Final day at Hampden Park. The trains involved were the 1.24pm special from Glasgow Central to Mount Florida and the 1.27pm regular timetable train from Glasgow Central to Kirkhill. All trains were numbered for ease of identification, the 1.24pm carrying the number 68 while the 1.27pm was 69. The accident occurred in the deep walled cutting between Pollokshields East and Queen's Park. The 1.24pm, consisting of eight non-corridor coaches weighing 230 tons, was halted with a brake failure shortly after passing through Pollokshields East. The 1.27pm was mistakenly allowed to enter the section already occupied by the stationary special with which it collided at about 20mph. The last four compartments of the rear coach of the special were destroyed, three passengers were killed, seventy-four were taken to hospital and a further sixty-six received minor injuries. Although the line was blocked by the accident it was found possible to open the Inner Circle temporarily for return football traffic between 5pm and 6pm. Signalling between the two signal boxes involved, Pollokshields East and Queen's Park, was by means of the original Tyer's Caledonian two position block instruments which were not interlocked to the starting signals, although the Pollokshields East Junction Outer Circle home signal was controlled by track circuits installed on the closure of the intermediate signal box at the Queen's Park end of Pollokshields East station some thirty years earlier.

The first train, number 68, was offered and accepted between the two signal boxes at 1.31pm and at 1.33pm was correctly signalled into the section. At 1.34pm, although he had not been informed that the first train had arrived safely at Queen's Park, McLellan, the Pollokshields East Junction signalman, offered the special, number 69, to Kelly, his colleague at Queen's Park, who telephoned him immediately to say that he (McLellan) had already sent a train into the section. McLellan denied that he had sent a train forward and Kelly, a junior signalman, allowed himself to be persuaded by McLellan, his senior, cancelled the train which his instrument told him was in the section and accepted train number 69 into the already occupied section. Train 69 was only 30 yards from the rear of train 68 when the latter came in sight of the driver and there was insufficient time to make an effective brake application. The locomotive and coaches of train 69 suffered little damage, but train 68 was pushed forward 81 feet, the rear bogey of the last coach being the only derailment.

An important factor which was revealed at the inquiry was the fact that Queen's Park signal box (as mentioned earlier, a simple 8-lever block post used solely for passing traffic) should have been in the charge of an experienced signalman, T. Tugwell, and that, although he had recently been satisfactorily examined, Kelly should not have been in sole command until

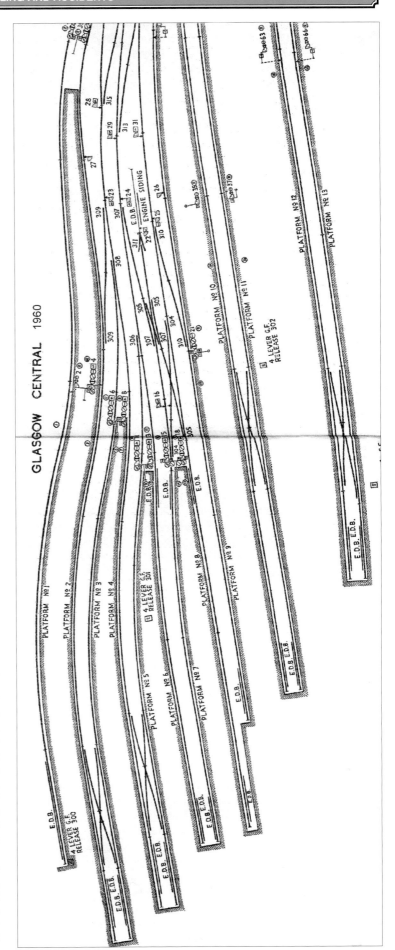

GLASGOW CENTRAL 1960

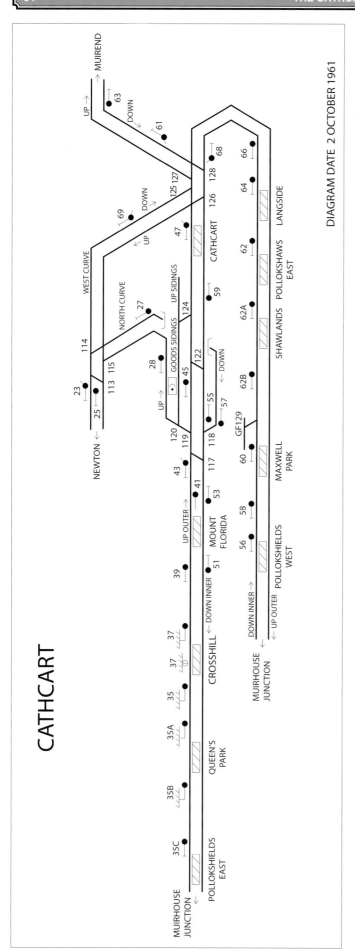

CATHCART

DIAGRAM DATE 2 OCTOBER 1961

the following Monday. Tugwell had, however, absented himself in order to attend a football match leaving Kelly in charge on one of the busiest days of the year.

The evidence of the train register books, recording every bell signal sent and received in the signal boxes, was of vital importance in deciding exactly what had occurred between the two signalmen. In Pollokshields East Junction this book was the sole responsibility of a seventeen-and-a-half-year-old boy, R. Morrison, who had worked with the railway for two years, while in Queen's Park the book was kept by the signalman. The relevant entries for the two trains are shown in the table.

The Pollokshields book recorded signals being received from Queen's Park that both trains had safely arrived through the section. Morrison admitted that he had anticipated the times, writing them in the book as the trains actually passed Pollokshields box. He also admitted that it was sometimes his practice to do this.

Two other officials in the boxes at the time were unable to add much to the facts already known. Inspector C. Potts was in Pollokshields box to regulate the traffic, but during the vital few minutes he was making tea and was unable to confirm or deny what had allegedly occurred. Stationmaster R. H. Ballentine, who was in the Queen's Park signal box, confirmed hearing the telephone conversation during which Kelly was persuaded that Train No. 68 had not been sent from Pollokshields East. Kelly remarked to Ballentine that he thought the signal must have been a mistake and that the signal he had received should probably have been sent on the Inner Circle instrument.

Colonel R. J. Walker, reporting on the Inquiry, attended in Pollokshields East Junction a few weeks after the accident during a period of early morning peak traffic which was less heavy than on the Cup Final Saturday. His report is interesting in giving an insight into the working of the busiest signal box on the Cathcart Circle which, in 1951, was still operating on the same principles and with the same equipment as when it was opened in 1886.

There were periods of intense activity when the signalman was either sending or receiving bell signals on the three block

POLLOKSHIELDS EAST JUNCTION

	Accepted from Eglinton Street	Train entering section received from Eglinton Street	Train out of section given to Eglinton Street	Accepted by Queen's Park	Train out of section received from Queen's Park
No. 68	1.31	1.32	1.33	1.31	1.34 (*Subsequently altered to 1.37*)
No. 69	1.33 (*Subsequently altered to 1.36*)	1.38	1.39	1.38 (*Subsequently altered to 1.37*)	1.41

QUEEN'S PARK

	Accepted from Pollokshields East	Train entering section received from Eglinton Street	Train out of section given to Pollokshields East	Accepted by Crosshill
No. 68	— — 1.30 — — — — — 1.33 — — — error			1.33
No. 69	1.34	1.37		

ABOVE: The control panel in Cathcart power signalbox in December 2009. The panel to the right controls the Neilston branch and was installed in 1982. Built into the panel at bottom left is the block instrument to Westburn Junction near Newton, which has not been used since the line closed in 1966.

J. KERNAHAN

FACING PAGE: Cathcart power signalbox opened on 2nd October 1961. It is due to close in 2012 when its area of control will be transferred to the West of Scotland Signalling Centre at Cowlairs.

J. KERNAHAN

ABOVE: WD 2-8-0 No. 90039 with a train of ex-LNER corridor coaches approaches Eglinton Street from Pollokshields East Junction in 1960. The Caledonian lower quadrant signals are still in use, but the new colour light signal which will come into use on 2nd January 1961 is installed and newly painted.

J. R. HUME

BELOW: BR 2-6-4T No. 80007 hauls an Inner Circle train under the newly-installed electric catenary at Pollokshields East Junction on 14th April 1962.

H. STEVENSON

instruments more or less simultaneously, as well as pulling or restoring signal levers and giving or removing descriptions on train describing apparatus. At the same time a train standing at the Inner Circle Down Home signal was operating an annunciator in the box, making a loud and persistent buzzing sound while any one or all of three omnibus circuit telephones were ringing with the code calls for other signal boxes. The noise of bells, gong and buzzer was considerable and the speed and precision required of the signalman were such that only a skilled and experienced man could have been expected to compete with his task successfully in the circumstances.

The inquiry came to the inevitable conclusion that the collision was caused by the combined mistakes of the two signalmen and the mutual misunderstanding of the telephone conversation which took place between them. It also highlighted many operating irregularities, such as the habit of the train register boy in anticipating bell signals and that of signalmen changing shifts at other than the appointed time, which must have contributed in part to the accident. Colonel Walker also commented that the intensity of traffic in the area had now outstripped the original two position block instruments, but this had already been recognised by the railway authorities, a scheme for re-equipping the whole area with modern three position instruments being in progress at the time. Ironically, two of the three instruments were lying in Pollokshields East Junction box awaiting connection on the day of the accident.

The third major accident on the Cathcart Circle occurred as a consequence, albeit rather indirect, of the electrification of the Caledonian main line between Glasgow and Carlisle. The electric locomotives on the main line operate only at 25Kv and to provide a relief route via the western half of the Cathcart Circle, this section was converted from 6.25Kv in September 1973. A neutral section at Pollokshields East between the station and the junction necessitated an alteration to the signalling on the Inner Circle at that point. The existing platform starting signal was sited in such a position that trains starting from it would not have gained sufficient power to pass through the neutral section. Accordingly the signal was moved to a position 132 feet before the end of the platform. There was, however, the very real danger that the driver of a train stopped at the platform could all too easily receive the bell signal to start from the guard and through force of habit start off past the red signal, particularly if he had brought his train to a halt too near to the signal.

This was exactly what happened shortly after 2.15pm on 11th June 1974 when the 14.04 Newton to Glasgow Central electric multiple unit passed the signal at red and collided on Pollokshields East Junction with the 14.16 Glasgow Central to East Kilbride triple diesel multiple unit, only narrowly missing a head on collision. Thus, despite the replacement of the original manual signalling apparatus prior to electrification with modern colour light signalling with automatic warning system and the most up to date track circuiting, and the further improvements by moving the control of the area to one panel in the sophisticated Central signalling centre less than a year before the accident, human error could still result in disaster. One passenger was killed in the accident and thirty-five were injured, four of them seriously.

All the evidence produced at the inquiry, conducted by Major C. F. Rose, indicated that the driver of the electric train had passed the starting signal at danger. All the signalling and automatic warning system equipment was proved to be working correctly and it was unfortunate that the diesel train

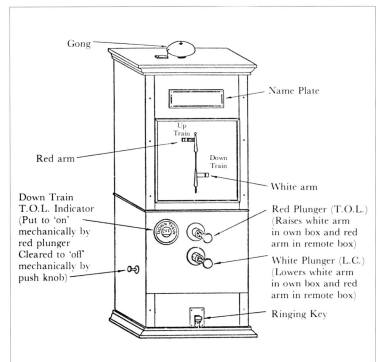

TYER'S TWO POSITION BLOCK INSTRUMENT

These signalling instruments were used throughout the Caledonian system, including the Cathcart Circle, and were in use at Pollokshields East Junction and Queen's Park signal boxes at the time of the 1951 accident. A sketch of an instrument is given above. One instrument in each box controls the movements through the section for both Up and Down lines. The instrument in the remote box is therefore identical with that shown in the drawing, with the exception that the red arm is marked 'Down Train' and the white 'Up Train'.

The method of operation between two signal boxes, A and B, excluding the usual 'call attention' signals, is as follows:

A offers the train on the ringing key.

B accepts on the white plunger. This lowers the red arm in A and the white arm in B.

A gives 'Train Entering Section' on the ringing key.

B acknowledges on the red plunger. This raises the red arm in A and the white arm in B and places the 'Train on Line' indicator in B to 'On'.

B gives 'Train out of Section' on the ringing key and removes the 'On' indication by pushing the push knob.

The points to note are that:

(i)   when the indicator in B is changed to 'On' by the operation of the red plunger, it does not correspondingly change the indicator in A. The latter indicator is used for trains in the opposite direction, when A is the receiver and B the sender.

(ii)   B is prevented by a mechanical interlock in the instrument from accepting a train by means of the white plunger so long as the 'Train on Line' indicator shows 'On'.

(iii)   there is nothing to prevent B, however, from removing the 'On' indication by means of the push knob at any time.

had not been running even a few seconds later as the passage of the electric train over the junction reset the junction signal for the diesel train to red and would have caused the diesel driver to make a much earlier emergency brake application, thus substantially reducing the impact of the collision.

The driver of the electric train explained that he had drawn up beyond the signal as he was worried that, with the shortening of the platform, he would not otherwise bring his full train into the platform. To avoid this temptation in the future it was suggested that the signal be moved nearer the junction, but the neutral section requirements ruled this out. It was also not possible to provide a repeater signal forward of the signal as this would be an incorrect use of a repeater. The solution arrived at was to physically reduce the Inner Circle platform length at the Glasgow end by removing a section and replacing it with a ramp, thus removing any incentive to a driver to bring his train to a stand in advance of the signal, and to increase the length of the Queen's Park end over the site of the signal box.

ABOVE LEFT AND LEFT: The block instruments, switches and illuminated diagram in the power signalbox at Muirhouse Junction opened on 7th August 1961.

J. KERNAHAN

BELOW: The signalling diagram covering the Cathcart Circle and adjacent lines in 2010.   J. KERNAHAN

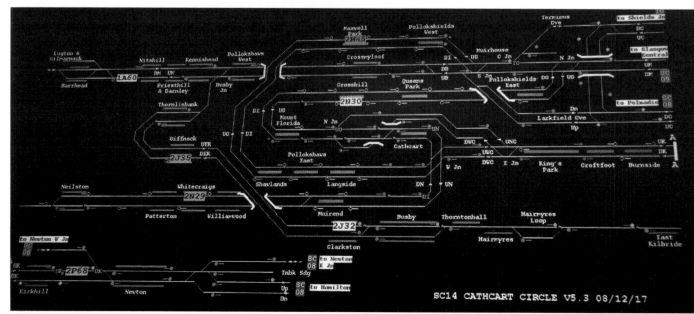

SC14 CATHCART CIRCLE V5.3 08/12/17

CHAPTER 8

MOTIVE POWER AND OPERATION

Throughout the seventy-six years of steam operation, small engines, principally the neat 0-4-4 tanks of Dugald Drummond and John Farquharson McIntosh, were associated with the line.

The first locomotives to work the line were probably the '171' Class 0-4-4 side tanks introduced by Drummond in 1884 and modelled on his 1880 North British 'R' Class 4-4-0 tanks. Despite having a different wheel arrangement the principal dimensions were the same, including the solid centre bogie wheels, a unique feature on CR 0-4-4 tanks.

The tank engines best known on the Cathcart lines were J. F. McIntosh's '104' 0-4-4s built at St Rollox in 1899. The twelve engines in the class (numbers 104–111 and 167–170) were designed specially for the Cathcart Circle and for Edinburgh's Balerno branch. Stations were situated very close together and to speed up the service by improved acceleration away from the stations, the coupled driving wheels were as small as possible at 4 feet 6 inches compared with 5 feet on the earlier '171' Class. Despite the smaller driving wheels the '104s' were much more powerful than the '171s', having a tractive effort of 16,376lbs compared with 11,968lbs. They were also much heavier at 51 tons 2.5cwt as against 37 tons 15cwt.

Other small locomotives occasionally used on the Circle included the Lambie condensing Class '1' 4-4-0 tanks, the first engines to be built for the Central Low Level lines and introduced in 1893. After the First World War certain changes were made to the permanent way and the bridges were strengthened to allow heavier locomotives to be used. The '104s' were relegated to station pilot and empty carriage duties.

The ubiquitous Caledonian Standard '439' Passenger 0-4-4 tanks now added the Cathcart Circle to the other branches throughout the Caledonian system which were under their control. Designed by McIntosh in 1900, the year after the introduction of the '104s', the '439s' had 5-foot 9-inch driving wheels, tractive effort of 16,603lbs and weighed 53 tons 19cwt. 0-6-0 tender engines were also used, including the superheated '30' Class introduced by McIntosh in 1912, and the impressive 4-6-2 tanks of William Pickersgill, normally associated with the fast routes to Edinburgh Princes Street and Wemyss Bay from Glasgow, made occasional appearances. The improvements in the line meant that it could be used for turning main line locomotives rather than sending them to the turntables at Cook Street and Polmadie. Thus the Cathcart Circle has seen such famous main line giants as *Cardean*, *Sir James Thompson* and members of Pickersgill's '60' Class working humble commuter trains between turns on the main line to Carlisle.

During Caledonian days Polmadie shed provided the motive power for the line, but, following the 1923 grouping, the old rival Glasgow & South Western Railway's shed at Corkerhill was allocated some turns on the Circle and some elderly G&SW engines found their way

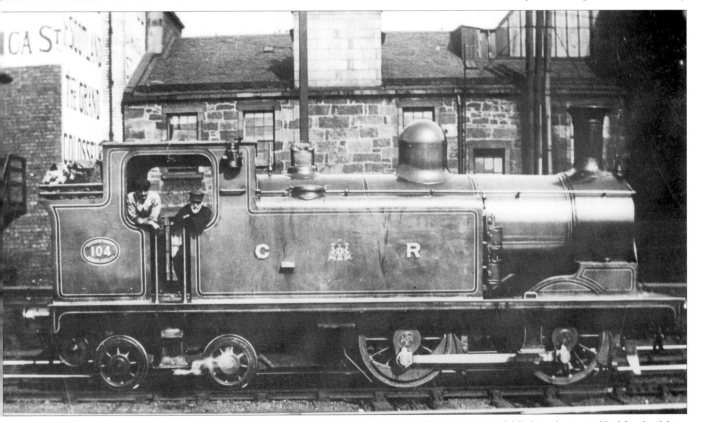

CR '104' 0-4-4T class leader, No. 104, at Glasgow Central. With their 4-foot 6-inch driving wheels these powerful little engines were ideal for the tight curves of the Balerno branch and their rapid acceleration suited the closely spaced stations on the Cathcart Circle. As the cab and bunker were the same width as the side tank all three were lined out as a single panel, giving the class a distinctive livery. The Westinghouse pump was mounted on the front of the tank rather than beside the cab door as in the other tank classes.

J. MACINTOSH COLLECTION

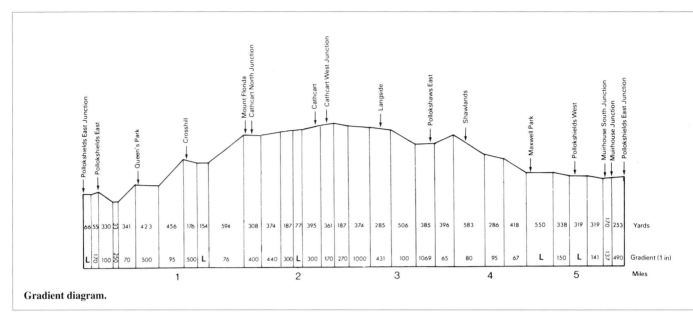

Gradient diagram.

to this new territory. In the 1930s, however, they were replaced at Corkerhill by Caledonian 0-4-4s and 0-6-0s which thus returned to their old hunting grounds.

Poor maintenance and sub-standard coal left the tank engines in an extremely run down condition after the Second World War and they were frequently unable to keep time with Circle trains. Many of the trains were now entrusted to the new LMSR 2-6-4 tanks and, following their introduction in 1951, the British Railways Standard 2-6-4 tanks. These engines handled the trains excellently, often hauling up to eight bogie coaches on Uplawmoor and Kirkhill services. More powerful engines, usually LMSR and BR Standard Class 5 4-6-0s, also made appearances. By the 1960s a Caledonian engine was a rare sight on the Circle, latterly being used only on off-peak services. One such train was the 10.30am Outer Circle which was regularly in the charge of '439' Class 0-4-4 tank No. 419, by this time British Railways No. 55189. The timetable allowed this train a pause of two minutes at Pollokshaws East, a feature not allowed on any other trains. It is a nice thought, although probably an erroneous one, that

Caledonian Railway '104' Class 0-4-4T, originally number 167, renumbered 15155 by the LMS. These tanks, with 4-foot 6-inch driving wheels, were specially designed for the Cathcart Circle and the Balerno branch in Edinburgh.

J. L. STEVENSON

he authorities had recognised that the little engine, now over fifty years old, was past its prime and needed a rest before tackling the 1 in 65 gradient, the steepest on the line, to Shawlands!

The last days of steam on the Circle were particularly interesting, not only on the passenger trains, but also on the freight and electrification engineers' trains. The local freight trips from Polmadie were normally worked by Caledonian 0-6-0s, more than likely a Drummond Standard Goods tender engine or a smaller '782' shunting tank, but Polmadie could provide almost anything for the mid-day freight. It was not unknown for a Class 7 'Britannia' Pacific or a 'Royal Scot' 4-6-0 to be used. Occasionally, however, things went too far, and on 3rd May 1960 LMSR Class 8F 2-8-0 No. 48773 was derailed in Maxwell Park goods yard. The locomotive was none the worse for its experience and, indeed, is still in existence, preserved and working on the Severn Valley Railway.

An interesting locomotive which worked the morning freight regularly for several months in the late 1950s was one of Matthew Holmes' 18-inch NBR Class 'C' 0-6-0s, introduced in 1888 and later classified 'J36' by the London & North Eastern Railway, No. 65216 (formerly NBR No. 628). This locomotive was one of twenty-five of the class which had served in France and Flanders with the Railway Operating Division of the Royal Engineers during the First World War and which had been given appropriate names on their safe return. 65216 bore the name *Byng* and was allocated latterly to Polmadie, in the heart of Caledonian territory! As late as January 1962, *Byng*'s sister, 65217 *French*, strangely also now from a Caledonian shed, Grangemouth, was a most unusual guest on the morning freight.

The heavy engineers' specials operated during electrification works were normally worked by British Railways Standard Class 5 4-6-0s, often in pairs, but these trains brought a great variety of motive power to the Cathcart Circle. The concreting trains were the preserve

of the steam engines, the largest used probably being 'Jubilee' Class 4-6-0 No. 45716 *Swiftsure* which appeared on 24th February 1961, but the lighter wiring trains were often worked by 350 hp diesel shunters (now Class 08) at that time in course of delivery new to Polmadie.

The rakes of coaches used on the original 1886 branch consisted of eight four-wheeled coaches, comprising three firsts, three thirds and two brake thirds, additional coaches being attached at peak hours. The detailed carriage diagram of the period is given in Appendix 11. When the Circle was completed, the trains were regularly made up of ten four-wheeled coaches painted all over in a brown livery. All the coaches were 30 feet in length (33 feet over the buffers). The third class coaches had five compartments, with wooden spar seating, while the more spacious first class coaches had four compartments, with upholstered seating, although the coaches used on Circle trains did not boast any armrests as did other Caledonian first class stock of the period. The brake thirds had three third class compartments in addition to the guard's accommodation. Occasionally at peak hours more luxurious Caledonian rolling stock found its way round the Circle, and the cream and brown livery of the coaches led them to be nicknamed 'The White Trains'.

Almost immediately after its formation, the LMSR constructed new rolling stock for the line which, while shorter than standard LMSR designs, were a considerable improvement on the Caledonian four-wheelers. Nine five-coach sets were delivered during 1926 and 1927, plus three spare coaches. Details of the coach numbers and delivery dates are given in Appendix 13. Sets of five were sufficient for Cathcart services, and indeed the length of the platforms, not to mention the capabilities of the 0-4-4 tanks, dictated that trains could not be much longer. As with the four-wheelers there was a greater proportion of first class accommodation (27.78 per cent of

CR '439' Class 0-4-4T No. 55169 approaching Shawlands with an Inner Circle train on 9th August 1956.   G. H. ROBIN

the seating accommodation of the complete train) than in most other suburban services. The sets were formed in the order: Brake third, Composite, First, Composite, Brake third.

All coaches were 54 feet in length, except for the composites which were only 51 feet. The brake thirds had seven compartments, the composites six third and two first class compartments, and the firsts eight compartments. Six-a-side seating was provided in the third class compartments, with five-a-side in the firsts. The coaches were steel panelled with steel-panelled ends, but retained wooden-framed windows. They cost £141,000.

The improvement in the third class seating in the new coaches over the old slatted wooden seating in the four-wheelers meant that there was no longer such a marked difference between first and third class accommodation and the popularity of the former fell away. Prior to the Second World War the first class compartments in the composite coaches were converted into third class, leaving only the eight compartments in the middle coach for first class passengers. These coaches, latterly joined by more modern equivalents constructed by British Railways, survived until electrification in 1962.

A feature of the operation of Caledonian lines out of the cities of Glasgow and Edinburgh was the semaphore route indicator, often known as the 'bow tie', carried by the locomotive on its lamp iron to indicate to signalmen the route which the train was taking. Although a Caledonian instigation, it did not die with the grouping, or with

LEFT: Fairburn 2-6-4T No. 42144 with a Cathcart Outer Circle train at Platform 10 in Glasgow Central on 2nd September 1954.   G. H. ROBIN/BY COURTESY OF THE MITCHELL LIBRARY, GLASGOW CITY COUNCIL

BELOW: Fairburn 2-6-4T No. 42191 passing Cathcart North Junction with a train for Neilston on 30th May 1957.
G. H. ROBIN

nationalisation, and until electrification it was regularly carried by he Cathcart Circle engines. The codes used were:

Original branch 1886–1894

Cathcart Circle 1894–1962

INNER CIRCLE   OUTER CIRCLE

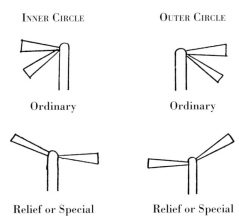

Ordinary   Ordinary

Relief or Special   Relief or Special

The Working Timetable required certain of the regular peak-hour additional trains which started or terminated at intermediate stations o carry the relief indicators.

The locomotives also carried route indicators by means of boards by day and lamps by night. Those used on the Cathcart Circle were:

By day

Inner Circle: Oval-shaped green board in front of chimney

Outer Circle: Oval-shaped white board in front of chimney

After sunset or during foggy weather

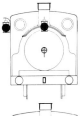

Inner Circle: Green lamp on right side of driving cab canopy and in front of chimney

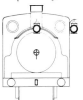

Outer Circle: White lamp on left side of driving cab canopy and in front of chimney

Like the semaphore indicators, the lamp codes were still in evidence until 1962 although, as there were no longer lamp irons on the cab sides, the codes were carried on the front buffer beam. Inner Circle trains carried one headlamp over the coupling and another over the right buffer. Outer Circle trains carried one headlamp over the coupling and another over the left buffer:

Inner Circle   Outer Circle

The digital headcodes used by electric multiple units are given in Appendix 14.

Diesel multiple units were used on Circle services for only four years between 1958 and 1962, but diesel locomotives were not used on passenger trains except for the occasional appearance of English Electric Type '1's (now Class 20) on football specials in 1962. The diesel multiple units were principally Cravens and Metropolitan

CR '439' Class 0-4-4T No. 55189 displays the semaphore route indicator clearly on the bunker as it passes Eglinton Street with the 5.39pm Inner Circle train on 8th September 1955. To the left is the island platform which permitted two city-bound trains to be held simultaneously for ticket collection.
W. A. C. SMITH/
TRANSPORT TREASURY

Cammell designs from Hamilton depot, but Derby-built units were not uncommon in the early 1960s. All the peak hour services remained steam hauled until electrification.

An interesting experiment was the running of a train, composed of a six-coach 'Cross Country' diesel multiple unit, on a Glasgow Easter Holiday Monday, 18th April 1960, direct from Cathcart Circle stations to the Ayrshire coast resorts at Prestwick and Ayr. Although the train was well patronised the idea was not repeated. Parcels traffic was important on the Circle, the boy porters at the stations being required to deliver the parcels to the houses, a task which regularly took longer than was possibly necessary due to lengthy visits to the kitchens of the houses of Langside and Pollokshields! Until it was unstaffed, the booking office at Maxwell Park contained the street plan of the area, showing the area for which the staff were responsible for delivering parcels. Parcels were normally carried by passenger trains, but the volume of this traffic at holiday times, when families often moved to the coastal resorts for up to two months, necessitated the running of special luggage trains during the evening breaks between passenger trains.

The greatest operating problem on the Cathcart Circle arose on the days of major football matches at Hampden Park. In addition to transporting thousands of Glaswegians from Central station to Mount Florida, the line was host to trains bringing supporters from all over Scotland. These trains normally left their passengers at King's Park and continued empty to the sidings at Muirend, Muirhouse or Kirkhill, depending on the direction from which they arrived, and brought a fascinating variety of 'foreign' locomotives to the line. To facilitate the running of the specials, particularly the Mount Florida to Glasgow trains, normal services on the Cathcart Circle were cancelled, and the return trains formed a queue, nose to tail, from Cathcart North Junction back along the Inner Circle as far as Pollokshaws East. In addition to these trains, Cathcart Goods Yard was also full, and more than twenty trains could assemble during the course of the football match. The normal block signalling over the Inner Circle was suspended and the trains were hand signalled into Mount Florida by an inspector. A failure in the middle of this operation would have been a disaster and spare engines were kept at Mount Florida and Cathcart, as well as at Maxwell Park, in case of trouble on the bank to Shawlands. Considering the number of passengers carried it is remarkable that the only major operating accident in running these specials was that in 1951 already mentioned.

Following the introduction of electric multiple units the operation of the specials became easier and it was no longer necessary to suspend normal services, although usually two Cathcart Circle trains were cancelled on these days. Originally a specific number of electric multiple unit specials were run to a timetable, but nowadays a number of units are provided to run round the Circle as often as required to clear the crowds.

From 1962 passenger services were handled entirely by the three-car electrical multiple units known familiarly as the 'Blue Trains' from the attractive lined Caledonian blue livery which they carried during the first ten years of their lives. Since 1966 they have been reliveried first in 'rail blue', then blue and grey and then into the orange livery of Strathclyde Regional Transport. Four of the units survived long enough to receive the more recent carmine and cream livery. Thus the Cathcart Circle has seen a great variety of colour in its rolling stock: Caledonian brown and white trains; LMSR and BR maroon, and latterly the green diesels for a short time before the coming of the Blue Trains. It is interesting to compare the electric units which were finally built with the ideas which had been projected in the past, particularly the three-car sets proposed in 1929. The designers in 1929 had favoured compartment stock to facilitate speed of loading

ABOVE LEFT: CR Class '439' 0-4-4T No. 15170 crosses Coustonholm Road, departing from Pollokshaws East with an Outer Circle train on 9th April 1948. The bridge over the road contains a passage for passenger access from the road. G. H. ROBIN/BY COURTESY OF THE MITCHELL LIBRARY, GLASGOW CITY COUNCIL

ABOVE RIGHT: CR Class '439' 0-4-4T No. 55189 arriving at Pollokshields West with an Inner Circle train on 13th September 1957. G. H. ROBIN/BY COURTESY OF THE MITCHELL LIBRARY, GLASGOW CITY COUNCIL

RIGHT: CR Class '300' 0-6-0 No. 57674 leaving Maxwell Park on the Outer Circle with a goods train. J. R. HUME

CR '439' Class 0-4-4T No. 55201 arriving at Pollokshaws East with an Inner Circle train in August 1948. The station bookstall replaced the original one which can be seen in the photograph on page 45.
G. H. ROBIN

ABOVE: CR Class '812' 0-6-0 No. 57581 leaving Glasgow Central, Platform 10, with a train for Kirkhill via the Outer Circle.   G. H. ROBIN

BELOW: BR Standard Class 5 No. 73060 at the special platform at Mount Florida built in 1938 for football traffic, sandwiched between two other returning special trains, on 23rd April 1955.   W. A. C. SMITH

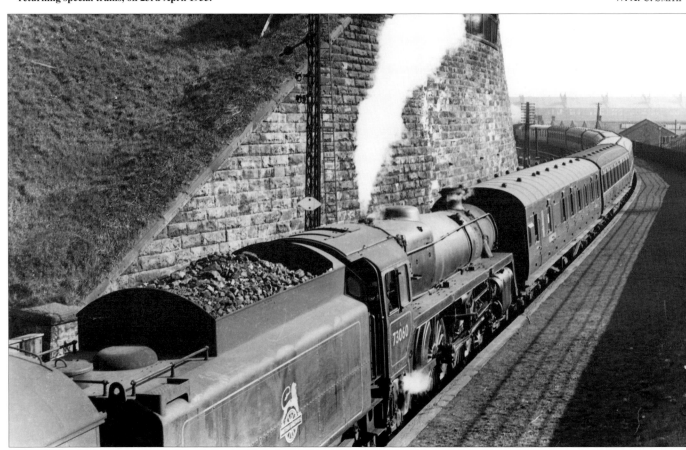

CR Class '439' 0-4-4T No. 55189 leaving Glasgow Central with the 2.30pm Outer Circle train on th November 1958. The buffer top of the Cathcart engine siding is adjacent to the second coach.

W. A. C. SMITH/
TRANSPORT TREASURY

nd unloading at stations, whereas the Blue Trains were built with entral vestibules. First class had accounted for nearly 31 per cent of the accommodation in the 1929 sets; the Blue Trains were second class only. One luggage compartment, situated in the middle power car, contrasted with two, one in each driving car, in 1929. Passengers n 1929 were also to be denied the fine forward views which could be obtained from the modern units, as the luggage compartments vere to intervene between the driver and the passengers. The Blue Trains were aesthetically very attractive and it was regrettable, but essential, that the wrap round windows of the driving cabs had to be replaced by smaller windows to reduce the danger to drivers from vandalism.

The ninety-one original 'Blue Trains', Scottish-built by Pressed Steel at Linwood, were originally designated as 'AM3' and latterly became Class 303. In 1967 they were joined by nineteen almost identical Class 311 units, numbered from 092, which were built by Cravens in Sheffield as fleet additions following the electrification of the Gourock and Wemyss Bay routes. The units underwent several alterations during their long lives, notably the removal of guards' compartments, installation of corridor connections between the coaches and the abolition of forward and rearward views for the passengers through the driving cabs. The installation of corridor connections was necessary following the inception of the open station system, which permitted the unstaffing of stations as economically required, and required ticket inspection and issue on board the train, one ticket collector being responsible for three coaches. The interiors were renewed. Although the new seating lacked the degree of comfort of the original and also provided less seats, this did give additional space for standing passengers. Trains were also changed to one-man operation, which required the installation of monitors and mirrors at the stations to permit the driver to see when it was safe to close the doors.

The last 303 units were withdrawn in 2002, and since then services on the Cathcart Circle, Newton and Neilston lines have been operated almost exclusively by Class 314 units. These were built in 1979 by British Rail Engineering Limited at York for the newly reopened lines through Glasgow Central Low Level. Each of the sixteen units can seat 220 passengers, slightly less than the 303s, and normally operate as single three-car units, although at peak times two units work in multiple. The normal off-peak service requires seven units so that Class 314s also work on services to Wemyss Bay and Gourock.

These units are now the oldest in Scotland, but it is intended that they will be given life extension overhauls permitting them to remain in service until 2014.

Electrification brought the introduction of the finest service ever known on the line, with four trains an hour in each direction at stations between Pollokshields West and Cathcart, and six trains an hour at stations between Mount Florida and Pollokshields East. The basic service was half-hourly, and trains left Glasgow Central at the following times after each half hour:

03	Kirkhill via Maxwell Park
15	Outer Circle
19	Inner Circle
23	Motherwell via Queen's Park and Kirkhill
29	Neilston

This pattern lasted until May 1974 when the electrification of the Lanarkshire lines to Motherwell and Hamilton led to a complete recasting of services. Still on a half-hourly frequency, the trains now left Glasgow Central at the following times after each half hour:

04	Outer Circle
07	Inner Circle
12	Newton via Queen's Park and Kirkhill
22	Kirkhill via Maxwell Park
27	Neilston

The electrification of the West Coast main line in 1974 meant that it was no longer necessary for services on the Circle to continue beyond Newton to Motherwell, and following the recasting of services on the reopening of the Glasgow Central Low Level lines in 1979 the Kirkhill services were extended to Newton. Since the mid 1980s the basic service comprises half-hourly trains between Glasgow and Neilston, and hourly services to Newton via Queen's Park, Newton via Maxwell Park, Cathcart Inner Circle and Cathcart Outer Circle, thus giving a half-hourly service from all stations except Cathcart to Pollokshields East which have four trains per hour.

In addition to the stopping passenger trains there are two services which operate on Saturdays only via Queen's Park and Kirkhill to allow drivers to retain route knowledge in case of diversions. These are the 04.26 Glasgow Central to London Euston, which brings a Pendolino on to the Circle, and the 21.02 Glasgow Central to Edinburgh via Holytown, worked by a Cross-Country Voyager.

Glasgow Corporation Transport and British Railways

Your New BLUE TRAIN BUS

Service Between

CASTLEMILK

and Glasgow

8**D** single fare - Castlemilk to the City.

Begins Monday 5th November

Every BLUE TRAIN BUS from Castlemilk connects with electric trains at King's Park station - there is NO waiting.

Sunday services were introduced in 1962 to all lines at approximately half of the weekday services, although Motherwell and Neilston enjoyed half-hourly services. The frequency has altered over the years, with Neilston services totally withdrawn for a period from 28th February 1965. At present the Newton and Neilston services are the same as on weekdays, but there are no Circle services, resulting in the western side of the Circle having only one train per hour.

A short-lived experiment was the integration of a bus service with the electrified railway. This road/rail integration was not new, as the Caledonian Railway had operated a motor bus service between Cathcart and Clarkston stations and the village of Eaglesham. The 'Blue Train Bus', Glasgow Corporation service Number 70 met all trains at King's Park and operated through the Castlemilk housing scheme, with a single fare of 8d to Glasgow and 7d to an intermediate station, which was the same as the rail fares from King's Park excluding the bus journey. The experimental service was not a success, and it lasted for only seven months from 5th November 1962 to 3rd May 1963.

The freight handled on the line consisted principally of household coal for the area, which was carried to the four mineral depots at Mount Florida, Cathcart, Pollokshaws East and Maxwell Park. The extension of smokeless zones to the district, together with the advent of coal concentration schemes, resulted in all the mineral depots being closed by the mid 1960s, and there is now no freight service on the line. For over forty years until its closure in 1964 Maxwell Park also handled motor cars bound for the showrooms of Messrs A. & D. Fraser which had opened on an adjacent site in 1919.

Prior to electrification, when it was still the custom for large numbers of Glaswegians to travel by rail to their holiday destinations, there was a great demand for trunks being sent in advance under the PLA (Passengers Luggage in Advance) system. For 2/9 (14p) passengers could have their luggage collected by road from their houses and taken to their destination station (CL) or alternatively taken from their home station and delivered by road to their hotel (DL). For 5/6 (27.5p) the full PLA service had the luggage uplifted by road, transported by rail from home to holiday station and delivered by road to the hotel. The large quantity of luggage involved resulted in special parcels trains being run during the evenings at peak holiday times.

BELOW: The connecting motor bus provided by the Caledonian Railway for a few years between Cathcart and Clarkston stations and the village of Eaglesham. Built by Durham-Churchill in 1906 it was one of three buses which operated the route until 31st January 1909, after which it was adapted for rail operation between Connel Ferry and Benderloch.

E.R.O. 4091

LMS Issued at _Langside_ Station
EXCESS FARE TICKET

W 001503   Date 29th March 19 69

Ticket held* _____ No. _____
Excessed from _Newlands_
To _Langside_
Train 1502   Available until _day of issue only_

Cause of Excess	Class	No. of Passengers		£	s.	d.
		Single	Return			
Without Tickets:— (a)* SCS	2	ONE				4
(b) Workman						
Ticket short of destination						
Ticket out of date						
Difference between						
Third Class to First						
*Give description						

NOT TRANSFERABLE   W McKnight   Collector
Issued subject to the Bye-Laws, Regulations, Notices and Conditions published in the Company's Bills and Notices.

ABOVE: CR '439 Class 0-4-4T No. 55167 between Pollokshields West and Maxwell Park with the 5.39pm Inner Circle train on 26th April 1956. This was a popular service for homeward-bound office workers.
W. A. C. SMITH

BELOW: The 'Blue Train Bus', Glasgow Corporation Transport route 70, connected King's Park station with the Castlemilk housing scheme for seven months from 5th November 1962.
W. S. SELLAR

Pollokshields West on the last day of operation by steam and diesel traction, 26th May 1962. Two twin diesel multiple units form an Outer Circle service.

J. L. Stevenson

CHAPTER 9

MAXWELL PARK – A PERSONAL REMINISCENCE

In November 1892 advertisements appeared in *The Glasgow Herald*, the *North British Daily Mail* and the *Scottish Leader* inviting tenders for the construction of the station buildings on the extension line. This involved the buildings at the six stations between the new station at Cathcart and Pollokshields West. Drawings could be inspected and duplicate copies of the schedule of the works embraced in the contract could be obtained from the offices of the engineers, Messrs Wharrie, Colledge and Brand, 109 Bath Street, on payment of one guinea (£1.05). The partners of Alexander Eadie and Son of Cathcart Road invested their guinea, and put in their tender. Although tenders had to be lodged by 2nd December 1892, it was not until 20th March 1893 that they found they were successful, and work was immediately commenced on the construction of the buildings. As their tender was £8,050, plus £213:18/- for the painting contract which was awarded to Mr George W. Sellars, the total cost of the six buildings was £8,263:18/-. The cost of the Maxwell Park building was probably slightly greater than one sixth of this amount, £1,377, as both Pollokshields West and Maxwell Park were more complex structures than the other four buildings.

Unlike all other buildings on the Circle, Pollokshields West and Maxwell Park were of two-storey construction. Steel latticed footbridges from the streets which ran along the cuttings adjacent to the line led to the upper floor where there was situated the booking office and, opposite it, a broad flight of stairs giving covered access to the island platform. A feature of the slated roof of both stations was scalloped snowboarding. Circle station buildings comprised a solid base on which was built a supporting structure of steel or iron posts at regular intervals from which sprang broad timber brackets. On top of these was a timber and glazed canopy which, when built, would have been relatively lightweight. The walls were built of timber studs with timber cladding which allowed numerous doors and windows to be installed in an arrangement to suit the individual layout required at each station. The roofs were shallow and slated, the two gable ends terminating in timber infills. Maxwell Park had five fireplaces which required two chimney stacks. The westerly one had three chimneys, for the fires in the booking office and, at platform level, in the ladies' waiting room and the station master's room, which were back to back, and the easterly one, the stack for which bisected the internal stairway, for the fires in the porters' room and the general waiting room, which were also back to back. In addition to the four rooms at platform level which had fireplaces, at the westerly end was the gentlemen's toilet, while under the stairs, accessed only from the Outer Circle side, was a small cellar. All other rooms were accessed from both platforms, with the exception of the station master's room which had a door on the Inner Circle side only. The ladies' waiting room was designated originally for the use of first class lady passengers only. There was a ladies' toilet accessed from inside the ladies' waiting room. No provision seems to have been made for ladies travelling third class! During the 1930s the base of the building at platform level was altered to be of

Fairburn 2-6-4T No. 42244 leaving Maxwell Park with the 9.30pm Outer Circle on 25th February 1958. W. A. C. SMITH

CR 'Jumbo' 0-6-0 No. 199, which later became British Railways 57373, at Maxwell Park goods yard around 1925 with a train delivering cars to the adjacent showroom of A. & D. Fraser. Tank wagons delivering fuel for the cars can be seen in the right of the photograph.

A. GREIG COLLECTION

attractive red brick on a sandstone base. Pollokshields West was not similarly altered.

At the time of the opening of the station there was very little potential traffic. While Maxwell Park itself, a gift from Sir John Stirling Maxwell for the recreation of the people of the district, had opened on 25th October 1890, the only building visible from the new station was likely to have been the impressive Pollokshields Burgh Hall which had opened on the same day. Villas already existed to the north of Glencairn Drive, but the newly constructed Terregles Avenue and Fotheringay Road which flanked the cutting in which the railway ran between Maxwell Park and Pollokshields West still awaited housing development. They were built with pavements immediately adjacent to the cutting, so that no houses would be built backing onto the railway.

A goods yard was provided on the Shawlands side of the Springkell Avenue bridge, and in 1894 Springkell Avenue gave access only to the goods yard. There were no houses on the Inner Circle side of the railway between Shawlands and Pollokshields West stations. A house for the station master at Maxwell Park was built by Alexander Eadie & Son early in 1895. It was situated immediately beside the Outer Circle, opposite the goods yard, and accessed by a path leading from Springkell Avenue. At that time there were no houses adjacent to it. It is likely that the principal goods handled in the new station's yard were the sandstone building blocks to construct the villas and flats which subsequently housed the passengers. When the station

was built the southern entrance was not open, a substantial wooden door at the building entrance remaining locked, as the only possible source of traffic was from the north. By 1908 most of the houses had been built and the southern entrance was opened, but the wooden door remained in place until the 1970s. Thereafter it was stored in the general waiting room which by that time was no longer in public use. The principal traffic for the goods yard now became coal for the fires in the many houses, but a new source of traffic came with the opening in 1920 of a garage by A. & D. Fraser who at one time were Scotland's largest Nuffield distributor. Archie and David Fraser had founded their business in 1919 in modest premises at Herriet Street, but had the foresight to move to premises adjacent to a railway line to ease delivery of the new vehicles. As the area was undeveloped it was easy for the business to expand, which it did, eventually occupying a building 300 feet long and with 57,000 square feet of floor space along the entire length of Maxwell Park goods yard. The business, which started selling Morris cars in 1922, continued to expand from the Maxwell Park base, with a city-centre showroom in Bothwell Street and further branches in Hamilton, Kilmarnock, Troon and Ayr. Lengthy trains bringing new cars to the showroom became a feature for the goods yard which also handled petrol tankers to provide fuel for the cars.

A notable passenger who used Maxwell Park from 1902 was the Caledonian locomotive superintendent, John F. McIntosh. He had lived close to the Cathcart Circle from around the time of

A further view of new cars being unloaded at Maxwell Park goods yard. A passenger train composed of four-wheel coaches hauled by a CR 0-4-4 tank engine can be seen in the top left, while the Outer Circle home signal, at that time with two co-acting arms, can be seen above the chimney of the goods yard office building.

MAP: Maxwell Park station in 1894.

PLANS: Maxwell Park station building.

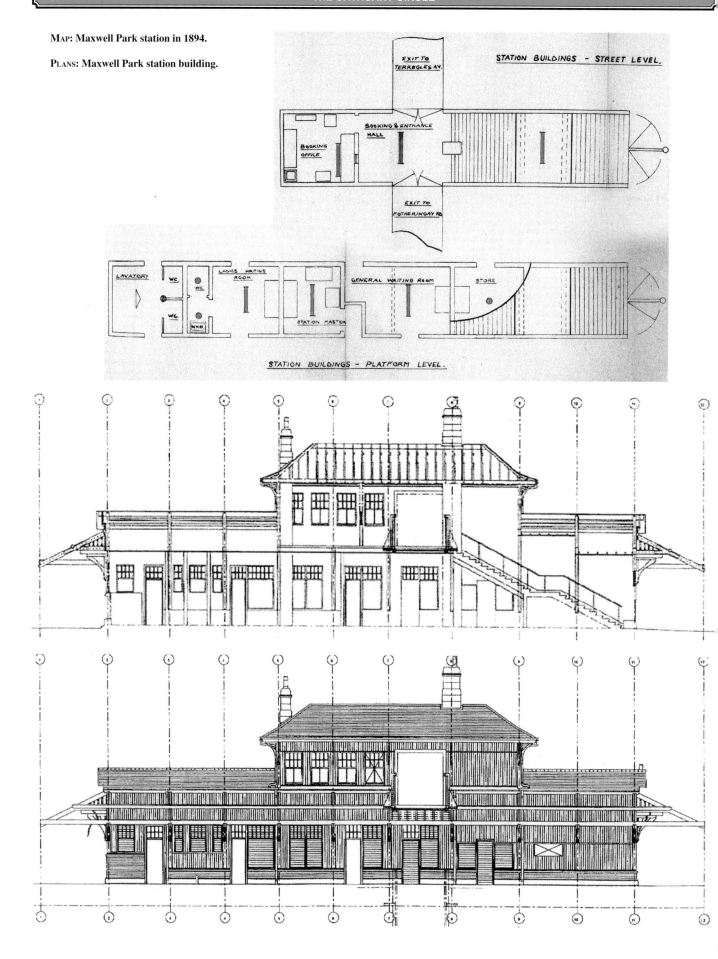

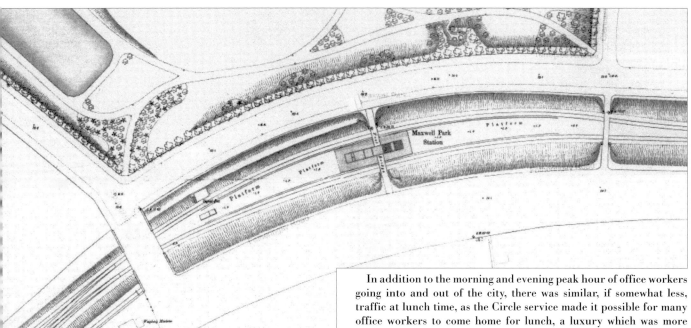

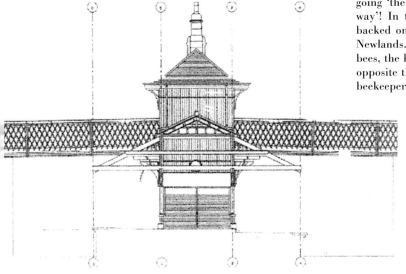

the opening of the original line, since he is recorded as resident at 5 Hampden Terrace, adjacent to Mount Florida station, on the day of his marriage to his near neighbour Jeannie Logan of 1 Hampden Terrace on 5th December 1888. Around the time of his appointment as locomotive superintendent in 1895 he moved to 67 Albert Road, where he is likely to have used Queen's Park, but the final sixteen years of his life were spent at 38 Dalziel Drive. One can imagine him strolling daily through Maxwell Park to the station where probably few of his fellow passengers would be aware that they were travelling with the designer of the locomotive which was hauling them! Of a quiet summer evening he could well have sat in his garden listening to the bark of one of his '104' Class 0-4-4 tanks attacking the climb from Maxwell Park to Shawlands. He retired as superintendent in May 1914, and continued to live at Dalziel Drive until his death in February 1918.

In addition to the morning and evening peak hour of office workers going into and out of the city, there was similar, if somewhat less, traffic at lunch time, as the Circle service made it possible for many office workers to come home for lunch, a luxury which was more easy to achieve a hundred years ago when offices closed for lunch for longer than an hour. A further benefit was that, as season tickets granted unlimited travel, there was effectively no cost for this, nor was there any additional cost to a season ticket holder in going back into town in the evening to the theatre or the cinema. Not only local residents used the trains. Crossmyloof Ice Rink had opened in 1908, customers using the trains in the evenings, while pupils attending nearby Craigholme School for girls and Hutchesons' Boys' Grammar School arrived in the middle of the morning rush and went home from the station in the afternoon. Craigholme School had opened in the same year as the station at 63 Dalziel Drive, moving to St Andrews Drive in 1939. Hutchesons' Boys' Grammar School was founded in 1641 and moved from premises in Crown Street to a new building at Crossmyloof in 1959, although the primary school had used the new building since 1957. The school became co-educational, as Hutchesons' Grammar School, in 1975.

Brought up in Shawlands, and somewhat confusingly having Pollokshaws East as my home station, I have known the Circle from my earliest days, and recollect the excitement of being allowed, accompanied by parent of course, to go into town 'the long way', via Cathcart, giving an extra ten minutes excitement in the train over going 'the short way'. We always seemed to come home 'the short way'! In the 1950s my father had an allotment, or 'plot', which backed onto the line between Pollokshaws East and Langside and Newlands. In addition to growing vegetables and flowers he kept bees, the hives being at the foot of the plot next to the railway, just opposite the Pollokshaws East Inner Circle starting signal. Another beekeeper close by was a Polmadie driver who kept his bees on the railway embankment near Langside and Newlands station. While the plot was a perfect spot for watching trains, there were few to see as times spent there tended to be Saturday and Sunday afternoons and summer evenings, all times when the line was closed! School holidays did give an opportunity to see the trains and the occasional Saturday afternoon when there was a major football match provided the wonderful spectacle of trains passing frequently and then lining up nose to tail on the Inner Circle awaiting the homeward traffic at the end of the game.

In 1958 I transferred from the local school to Hutchesons' Boys' Grammar School and for this first year at the school used Pollokshields West station as it was closest to the primary section. It was in this year that I was first introduced, through my fellow pupils and the proximity of the former Glasgow & South Western main line, to the delights of watching main line trains. It was just possible, if the teacher's eye was averted, to see the southbound Thames–Clyde Express around 9.30am heading south, usually double headed by a 2P and a 'Royal Scot'. At this time I started going into town to watch trains on Saturday mornings and in the evenings, the latter being to see the departure of the 6.45pm mail train from Platform 11 and the 6.50pm to London from Platform 1. Usually these would be hauled by 'Princess Coronation' Pacifics, but in later years the English Electric Type 4 diesels took over. My journeys on the Cathcart Circle were on the 6.5pm Outer Circle, initially still steam worked and giving the inexplicable thrill of travelling non-stop through Shawlands and Maxwell Park, and home on the last train of the day, the 7pm Inner Circle, which by that time was worked by a diesel multiple unit.

In September 1959 I moved to the senior school, the entrance to which was closer to Maxwell Park, and so began my association with that station. The next few years proved to be a fascinating time on the Circle. I was able to enjoy the final years of the atmosphere of what in some places, like Langside and Maxwell Park, felt almost like

ABOVE: On the first day of 'The Sixties', 1st January 1960, the 12.30pm Outer Circle passes Maxwell Park signalbox. This service was normally worked by steam but, as a reduced service was operating on a holiday, it consisted of two twin diesel multiple units, the leading one built by Cravens. As there is no signalman present, it is likely that the signalbox was switched out, with Cathcart West Junction working to Muirhouse Junction.

W. A. C. SMITH/TRANSPORT TREASURY

a country branch line in the outskirts of the city, while witnessing the engineering work involved in electrification, modernisation of the stations and installation of colour light signalling. School friends from Langside and I were able to travel home for lunch, timed to perfection. School finished for lunch at 12 noon, and a run to Maxwell Park enabled us to catch the 12.7pm Inner Circle, into Pollokshaws East at 12.12. My mother had lunch on the table for my father (who was also able to travel home for lunch from work in the city by the same trains) and me at 12.20. We left home at 12.40, caught the train at Pollokshaws East at 12.49, Maxwell Park was reached at 12.53, and another run along Fotheringay Road trying in vain to keep up with the departing train, enabled the desk to be reached in time for classes recommencing at 1pm! There were risks involved, of course, the biggest of which was the non-appearance of the 12.49 return train, which did happen on occasions during the period when electrification work was disrupting services! A lengthy run in those circumstances inevitably resulted in a late arrival back at school! After electrification the timetable was still suitable for lunch at home, but it is no longer possible with today's timetable.

The stations still had a character unchanged, probably, since the time of the opening of the line. In 1960 all stations except Crosshill and Queen's Park were lit by gas, and had coal fires in the waiting rooms. There was a lovely cosy atmosphere when waiting for trains in front of a roaring fire and listening to the crackle of the flames and the gentle hiss from the gas lamp. These were also the last years before Glasgow became a smokeless zone, and during periods of fog a reduced train service operated, known as the 'fog service'. This could result in no journeys home for lunch and lengthier waits than usual for the train home after school, but the additional times spent in front of the waiting-room fire were most enjoyable. Occasionally one of our number would be sent out to see if by any chance our train was signalled, the fog sometimes being so thick that a walk to the end of the platform was required.

While diesel multiple units took over most of the services during this period, a few services, particularly during the peak periods, remained steam hauled until the electric trains started in May 1962. The first day started with an adventure. A full weekday service was to operate on Sunday 27th May, so, to ensure that I travelled on the first train, I walked into town, intending to travel as far as Mount Florida on the 5.53am to Motherwell. It was advertised as departing from Platform 6, so, along with a dozen or so others, I joined the train at that platform, going right up to the front to enjoy the view from directly behind the driving cab. Only when the train ran non-stop through Pollokshields East and Queen's Park did we realise that we were on the 5.50am empty train to Neilston! An exhilarating

RIGHT: CR 'Jumbo' 0-6-0 No. 57360 at Maxwell Park with the 5.39pm Inner Circle train in April 1957.   J. L. STEVENSON

non-stop run ensued, and the unwitting passengers returned, without complaint, on the 6.24am from Neilston.

During 1963, having developed over the previous four years a friendship with the station staff, I started spending some of my leisure time at Maxwell Park station. In particular I was interested in the operation of the booking office, and soon learned how to sell tickets and keep the financial records. During the school summer holidays in 1962 and 1963 I had worked as an office boy in a chartered accountants' office in the city, enjoying 'real' commuting into town, and had begun to think that accountancy might be an interesting career. The first 'books' I ever kept were, totally unofficially, the scroll balance books at Maxwell Park, and I like to think that it was this which started me on the career which served me throughout my working life. Despite my love of railways, I never had any real desire to work on the railways, except, possibly, as a signalman! In 1963 there were five members of staff at the station, Tom McPherson the station master, Eddie McGuire and Gordon Sloan the clerks, and Louden Connolly and Hector Kerr the leading porters. Hector had been a signalman in Maxwell Park box prior to its closure in 1961 and his brother was a signalman in St Enoch box.

I was soon joined at the station by my friend Hamish Stevenson who also used the station on his journeys to school, keeping his bicycle in the porters' room every day when he travelled across the city to Glasgow Academy. It was from Maxwell Park that we set off for our trips to visit many railway lines, stations and sheds in what was both a fascinating and sometimes sad time. While many of our trips were to be last visits (and often for us at the same time first visits) to lines and stations due for closure, we would also be accumulating as much mileage as possible in the last years of steam. We had a particular interest in tickets and would visit as many stations as possible to obtain tickets for our collections. If we were lucky we would find some pre-nationalisation tickets, often old and worn in the ticket cases through

ABOVE: A clerk at work in Maxwell Park booking office on 1st February 1986, the year before the booking office closed. P. AITKEN

BELOW: Electric multiple unit 005 at Maxwell Park on 20th August 1965 on the 17.06 Motherwell to Glasgow, as indicated by the headcode 2H. The artistic work on the platform ramp was largely the work of Eddie Connolly who was relief porter at the station for several months in 1965. H. STEVENSON

BRITISH RAILWAYS **TRAIN ACCOUNT BOOK**

PAGE ①

STATIONS	Class and Desc.	Fare	DATE 1/1/64 NAME McGuire								DATE 2-2-64 NAME R...w							
			Commencing Number	Closing Number	Child	Non-Issued	No of Tickets	Debit £	s.	d.	Commencing Number	Closing Number	Child	Non-Issued	No of Tickets	Debit £	s.	d.
EGLINTON STREET	2ND O/S.	6d									576							
QUEEN'S PARK		6d	2410½				1			3	2410½	2412½			2		1	
POLLOKSHIELDS WEST		3d	6953				1			3	6953	6961			8		2	
" " CHILD		2d									8407	8409			2			4
BLANK CARD		—																
" CHILD		—									171							
PAPER TICKET		—									8969							
										6							3	4
QUEEN'S PARK	2ND C/R	1/-									383							
" CHILD		6d									240	242			2		1	
POLLOKSHIELDS WEST		6d	7154				1			6	7154	7156			2		1	
" CHILD		3d																
BLANK CARD		—									472							
" CHILD		—									061							
PAPER TICKET		—									7943							
										6							2	-
SPECIAL CHEAP SINGLES	2ND																	
GLASGOW CEN [CARD]			9335		1		1½	1		1½	9335	9340½			5½	4	1	½
BURNSIDE		10d									862	865			3		2	6
" CHILD		5d									1249	1252			3		1	3
CROFTFOOT		8d									479	481			2		1	4
" CHILD		4d									347	356			9		3	
CATHCART ZONE		7d	2234		1		2	1		2	2234	2241			7		4	1
" CHILD		4d	2058		1		1			4	2056	2059			3		1	
GLASGOW CEN [ULT]		9d	33098	33106			8	6		-	33106	33155			49	1	16	9
GLASGOW CEN CHILD		5d																
KING'S PARK		7d									731	735			4		2	4
" CHILD		4d									305							
KIRKHILL		1/-									224½	226			1½		1	6
LANGSIDE		5d									1559	1560			1			3
" CHILD		3d																
MOTHERWELL		2/-									041							
POLLOKSHAWS EAST		4d	2824		1		2			8	2824	2830			6		2	
" CHILD		2d	2424		1		1			2	2424							
WILLIAMWOOD		9d									125½							
" CHILD		5d																
WHITECRAIGS		9d									032							
" CHILD		5d									305							
BLANK CARD		—	664		1		1			5	664	665			1			5
" CHILD		—									685							
								9	62							3	06½	
DBP 3mile SINGLE		3d			1						—							
" " RETURN		5d			1						336							
" 6 mile SINGLE		8d			1						101							
" " RETURN		1/-			1						150							
" BLANK SINGLE		—			1						104							
" BLANK RETURN		—			1						250							
PT BLANK SINGLE		—									010							
" BLANK RETURN		—									233							
" BLANK RETURN CHILD		—									002							
" GLASGOW RETURN		5d									080	082			2			10
TOTAL C/F TO PAGE 2								10	0½							3	6	8½

lack of use. Investigation of the contents of station lofts could be a somewhat dangerous, and inevitably filthy, exercise, but could prove very rewarding! There was nothing of interest in Maxwell Park's loft but Pollokshields West revealed a set of Caledonian Railway special traffic notices dating from 1912. We would occasionally find pre-grouping posters and timetables, and often saw ideas for decorating Maxwell Park in novel ways! The idea for painting the steps inside the building came from Doune, and the flower-filled hanging half-tyres under the main station nameboards from Logierieve! The staff became enthusiastically involved in developing the gardens, and in particular Eddie Connelly, who came for several months on relief, was an expert in making a model wasp, complete with cardboard wings, out of the end of the station broom!

Strangely, there were no timetables available for distribution to passengers in the mid sixties, although each station had printed posters showing the times of all trains for display at the entrances and on the platforms. A further one was pinned inside the booking office for the staff. We rectified this by producing typed duplicated timetables, incorporating a photograph of the station, which were given free to passengers, although we did encourage, if asked, donations for the station gardens fund.

Each week we would await the arrival at the station of two booklets which were probably of very little interest to the staff but of great interest to us. These were the 'SW' and 'Sc2' notices. The first gave warning of impending signalbox closures, sometimes necessitating a visit for final photographs while the latter gave the timetables for any

ABOVE: English Electric Type 1 (later Class 20) No. D8120 passing the station master's house at Maxwell Park with the 5.54pm football special from Glasgow Central to Mount Florida on 2nd May 1962.

W. A. C. SMITH/TRANSPORT TREASURY

RIGHT: Maxwell Park's brief day as a terminus. On 1st May 1961 an Inter City diesel multiple unit reverses on the crossover, operating a shuttle service to Glasgow due to the reconstruction of the bridge carrying the Circle over the GB&K line at Shawlands not having been completed the previous weekend. An engineers' electrification train sits in the goods yard.   W. A. C. SMITH

FACING PAGE: Scroll balance book for Maxwell Park station, February 1964.

special trains operating south and west of Glasgow in the next week, which might well produce interesting engines!

There were changes in the station staff. Tom McPherson went on to become station inspector at Queen Street, being replaced by John Coughtrie, who came from the remote station at Barrhill in Ayrshire. The number of clerks was reduced to one, the post being filled by Georgina (Georgie) Oliver, while Louden Connolly moved to head office to be replaced by Jimmy Burns transferred from St Enoch.

The abolition of the station master's post in 1966 on the formation of the area management scheme provided us with an excellent opportunity as it appeared that, unlike Mount Florida and Queen's Park where offices were required for the area management staff, there was no apparent use for the station master's room at Maxwell Park. Accordingly it was used for the next five years as an unofficial railway museum where the various items 'saved' on the closure of lines and stations were kept. There had been an earlier attempt to create a museum after we discovered in the cellar under the stairs the complete set of original platform signs for Porters' Room, General Waiting Room, Station Master's Room, Ladies Waiting Room (First Class) and Gentlemen. These formed the principal 'exhibits' in a museum created in the oil store at the Shawlands end of the platform, which, as the station was no longer responsible for filling the oil lamps behind semaphore signals, was available for this new purpose. To our great disappointment, we arrived one day to find that the oil store, complete with the precious relics, had been demolished! The former station master's room was a safer option and the principal items kept there were two Caledonian and two Glasgow & South Western Railway block signalling instruments, the Caledonian ones from Dunrod and Wemyss Bay and the Glasgow & South Western ones from Stoneybrae in Paisley. The clock from Shields Junction

No. 2 signalbox was also put back to work and, mounted high on one wall, Maxwell Park's own Caledonian Railway lower quadrant distant signal for the Outer Circle, restored to its original red colour. Colourful Glasgow & South Western posters advertising Clyde Coast resorts decorated the walls. The largest item was the panel from Galashiels signal box, obtained following its closure in 1969. This was an early power signalling installation dating from January 1937. It was so heavy that we had to muster as many friends as possible to get it down the stairs from the van used for its delivery and along the platform into its new home. Twelve of us were involved in this operation!

I interrupted my accountancy studies, started in 1964, for three years from 1966 to study law at Glasgow University. The station master's room, quiet apart from the perfectly acceptable sounds of trains passing on each Circle every quarter of an hour and the sonorous ticking of the signalbox clock, provided a perfect location for studying, being kept cosy and warm by the solid fuel stove. There was also the temptation of the daily purchase of a bar of chocolate from Bunty in the bookstall. After she closed at lunchtime, remaining newspapers were transferred to the booking office for collection.

During my time at Maxwell Park, I was introduced to the signalmen at the new power signalbox at Muirhouse Junction and learnt the rudiments of signalling. There was no great difficulty in signalling the electric trains, although you had to be careful not to send an Inner Circle train round the Outer! More interesting were the trains to and from Strathbungo Junction where you had to use the block instruments and operate the points. The real excitement came on the rare occasions when a train came from Terminus Junction as, in addition to the operation of more points and the other block instruments, it was unusual to be able to allow the train through the

Part of the decoration of Maxwell Park in the summer of 1965. The oil store housed the first small 'museum' before it was demolished, complete with contents. The idea for planting flowers in a painted half-tyre hung under the nameboard came from Logierieve station, while the half-painted posts with black tops emulated Doune.

J. KERNAHAN

junction without stopping due to a conflicting move by an electric service. There was a real feeling of power in turning the switch to allow the train to proceed and watching the engine starting to lift its heavy train at your command!

Eventually all things come to an end, and in 1971 I qualified as a chartered accountant, married and set up house in Larbert. The museum was disbanded and most items transferred to the Scottish Railway Preservation Society's museum, then situated at nearby Falkirk and now at Bo'ness.

Along with the other stations between Langside and Pollokshields West, Maxwell Park was unstaffed from 13th April 1987 and, while there had not been a great deal of maintenance done on the station during the seventies and the eighties, a real deterioration to the building set in after that date. In early 1989 a contract was let to demolish Maxwell Park and Pollokshields West, the buildings at Langside, Pollokshaws East and Shawlands having already disappeared. Work started on Sunday 28th May on Pollokshields West, and the street level building and part of the platform canopy were removed before instructions were received to stop the work immediately as the necessary Conservation Area Consent had not been obtained. The building remained in a fairly dangerous condition for nearly three years, during which time it was suggested that it might be necessary to close the station permanently due to the cost of rebuilding, estimated at £440,000. In March 1992 the local authority reluctantly gave permission and Pollokshields West was demolished, to be replaced by a wall-less waiting shelter, but Maxwell Park remained, having been 'B' listed in 1990. All windows had been boarded up, and the doors to all the rooms locked. However, a few years after unstaffing I paid a visit to the station with my daughter and found the doors to several of the rooms lying

open! We, of course, investigated, and soon I heard my daughter exclaim 'I've just found your writing, Dad!!' She had discovered in the porters' room the scroll balance book from December 1963 and January 1964, which contained my first attempts at book-keeping, and supplied evidence of the time I had spent at the station when I should have been studying for my 'Highers'! Interestingly the book disclosed that on Christmas Day 1963 there were both early- and late-shift clerks on duty, the early shift taking in £6:11/7. This sum was somewhat falsely high as someone purchased a £4 three-monthly season to Glasgow on Christmas morning! The back shift earned a more modest £3:9/10.

No new use could be found for Maxwell Park station. It appeared in the Scottish Civic Trust's 'Buildings at Risk' bulletin and Glasgow City Council's 'Surplus Buildings Register'. For both publicity purposes and in an attempt to find a possible tenant for the building, an Open Day was held by Scotrail on 20th June 1993. I was honoured to be asked to perform the opening ceremony. A Class 101 diesel multiple unit ran a shuttle service round the Inner Circle to take visitors from and back to Glasgow Central, while on view on the Outer Circle were a Class 90 electric locomotive and Class 26 and 37 diesel locomotives together with Class 303 electric unit 048, restored as far as possible to original condition and in the Caledonian blue livery of the first 'Blue Trains'. Eddie Connolly, one of the staff stalwarts of the sixties at the station, was present, and it was a great pleasure for Hamish and me to meet him there again. The event was unsuccessful in finding a new user for the building, and deterioration continued, particularly to the glass in the canopies which eventually was largely removed by 1996. In 1998 a Listed Buildings Repairs Notice was served so something had to be done!

Under Railtrack's station regeneration programme the station was

The arrival of the panel from the early power signalbox at Galashiels installed by the LNER. Following closure of the Waverley Route in 1969 the panel was kept in the small museum in the former station master's room for a few years. It was so heavy it took twelve enthusiasts to carry it!   J. KERNAHAN

The external refurbishment of the station building at Maxwell
Park which took place during 2000.   J. KERNAHAN

ubstantially refurbished externally at a cost of £525,000, although his left the interior at platform level as an empty shell, accessed by only one door from the Outer Circle side and with no windows other han two sections adjacent to the door which are covered by external hutters and small areas on both sides located at a high level. The very effective natural lighting of the staircase was lost when the buildings were boarded up and these windows have not been re-instated. The project won a Commendation in the RIAS Regeneration of Scotland Awards for 2000. The slatted wooden bench seats from the waiting room were saved, and can now be found in use at Birkhill station on the Bo'ness and Kinneil Railway. The former booking office was enlarged and a rear extension constructed, apparently with the intention of creating access to the lower level by means of a spiral staircase which was not constructed. The building was repainted in the attractive red and cream colours of the Strathclyde Passenger Executive and looked extremely smart on the morning of 25th August 2000 when the plaque on the Inner Circle side, at the site of the former station master's room (and our museum!) was unveiled by Tom Winsor, the Rail Regulator.

A new use for the building continued to be sought, but the lack of a water supply with resultant lack of toilet facilities has proved a major obstacle. Although there was a water supply to both levels of the building until unstaffing, it appears to be impossible, or exceedingly difficult, to restore the supply. Accordingly the buildings at platform level remain unused, but in January 2009 the former booking office was given a new lease of life as a community meeting room. The work involved laying a new floor and carpeting, renewing the electricity supply with wall lighting and installation of tongue and groove panelling. This was done under First Scotrail's 'Adopt-a-Station' scheme and the work in creating the new room was masterminded by Pollokshields Heritage, with help from the Glasgow Buildings Preservation Trust and financial assistance from Glasgow City Council and The Railway Heritage Trust. I was delighted to perform the opening ceremony and presented for display in the room a few items which were being returned 'home' after several years in my safekeeping. As well as Tom McPherson's station master's hat, a framed page from the scroll balance book mentioned earlier and several photographs and tickets, the original framed map of the area, hand drawn probably some time at the beginning of the twentieth century by a member of staff, was restored to the exact spot, above where the sink used to be, from whence I had 'borrowed' it on the unstaffing in 1987.

The station is now neat and tidy, with a well glazed canopy, five cycle storage racks, and with gardens also making a welcome reappearance, thanks to Pollokshields Heritage. Much of the atmosphere of the country station was lost on electrification, and with the closure of the bookstall, but most of all with the withdrawal of staff. The station is covered by closed circuit television, particulars of train running is provided on electronic information boards and tickets are purchased from a machine on the platform.

Every time I visit Glasgow, I return for a short time to Maxwell Park, remember the happy times spent there, and in particular the friendly staff and passengers, and rejoice that the building, beautifully restored, is still in existence. It was so nearly lost!

Dusk falling at Maxwell Park on 15th December 2009 shows the heritage lighting installed at the time of refurbishment in 2000 and the more recently installed passenger information screen.

J. KERNAHAN

ABOVE: The last appearance of a blue 'Blue Train' on the Cathcart Circle. The last unrefurbished unit, 048, retained its original seating with full forward views for passengers behind the driving compartments and was restored for a short time to its original lined Caledonian Railway blue. It is seen at the Open Day held at Maxwell Park on 20th June 1993. Sadly it was not possible for unit 048 to be preserved.

RIGHT AND BELOW: Maxwell Park in the twenty-first century. The staff have been replaced with closed circuit television, electronic train information screens and a ticket vending machine.
ALL J. KERNAHAN

♿ Maxwell Park

- An unstaffed halt with stairs down to an Island platform
- There is a customer help point on platform fitted with an induction loop
- The station has a ticket vending machine
- There are 5 cycle racks
- CCTV in operation

This plaque was unveiled
by
Tom Winsor, Rail Regulator
on
25 August 2000
to mark the completion of
the Station Regeneration Programme
refurbishment work at
Maxwell Park.

RAILTRACK | Scotland

The refurbishment of the station building was celebrated with the unveiling of a suitable plaque on 25th August 2000 by the Rail Regulator, Tom Winsor, seen with representatives of Pollokshields Heritage, Railtrack and the contractors who undertook the work.

ALL J. KERNAHAN

The Inner Circle platform after the completion of the refurbishment work, showing the reglazed canopy and the heritage lighting, emulating the gas lamps of an earlier age.

J. KERNAHAN

CONCLUSION

A century ago the Cathcart Circle passengers, virtually all wearing hats, the ladies long dresses and the gentlemen carrying rolled umbrellas, would crowd into the compartments of the four-wheeled coaches for their journeys 'into town'. Fifty years later, much of the experience they had daily at the stations remained unaltered. The queue at the booking office window, the aroma of the highly polished linoleum on the counter, the double 'clunk' of the dating press as a ticket was purchased and, if it was a dark winter's day, the smell and hiss of the gas lamps and the crackle of the waiting room fire would be much the same as Edwardian travellers had known. By this time there were more compartments in the coaches and, if one was fortunate, it was possible to get a compartment to oneself. This meant that, using the large leather strap provided, it was possible without annoying other passengers to lower the window. Ignoring the cautionary notice warning passengers 'do not lean out of the window' (occasionally irreverently amended to read 'do not clean soot off the window'), one could enjoy from a compartment at the front of the train the sight and sound of the steam engine at work and look out by night for the beautiful blue/green colour of the signal as the signal spectacles were illuminated by the oil lamps behind them.

Today the experience is so very different, and the line is akin to a glorified tramway. Indeed, there are occasional attempts to convert the Circle and its associated lines to a light rapid transit modern tramway.

In reply to a letter to the editor of the *Glasgow Herald* in January 1953 complaining about the poor timekeeping prevalent on the Cathcart Circle at the time, an enthusiastic supporter of the line hoped that it would 'be a long time before it was reduced to a punctual, fool-proof, characterless, push-button electric railway.' The newspaper's 'Editorial Diary', following the correspondence, also came out out in favour of the railway as it was. 'It is worthy of respect and devoted preservation as an ancient monument.' That was just under sixty years after the opening of the Circle. Almost a further sixty years have passed, and effectively the railway has become what was feared. The trains run punctually, the modern electronic signalling is operated by a push-button system and is as fool-proof as humanly possible, the unstaffed stations are devoid of 'characters', and the line is, of course, electrified. The newspaper's correspondents in 1953 would never have contemplated the stations monitored by close circuit television and the staff replaced by a ticket issuing machine, a remotely controlled public address system and an electronic train information system.

There is still an incline at Cathcart where John McGaw climbed to the new Cathcart station on that May morning in 1886, but it now leads to Victoria Mansions, modern executive flats built on the site of the original passenger and goods station. The sites of the other goods stations at Mount Florida, Pollokshaws East and Maxwell Park, and the area at Langside where its goods station would have been built, are now also occupied by housing, thus finally achieving the aim of the Cathcart Circle's promoters that housing would follow the railway.

Provost Browne and his fellow promoters of the Cathcart District Railway would have no difficulty today in recognising the Cathcart Circle which they founded in the last decades of the nineteenth century and, while they might be saddened to see some of the stations reduced to unstaffed halts, they would be pleased to know that their railway was continuing into the twenty-first century to serve the suburbs which it was instrumental in creating.

Maxwell Park after refurbishment in 2000. Much of the foliage surrounding the station has now been removed.   J. KERNAHAN

English Electric Type 4 diesel (later Class 40) No. D364 climbs towards Shawlands from Pollokshaws East with a returning football special from King's Park.
J.Kernahan

APPENDIX 1
CHRONOLOGY: CATHCART CIRCLE

Nov	1864	Kilmarnock District Railway, via Cathcart, proposed.
15 Nov	1879	Three competing schemes for lines between Glasgow and Cathcart proposed.
7 Sept	1880	Cathcart District Railway Act passed.
16 Dec	1880	First meeting of directors of Cathcart District Railway Company.
12 April	1882	First meeting of shareholders of Cathcart District Railway Company.
20 Jan	1883	First turf cut.
1 March	1886	Cathcart Junction to Mount Florida opened to passengers (single line only between Crosshill and Mount Florida).
25 May	1886	Mount Florida to Cathcart opened to passengers as double line (double line completed between Crosshill and Mount Florida).
2 Aug	1886	Cathcart Junction to Cathcart opened to goods.
19 July	1887	Act authorising extension passed.
9 Oct	1890	Tender for construction of extension let.
19 March	1894	New station on extension line at Cathcart opened.
2 April	1894	Extension line from Cathcart to Muirhouse Junction opened to passengers and goods.
1 Aug	1901	Langside station renamed Langside and Newlands.
1 July	1903	Cathcart Junction renamed Pollokshields East Junction.
1 Jan	1917	Pollokshields East and Crosshill stations closed as wartime economies.
1 March	1919	Pollokshields East station reopened.
1 June	1919	Crosshill station reopened.
21 Feb	1923	Last meeting of directors of Cathcart District Railway Company.
16 March	1923	Last meeting of shareholders of Cathcart District Railway Company.
20 Sept	1940	Pollokshields East Junction accident.
10 Dec	1945	Pollokshields East murder.
21 April	1951	Queen's Park accident.
27 April	1956	Electrification authorised.
25 Jan	1958	Cathcart station partially destroyed by fire.
7 July	1958	Diesel multiple units introduced on off-peak services.
6 March	1961	Cathcart West Junction altered to permit running from Kirkhill line to west side of Cathcart Circle.
10 Dec	1961	Electric power switched on.
27 May	1962	Electric services commenced.
		Langside and Newlands station name reverted to Langside.
		Sunday services introduced.
7 March	1965	Stations unstaffed on Sundays.
28 March	1966	Glasgow South Area Manager's office opened.
13 Aug	1966	Langside station partially destroyed by fire.
11 June	1974	Pollokshields East Junction accident.
21 April	1976	Pollokshields East station partially destroyed by fire.
13 April	1987	Langside, Pollokshaws East, Shawlands, Maxwell Park and Pollokshields West stations unstaffed and other stations staffed only on early shifts.
25 Aug	2000	Refurbished building at Maxwell Park opened.
15 Jan	2009	Former booking office at Maxwell Park opened as small community meeting room.

APPENDIX 2
CHRONOLOGY: LANARKSHIRE & AYRSHIRE RAILWAY

20 Aug	1883	Barrmill and Kilwinning Railway authorised.
3 Sept	1888	Opened from Barrmill to Ardrossan. Name changed to Lanarkshire & Ayrshire Railway.
1 April	1903	Giffen Junction to Clarkston East Junction opened for goods.
1 May	1903	Giffen Junction to Cathcart opened for passengers.
		Barrmill Junction to Giffen Junction closed entirely.
1 July	1903	Muirend station opened.
20 Sept	1903	Lugton East Junction to Lugton Junction opened.
6 Jan	1904	Newton to Cathcart and Clarkston West Junction opened for goods.
20 June	1904	Westburn Junction to Kirkhill Junction opened for goods.
1 Aug	1904	Newton to Cathcart, and Westburn Junction to Kirkhill Junction opened for passengers.
	1907	Clarkston East Junction to Clarkston West Junction put out of use.
8 Oct	1928	King's Park station opened.
Feb	1929	Barrmill Junction and Giffen Junction signal boxes closed.
9 July	1929	Williamwood station opened.
	1930	Barrmill Junction to Giffen Junction lifted.
1 April	1931	Croftfoot station opened.
4 July	1932	Local services beyond Uplawmoor withdrawn.
27 Jan	1947	Kilwinning East to Stevenston closed.
16 June	1947	Link between G&SWR and L&AR lines at Stevenston opened.
17 Oct	1949	Lugton East Junction to Kilwinning East singled, worked by 'one engine in steam' principle.
17 Dec	1950	Barrmill Junction to Giffen Junction relaid and reopened.
		Lugton East Junction to Giffen Junction closed (lifting completed by July 1952).
30 March	1953	Kilwinning East to Giffen closed (lifting completed by April 1955).
2 April	1962	Neilston to Uplawmoor passenger services withdrawn.
14 Dec	1964	Neilston to Lugton Junction closed and immediately lifted.
1 Aug	1966	Westburn Junction to Kirkhill Junction closed.
6 May	1968	Stevenston to Ardrossan Montgomerie Pier closed.

APPENDIX 3
STATION OPENING AND CLOSURE DATES: CATHCART CIRCLE

		OPENED		CLOSED	
MILES	STATION	PASSENGERS	GOODS	PASSENGERS	GOODS
—	Glasgow Central	1.8.1879	—		—
0.25	Bridge Street	1.7.1879(2)	—	1.3.1905	—
1	Eglinton Street	1.7.1879	—	1.2.1965	—
1.5	Pollokshields East	1.3.1886(3)	—	(3)	—
1.75	Queen's Park	1.3.1886	—		—
2.25	Crosshill	1.3.1886(4)	—	(4)	—
2.75	Mount Florida	1.3.1886	2.8.1886		23.1.1961
3.5	Cathcart (original)	25.5.1886	2.8.1886	18.3.1894	5.4.1965
3.5	Cathcart (new)	19.3.1894	—		—
4.25	Langside (1)	2.4.1894	—		—
4.75	Pollokshaws East	2.4.1894	2.4.1894		1.6.1959
5	Shawlands	2.4.1894	—		—
5.75	Maxwell Park	2.4.1894	2.4.1894		6.1.1964
6.25	Pollokshields West	2.4.1894	—		—
7	Eglinton Street				
8	Glasgow Central				

NOTES:
1 Named Langside and Newlands 1.8.1901 to 26.5.1962.
2 Original Glasgow Paisley Kilmarnock & Ayr Railway station opened 21.7.1840.
3 Temporarily closed as wartime economy 1.1.1917 to 1.3.1919.
4 Temporarily closed as wartime economy 1.1.1917 to 1.6.1919.

To ensure continuing route knowledge, necessary in case of diversions, main line trains can be found on the Cathcart Circle. Within a thirty-minute period on the evening of Saturday 12th June 2010, empty workings through Pollokshields East were (FACING PAGE) East Coast electric set led by DVT No. 82231 and (ABOVE) Virgin Pendolino No. 390034 *City of Carlisle*.

BOTH J. KERNAHAN

APPENDIX 4
STATION OPENING AND CLOSURE DATES: LANARKSHIRE & AYRSHIRE RAILWAY

MILES FROM GLASGOW CENTRAL	STATION	OPENED PASSENGERS	CLOSED PASSENGERS
3.75	King's Park	8.10.1928	
4.5	Croftfoot	1. 4.1931	
5.5	Burnside	1. 8.1904	
6.75	Kirkhill	1. 8.1904	
4.25	Muirend	1. 7.1903	
5.5	Williamwood	9. 7.1929	
6.5	Whitecraigs	1. 5.1903	
7.5	Patterton	1. 5.1903	
11.25	Neilston	1. 5.1903	
14.25	Uplawmoor	1. 5.1903	2.4.1962
16.25	Lugton	1. 5.1903	4.7.1932
20.25	Giffen	3. 9.1888	4.7.1932
22	Auchenmade	3. 9.1888	4.7.1932
26.25	Kilwinning	3. 9.1888	4.7.1932
29	Stevenston	3. 9.1888	4.7.1932
30.25	Saltcoats	3. 9.1888	4.7.1932
31.5	Ardrossan Town	3. 9.1888	4.7.1932
31.75	Ardrossan Pier	30. 5.1890	18.4.1966

The 21.02 Cross-Country service between Glasgow Central and Edinburgh is routed through Queen's Park on Saturdays to maintain drivers' route knowledge. It is seen passing through the station on 12th June 2010.

J. KERNAHAN

APPENDIX 5
SIGNALBOX OPENING AND CLOSURE DATES: CATHCART CIRCLE

SIGNAL BOX	OPENED	CLOSED
Cathcart Junction (1)	1. 3.1886	7. 8.1961
Pollokshields East	20.12.1893	7. 8.1921
Queen's Park (2)	1. 3.1886	1.10.1961
Crosshill	1. 3.1886	1.10.1961
Mount Florida	1. 3.1886	6. 3.1938
Cathcart North Junction	1. 5.1903	1.10.1961
Cathcart (power box)	2.10.1961	
Cathcart (old station)	25. 5.1886	19. 3.1894
Cathcart (new station)	19. 3.1894	1. 5.1903
Cathcart West Junction	1. 5.1903	1.10.1961
Langside	2. 4.1894	23. 8.1927
Pollokshaws East	2. 4.1894	16.10.1961
Shawlands	2. 4.1894	23. 8.1927
Maxwell Park	2. 4.1894	16.10.1961
Pollokshields West	2. 4.1894	23. 8.1927
Muirhouse Junction (power box)	7. 8.1961	17. 9.1973
Muirhouse Junction (3)	1. 7.1879	7. 8.1961

NOTES:
1 Renamed Pollokshields East Junction 1.7.1903.
2 Upgraded to block post 15.2.1898.
3 Replacement box built 1893

Preserved Class 87 electric locomotive No. 87002 *Royal Sovereign* passes through Queen's Park on 11th July 2009 with a return railtour from Glasgow Central to Birmingham. Earlier in the day the train had gone round the Inner Circle hauled by Class 47 diesel No. 47760 *Roy Castle OBE* with 87002 on the rear to turn the train, thus reviving the use made of the Circle in earlier years to turn locomotives.

M. GIBB

APPENDIX 6
SIGNAL BOX OPENING AND CLOSURE DATES:
LANARKSHIRE & AYRSHIRE RAILWAY NORTH OF GIFFEN

SIGNAL BOX	OPENED	CLOSED
Kirkhill Junction	20. 6.1904	26.11.1961
Kirkhill	6. 1.1904	26.11.1961
Burnside	1. 8.1904	26.11.1961
Cathcart East Junction *	6. 1.1904	1.10.1961
Cathcart West Junction	1. 5.1903	1.10.1961
Muirend	1. 5.1903	16.11.1980
Clarkston East Junction	1.12.1902	29.10.1907
Clarkston West Junction	1. 5.1903	29.10.1907
Whitecraigs	1. 5.1903	23. 7.1961
Patterton	1. 5.1903	23. 7.1961
Lyoncross Junction	1. 6.1905	25.11.1953
Neilston	1. 4.1903	31.10.1982
Uplawmoor	1. 5.1903	11. 3.1953
Lugton East Junction	1. 4.1903	31. 5.1953
Lugton	1. 5.1903	1. 2.1927
Giffen Junction	1. 4.1903	26. 2.1929

NOTE:

*   Renamed King's Park on opening of King's Park station.

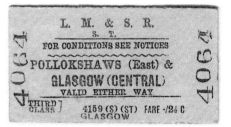

Diesel locomotives were never used on Cathcart Circle services, but did appear on football specials. English Electric Type 4 (later Class 40) No. D367 approaches Maxwell Park on the Inner Circle with a special comprising corridor stock.

                                                      J. KERNAHAN

APPENDIX 7
STATION TICKET CODE NUMBERS

For audit purposes each station had a code number which was printed in the bottom centre of the ticket. From January 1923 until April 1927 the LMSR used the former Caledonian Railway number prefixed with the letter C. From April 1927 a new series of numbers was introduced. The following numbers were used for Cathcart Circle stations.

STATION	CALEDONIAN RAILWAY	LMSR
Pollokshields East	125	4153
Queen's Park	126	4154
Crosshill	127	4155
Mount Florida	128	4156
Cathcart	129	4157
Langside and Newlands	313	4158
Pollokshaws East	312	4159
Shawlands	311	4160
Maxwell Park	310	4161
Pollokshields West	309	4162

Non-corridor stock is seen on a return football special from King's Park in May 1966 leaving Maxwell Park on the Outer Circle behind North British Type 2 No. D6122.

J. KERNAHAN

APPENDIX 8
PASSENGER JOURNEYS ORIGINATING AT CATHCART CIRCLE STATIONS

STATION	1913	1922	1949	1964	2008
Pollokshields East	48,783	64,833	16,201	109,766	193,339
Queen's Park	225,331	260,655	203,821	237,257	359,146
Crosshill	82,333	92,332	84,404	140,086	325,863
Mount Florida	480,873	501,442	438,697	408,385	824,444
Cathcart	625,935	420,060	209,639	454,278	382,029
Langside and Newlands	184,010	173,975	131,783	333,400	164,055
Pollokshaws East	236,084	212,957	84,349	299,698	164,293
Shawlands	170,748	170,645	69,029	166,772	98,657
Maxwell Park	219,438	179,775	198,815	179,965	231,679
Pollokshields West	198,416	180,208	154,908	229,887	141,050

NOTES:
Return tickets counted as two journeys.
Season tickets excluded.

On 15th January 2009 the former booking office at Maxwell Park was opened as a community meeting room, and the former station master's hat and a hand-drawn map of the area 'borrowed' over forty and twenty years previously were returned. Left to right: John Yellowlees (ScotRail), Ann Laing (Pollokshields Heritage), Jim Cornell (Railway Heritage Trust), Jack Kernahan (the author), Niall Murphy and Karin Currie (Pollokshields Heritage) and Tom Harris MP.

APPENDIX 9
CATHCART DISTRICT RAILWAY COMPANY LIMITED

DIRECTORS

George Browne	1880–1906	} First directors under Cathcart District Railway Act 1880, S.27
William G. Lindsay	1880–1881	
Robert G. Sommerville	1880–1889	} Replaced by Caledonian Railway Company directors
T. R. J. Logan	1881–1889	
A. F. Stoddart	1881–1882	
James King	1882–1886	
Alexander Crum	1886–1893	
Hugh Brown	1889–1906	Caledonian Railway representative
Joseph C. Bolton	1889–1901	Caledonian Railway representative
James Neilson	1893–1903	
James C. Bunten	1901–1901	Caledonian Railway representative
Sir James Thompson	1901–1906	Caledonian Railway representative
David Tod	1904–1910	
Sir Charles Bine Renshaw	1906–1918	Caledonian Railway representative
Henry E. Gordon	1906–1923	Caledonian Railway representative
T. R. J. Logan	1910–1912	
William Maclay	1912–1923	
Henry Allan	1918–1923	Caledonian Railway representative

SECRETARIES

J. M. Robertson	1880–1889
G. W. T. Robertson	1889–1923

AUDITORS

William G. Lindsay	1881–1905
James Grahame	1882–1917
Herbert J. G. Lindsay	1905–1910
Peter Rintoul	1910–1923
John G. Crum	1917–1923

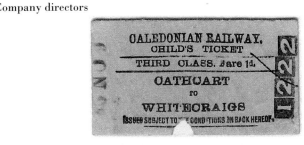

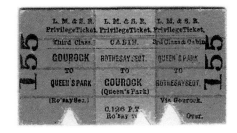

New planters are now installed at Maxwell Park, courtesy of Pollokshields Hertitage, restoring gardens to the station.

J. KERNAHAN

APPENDIX 10
CATHCART DISTRICT RAILWAY: STATISTICS

YEAR ENDED 31 JAN	MILES PASSENGER	GOODS	RECEIPTS £	UNAPPROPRIATED PROFIT/(DEFICIT) AT CLOSE OF YEAR £	DIVIDEND %
1887	35,968	622	10,573	23	0.5
1888	43,965	1,284	14,791	72	0.75
1889	48,256	1,384	17,380	370	1
1890	48,424	1,415	7,462	(7,532)	—
1891	48,144	1,364	7,787	(9,802)	—
1892	50,564	1,413	8,859	(11,022)	—
1893	51,912	3,987	9,727	(10,701)	—
1894	51,712	2,255	10,804	(9,248)	—
1895	124,804	2,257	14,365	(6,647)	—
1896	139,502	2,432	14,617	(4,599)	—
1897	146,759	4,030	17,307	189	—
1898	153,540	3,850	19,023	29	2
1899	152,522	4,951	20,675	87	2.25
1900	147,956	4,170	21,879	111	2.5
1901	158,178	3,733	21,974	331	2.5
1902	178,393	3,899	22,793	373	2.625
1903	175,297	5,414	20,788	72	2.125
1904	188,854	4,970	21,002	236	2
1905	196,574	4,244	20,352	74	2.25
1906	179,104	4,148	20,252	20	2.25
1907	183,660	4,404	22,145	206	2.375
1908	179,633	4,271	22,197	139	2.625
1909	171,909	4,030	22,037	37	2.5
1910	169,202	3,970	22,625	313	2.375
1911	170,954	4,054	24,277	71	3
1912	183,664	4,004	25,326	358	3.125
1912*	169,612	3,451	24,755	427	3.125
1913	189,105	4,358	30,999	614	3.625
1914	186,741	4,447	31,811	942	3.625
1915	182,991	4,666	31,047	652	3.75
1916	165,507	4,946	31,031	223	3.75
1917	150,111	4,859	31,031	349	3.875
1918	145,561	4,470	31,031	365	3.75
1919	149,401	4,245	31,031	1188	3.75
1920	167,545	11,548	31,031	306	3.625
1921	142,076	8,443	31,031	158	3.375
1922	165,771	2,589	31,031	35	5

NOTE:

*   Under the Railway Companies (Accounts and Returns) Act 1911, S. 1 (2), the accounting year for railway companies was changed to the calendar year. These figures relate to the eleven months ended 31st December, 1912, and the subsequent figures are for calendar years.

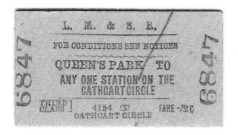

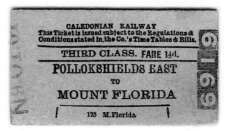

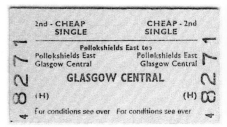

The building at the road-level entrance to Crosshill in August 1956. This contained the booking office which was later moved to the platform-level building and this building demolished.   A. GREIG COLLECTION

ANALYSIS OF INCOME

1st March 1886 to 31st December 1913

	£	%
Passengers	429,185	83.05
Parcels	16,624	3.22
Merchandise	17,980	3.48
Minerals	52,169	10.10
Mail	813*	0.15
	516,771	100.00

NOTE:

*   Contract at £30 per annum from December 1886.

CAPITAL

Ordinary Share Capital – Authorised and Issued

1880 Act – £10 shares		£175,000
1887 Act – £10 shares		109,000
		284,000

4 per cent Debentures	Authorised	Issued	
1880 Act	£58,330	158,330	
1887 Act	36,000	36,000	
1890 Act 'B'	100,000	63,000	
		157,330	
		441,330	

APPENDIX 11
CALEDONIAN RAILWAY CARRIAGE DIAGRAM, JANUARY 1893:
GLASGOW AND CATHCART

Each of the trains on this branch consists of three Firsts, three Thirds and two Brake Thirds; additional carriages are attached to some of the morning, mid-day and evening trains daily and also on the afternoon trains on Saturdays, as the traffic may require. All these trains are washed at Glasgow. Spares are washed at Cathcart.

CATHCART LEAVE	CENTRAL ARRIVE	No.	CENTRAL LEAVE	CATHCART ARRIVE	No.
6.32am	6.48am	1	6.10am	6.25am	1
7.25	7.42	2	7.16	7.30	1
8.02	8.18	1	7.48	8.03	2
8.15	8.33	2	8.22	8.37	1
8.28	8.49	3	8.40	8.55	2
8.47	9.04	1	8.56	9.11	3
9.02	9.19	2	9.10	9.25	1
9.20	9.37	3	9.25	9.40	2
9.35	9.52	1	9.55	10.10	1
10.05	10.23	2	10.27	10.42	2
10.32	10.49	1	10.55	11.10	1
11.02	11.19	2	11.25	11.40	2
11.32	11.48	1	11.55	12.10pm	1
12.02pm	12.19pm	2	12.23pm	12.38	2
12.32	12.49	1	12.41	12.56	3
12.48	1.05	2	12.55	1.10	1
1.02	1.19	3	1.10	1.25	2
1.30	1.47	2	1.25	1.40	3
1.49	2.05	3	1.53	2.08	2
2.05	2.22	1	2.10	2.25	3
2.32	2.48	3	2.26	2.41	1
3.02	3.19	1	3.00	3.20	3
3.31	3.48	3	3.28	3.43	1
4.02	4.18	1	3.55	4.10	3
4.29	4.46	2	4.26	4.41	1
4.45 S	5.02	3	4.55	5.10	3
5.02	5.19	1	5.06 S	5.21	1
5.17	5.33	3	5.27	5.42	2
5.30 S	5.47	1	5.40	5.55	3
5.47	6.04	2	5.55 S	6.10	1
6.00	6.17	3	6.10	6.25	2
6.13 S	6.29	1	6.22	6.38	3
6.32	6.48	2	6.40	6.55	1
7.02	7.19	1	7.06	7.21	2
7.32	7.49	2	7.27	7.42	1
8.02	8.19	1	7.55	8.10	2
8.32	8.50	2	8.25	8.40	1
9.02	9.19	1	8.55	9.10	2
9.32	9.49	2	9.25	9.40	1
10.17	10.34	1	10.15	10.30	2
10.37	10.54	2	10.40	10.55	1
11.02	11.19	1	11.10	11.25	2

S – Saturdays excepted

NOTES:

No. 2 – Forms No. 3 next day. Finishes on Saturday with the 1.53pm train, No. 1 takes up No. 2's run at 5.02pm and No. 3 takes up No. 1's run at 7.02pm on Saturdays.

No. 3 – Forms No. 1 next day.

Guards: David Paterson, Ewan McRae, Adam Scott, William Allan, William Hendry.

All trains call at Bridge Street, Eglinton Street and all stations on the Cathcart branch.

APPENDIX 12
COMPARATIVE JOURNEY TIMES TO GLASGOW (MINUTES)

STATION	STEAM TRAIN	TRAM	BUS	STEAM TRAIN	PROPOSED ELECTRIC TRAIN	ELECTRIC TRAIN	ELECTRIC TRAIN
	1910	1929	1929	1929	1929	1969	2010
Neilston	31	—	30	31	22	27	29
Whitecraigs	18	—	20	23	16	18	20
Cathcart	14	20	17	16	10	11	12
Kirkhill	25	—	—	22	16	19	21
Burnside	21	30	18	18	13	16	18
Pollokshaws East	13	17	15	15	10	10	13

BRITISH RAILWAYS

B 35069

SPECIAL CHEAP DAY TICKETS
FROM
EGLINTON STREET
BY ANY TRAIN EVERY DAY
(where service permits)

To	Return Fares 1st Class	2nd Class	To	Return Fares 1st Class	2nd Class
Bellshill	3/6	2/4	Lanark	8/-	5/3
Blackwood	8/-	5/3	Langside	—	10d.
Blantyre	3/-	2/-	Larkhall (Central)	4/9	3/2
Burnside	—	1/5	Law Junction	6/6	4/3
Cambuslang	2/3	1/6	Lesmahagow	8/3	5/6
Carfin Halt	4/6	3/-	Maxwell Park	—	9d.
Carluke	6/6	4/3	Motherwell	4/3	2/9
Carstairs	8/-	5/3	Mount Florida	—	9d.
Cathcart	—	10d.	Muirend	—	1/2
Cleghorn	8/-	5/3	Neilston (High)	—	2/4
Cleland	5/-	3/3	Newton	2/9	1/10
Coalburn	9/-	6/-	Patterton	—	2/-
Coatbridge (Central)	3/6	2/4	Pollokshaws (East)	—	10d.
Croftfoot	—	1/2	Ponfeigh	10/6	7/-
Crosshill	—	9d.	Rutherglen	2/-	1/3
Douglas (West)	10/6	7/-	Sandilands	10/3	6/10
Fauldhouse (North)	9/-	6/-	Shawlands	—	9d.
Flemington	4/6	3/-	Shotts	7/3	4/9
Hamilton (Central)	4/3	2/9	Stonehouse	6/9	4/6
Hamilton (West)	4/3	2/9	Strathaven (Central)	7/3	4/9
Happendon	10/6	7/-	Uddingston	2/9	1/10
Hartwood	7/3	4/9	Whitecraigs	—	1/6
Holytown	4/3	2/9	Williamwood	—	1/4
King's Park	—	1/-	Wishaw (Central)	5/-	3/3
Kirkhill	—	1/6			

Note—Passengers may alight at a station short of destination in either direction upon surrender of the ticket and commence the return journey from an intermediate station.

TICKETS OBTAINABLE IN ADVANCE
at station and are valid on the date for which issued

Children under three years of age, free ; three years and under fourteen, approximately half-fare.

All information regarding Excursions and Cheap Fares will be supplied on application at station or to R. B. Reid, District Passenger Manager, 87 Union Street, Glasgow. Telephone CITy 2911.

NOTICE AS TO CONDITIONS—These tickets are issued subject to the British Transport Commission's published Regulations and Conditions applicable to British Railways exhibited at their stations or obtainable free of charge at station ticket offices.

B.R. 35000—WA—October, 1962.

George Outram & Co. Ltd., Perth

Eglinton Street fares handbill from October 1962.

APPENDIX 13
LMS COACHING STOCK, 1926–27

Set No.	1	2	3
Delivered	April 1926	May 1926	June 1926
BT	16815	16835	16729
C	15799	15619	15867
F	15368	15389	15403
C	15597	15818	15702
BT	16236	16362	16836

Set No.	4	5	6
Delivered	July 1926	Sept 1926	Sept 1926
BT	16866	16870	16878
C	15872	15774	15883
F	15425	15426	15428
C	15768	15875	15790
BT	16757	16774	16787

Set No.	7	8	Spare
Delivered	Nov 1926	June 1927	July 1927
BT	16788	16893	17018
C	15794	15896	15982
F	15430	15456	15487
C	15892	15918	15990
BT	16882	16904	16920

Spare coaches delivered August 1927:   BT   17135
                                             C   16001
                                           F   15490

NOTES:

1 BT — Brake Third   7 third class compartments
    C — Composite   6 third and 2 first class compartments
    F — First   8 first class compartments

2 These coaches were renumbered in 1933
    BT — 19 coaches   20103–20121
    C — 19 coaches   16007–16025
    F — 10 coaches   10017–10026

An electrification engineers' train passes through Maxwell Park on 29th April 1961 hauled by recently-delivered diesel shunter No. D3914.

W. A. C. SMITH

Appendix 14
Electric Multiple Unit Headcodes

The two character headcodes used on the introduction of electric services on 27th May 1962 were:

First Digit	2	Ordinary passenger train	
	3	Empty coaching stock train	
Second digit	1	Inner Circle	
	2	Outer Circle	
	3	Kirkhill via Maxwell Park	
	4	Kirkhill via Queen's Park	
	6	Neilston	
	7	Inner Circle Relief	
	8	Outer Circle Relief	
	D	Motherwell via Queen's Park	
	H	Motherwell via Maxwell Park	

From 18th April 1966 four character headcodes were introduced, but as the electric units were only equipped to display two digits, only the last two, for the route, were displayed, thus causing little change from the previous system.

First digit (not displayed)	1	Express passenger train
	2	Ordinary passenger train
	3	Empty coaching stock train
Second digit (not displayed)	C	Steam or diesel ⎫ via Muirhouse Junction and Circle lines
	E	Electric ⎭
Third and fourth digits	19	Motherwell via Maxwell Park
	20	Motherwell via Queen's Park
	21	Cathcart Inner Circle
	22	Cathcart Outer Circle
	23	Kirkhill via Maxwell Park
	24	Kirkhill via Queen's Park
	26	Neilston
	27	Mount Florida via Queen's Park
	28	Mount Florida via Maxwell Park

OUTER CIRCLE (via Queen's Park)

MONDAYS TO SATURDAYS ONLY

	E am	D am		am	am		D am		am	E am		am	am
Glasgow (Central) leave	7 18	7 30	..	7 45	7 50	..	8 6	..	8 18	8 22	..	8 30	..
Eglinton Street ,,											..	8 35	
Pollokshields (East) ,,		7 35							8 24	8 28		8 37	
Queen's Park ,,	7 24	7 37					8 12		8 26	8 30		8 39	
Crosshill ,,		7 39							8 28	8 32		8 41	
Mount Florida ,,	7 27	7 41		7 53									8 58
Cathcart ,,		7 44		7 56	8 2			8 18	8 31			8 47	8 58
Langside and Newlands ,,		7 47			8 5			8 21	8 39			8 50	9 1
Pollokshaws (East) ,,		7 49			8 7			8 23	8 42			8 53	9 4
Shawlands ,,		7 51			8 9			8 25	8 44			8 55	9 6
Maxwell Park ,,		7 53			8 11			8 27	8 46			8 57	9 8
Pollokshields (West) ,,		7 55			8 13			8 29	8 48			8 59	9 10
Eglinton Street ,,					8 16				8 51			9 5	9 16
Glasgow (Central) arrive		8 1			8 21			8 35	8 56			9 5	9 16

	D am	D am		D am	D am		D am		E pm	DE pm		DS pm	S pm
Glasgow (Central) leave	9 30	10 30	..	11 10	11 30	..	11 54	..	12 5	12 11	..	12 14	12 17
Eglinton Street ,,													
Pollokshields (East) ,,	9 35	10 35			11 35		11 59						
Queen's Park ,,	9 37	10 37		11 16	11 37		12 1p		12 11				
Crosshill ,,	9 39	10 39			11 39		12 3						
Mount Florida ,,	9 41	10 41		11 19	11 41		12 5		12 14				12 25
Cathcart ,,	9 44	10 44			11 44		12 8			12 20		12 23	
Langside and Newlands ,,	9 47	10 47			11 47		12 11						
Pollokshaws (East) ,,	9 49	10 51			11 49		12 14						
Shawlands ,,	9 51	10 53			11 51		12 16						
Maxwell Park ,,	9 53	10 55			11 53		12 18						
Pollokshields (West) ,,	9 55	10 57			11 55		12 20						
Eglinton Street ,,													
Glasgow (Central) arrive	10 1	11 3			12 1p		12 26						

D—Diesel Service. E—Saturdays excepted. S—Saturdays only. p—p.m.

2 Continued on next page.

1960 Timetable.

APPENDIX 15
DEVELOPMENT OF MUIRHOUSE JUNCTION

The following plans, copied from contemporary drawings and signal diagrams, show the development of Muirhouse Junction from 1861 until the present day. Each plan is accompanied by a small map of the whole junction area to indicate which part is illustrated, and a short description. For ease of comparison, all the diagrams have been redrawn with north or north-east towards the top of the page.

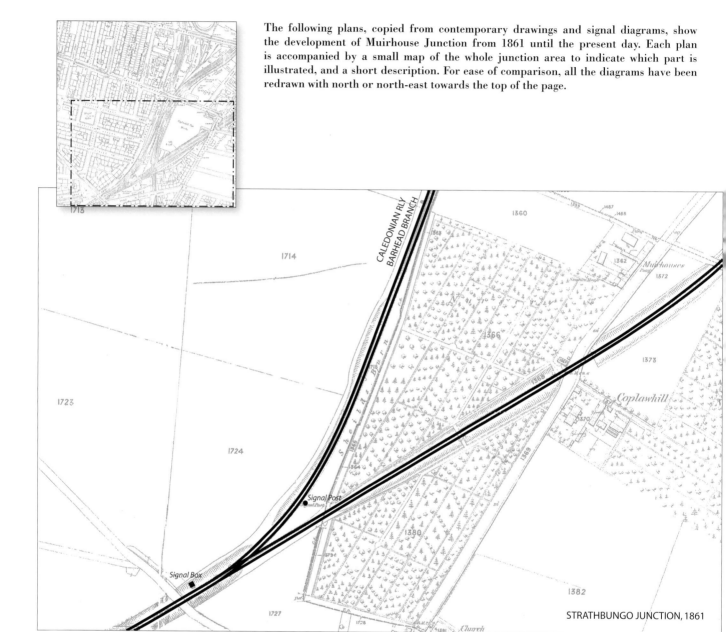

STRATHBUNGO JUNCTION, 1861

Line through Strathbungo on the Glasgow South Side to Barrhead line opened 27th September 1848. Single line between Strathbungo and General Terminus opened 30th March 1849 for goods only. By 1861 this line had been doubled. Small signalbox to the north of the junction at Strathbungo (ABOVE).

By 1876, the track had been laid and a single line connection made at Strathbungo for the Central Station Extension Line (RIGHT).

In 1877 a siding was laid from the north of the General Terminus branch to Muirhouse (FAR RIGHT).

STRATHBUNGO JUNCTION, 25 JULY 1876

CALEDONIAN STRATHBUNGO BRANCH

TO GLASGOW

DARNLEY ST

SIGNAL CABIN

NITHSDALE RD

PROPOSED TEMPORARY SIDING

STRATHBUNGO JUNCTION, 12 OCT 1877

CALEDONIAN BRANCH

DARNLEY ST

SIGNAL CABIN

NITHSDALE ROAD

BOOKING HALL

WAITING ROOM

WAITING ROOM

PLATFORM

PLATFORM

MORAY PLACE

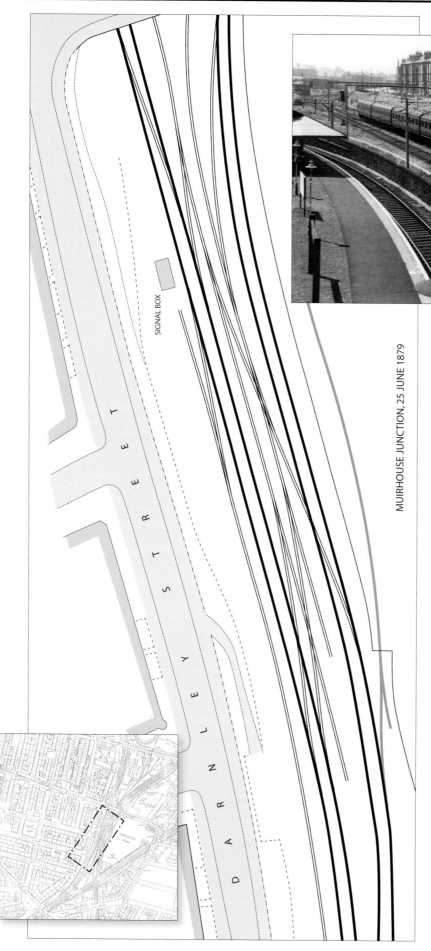

SIGNAL BOX

S T R E E T

D A R N L E Y

MUIRHOUSE JUNCTION, 25 JUNE 1879

BR Standard 2-6-4T No. 80130 passes Muirhouse Junction on 26th May 1962, the last day of steam operation, with an Outer Circle train. Pollokshields East station retains gas lighting despite the fact that electric trains will start operating on the following day. J. L. STEVENSON

On 1st July 1879 the Central Station Extension Line opened between Strathbungo Junction and Eglinton Street (LEFT). A replacement signalbox was built at Strathbungo Junction and new signalboxes built at Muirhouse and Eglinton Street (main running lines shown in black, sidings in outline).

On 5th December 1879 a short-lived siding was put in to the south of the Central Station extension line, approximately on the site of the Inner Circle rail at Pollokshields East for Messrs Paterson's traffic (shown in grey).

On 25th March 1886 Cathcart Junction signalbox was formally opened to traffic, although use by contractor's trains had been authorised on 21st December 1885 (RIGHT) (new lines shown in grey).

Plan dated 16th October 1890 shows the intended junction of the Cathcart Circle extension at Strathbungo Junction rather than Muirhouse Junction (FAR RIGHT). This required the reconstruction of the junction between the Terminus line and the Central Extension line (new lines in grey, lines to be lifted in broken outline).

On 20th October 1892 the Strathbungo Junction to Terminus branch was formally authorised for passenger traffic.

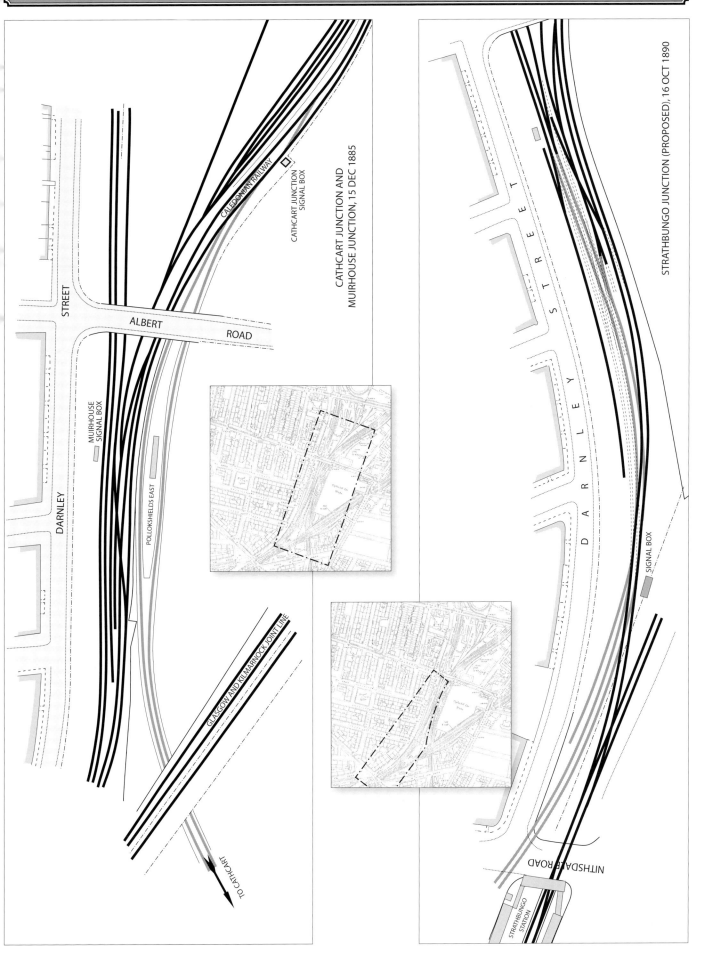

CATHCART JUNCTION AND
MUIRHOUSE JUNCTION, 15 DEC 1885

CALEDONIAN RAILWAY

CATHCART JUNCTION
SIGNAL BOX

STREET

DARNLEY

ALBERT   ROAD

MUIRHOUSE
SIGNAL BOX

POLLOKSHIELDS EAST

GLASGOW AND KILMARNOCK JOINT LINE

TO CATHCART

STRATHBUNGO JUNCTION (PROPOSED), 16 OCT 1890

D A R N L E Y   S T R E E T

SIGNAL BOX

NITHSDALE ROAD

STRATHBUNGO
STATION

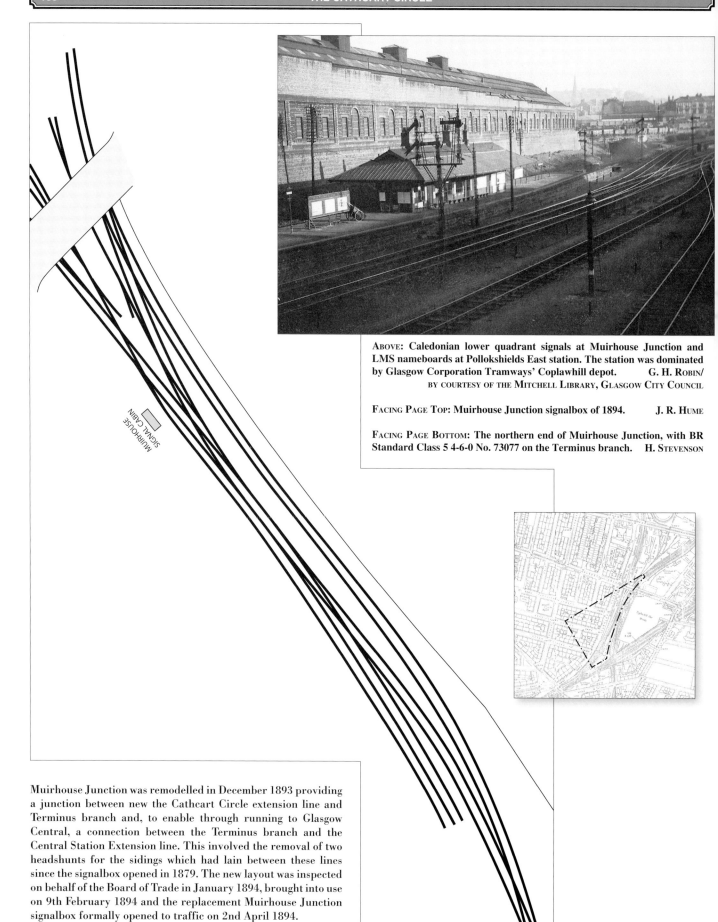

MUIRHOUSE SIGNAL CABIN

ABOVE: Caledonian lower quadrant signals at Muirhouse Junction and LMS nameboards at Pollokshields East station. The station was dominated by Glasgow Corporation Tramways' Coplawhill depot.　　G. H. ROBIN/
BY COURTESY OF THE MITCHELL LIBRARY, GLASGOW CITY COUNCIL

FACING PAGE TOP: Muirhouse Junction signalbox of 1894.　　J. R. HUME

FACING PAGE BOTTOM: The northern end of Muirhouse Junction, with BR Standard Class 5 4-6-0 No. 73077 on the Terminus branch.　　H. STEVENSON

Muirhouse Junction was remodelled in December 1893 providing a junction between new the Cathcart Circle extension line and Terminus branch and, to enable through running to Glasgow Central, a connection between the Terminus branch and the Central Station Extension line. This involved the removal of two headshunts for the sidings which had lain between these lines since the signalbox opened in 1879. The new layout was inspected on behalf of the Board of Trade in January 1894, brought into use on 9th February 1894 and the replacement Muirhouse Junction signalbox formally opened to traffic on 2nd April 1894.

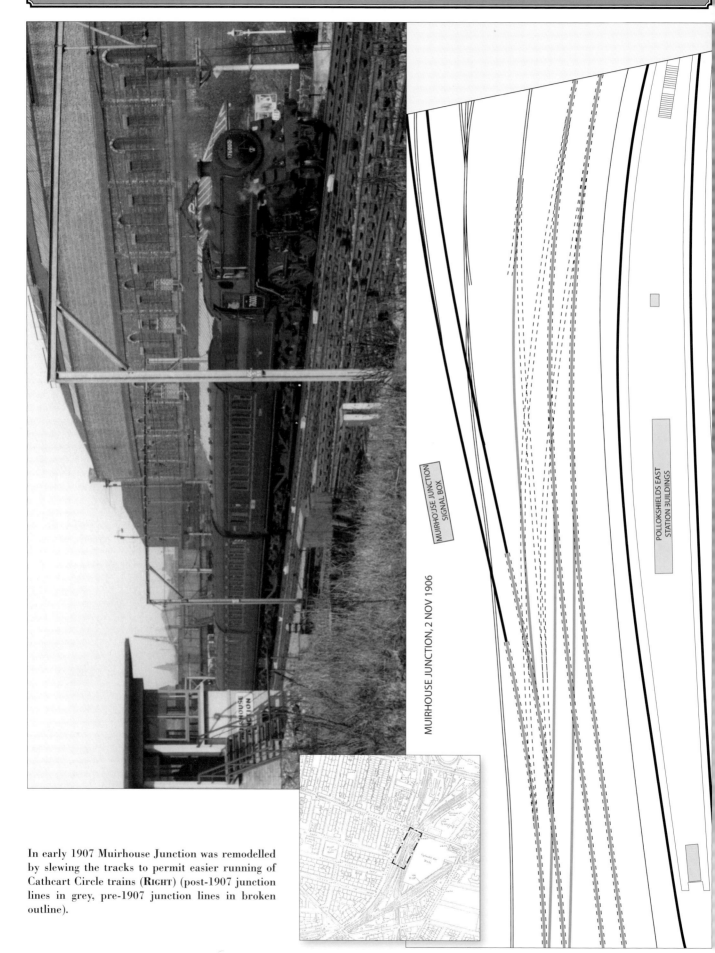

MUIRHOUSE JUNCTION SIGNAL BOX

MUIRHOUSE JUNCTION, 2 NOV 1906

POLLOKSHIELDS EAST
STATION BUILDINGS

In early 1907 Muirhouse Junction was remodelled by slewing the tracks to permit easier running of Cathcart Circle trains (**Right**) (post-1907 junction lines in grey, pre-1907 junction lines in broken outline).

FACING PAGE: BR Standard Class 4 2-6-0 No. 76000 passes the new Muirhouse Junction signalbox on a football special on 14th April 1962.

H. STEVENSON

ABOVE: CR 'Jumbo' 0-6-0 No. 57444 between Muirhouse Junction and Pollokshields West with empty stock for a football special on 20th April 1957. Strathbungo Junction signalbox on the right did not control Cathcart Circle traffic, although it was proposed in 1890 that the extension line would join the line to Glasgow Central immediately opposite the signalbox.

W. A. C. SMITH

THIS PAGE: Muirhouse Junction, viewed from the north, as it was between 1907 and 1961. The foundations for the new power box can be seen to the south of the signalbox.   G. H. ROBIN/BY COURTESY OF THE MITCHELL LIBRARY, GLASGOW CITY COUNCIL

FACING PAGE: Ex-LMS 4-6-0 No. 44956 heads a goods train past the new power box that opened in 1961   J. L. STEVENSON

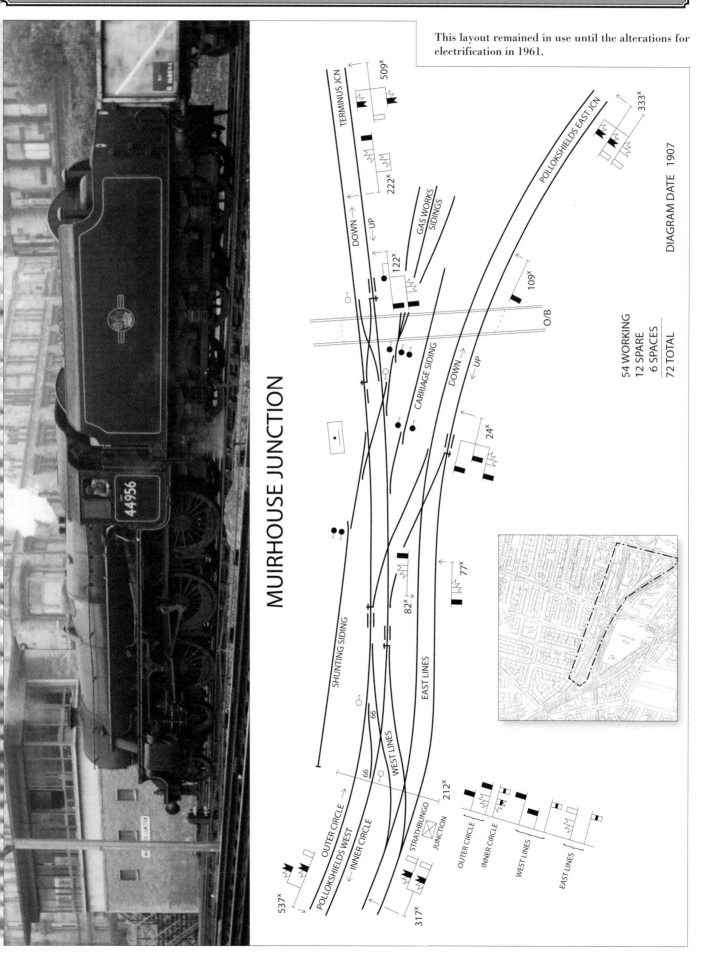

This layout remained in use until the alterations for electrification in 1961.

MUIRHOUSE JUNCTION

TERMINUS JCN

509ˣ

222ˣ

POLLOKSHIELDS EAST JCN

333ˣ

DIAGRAM DATE 1907

DOWN →
← UP

GAS WORKS SIDINGS

122ˣ

CARRIAGE SIDING

DOWN →
← UP

109ˣ

O/B

54 WORKING
12 SPARE
6 SPACES
72 TOTAL

24ˣ

77ˣ

82ˣ

SHUNTING SIDING

66

EAST LINES

WEST LINES

66

OUTER CIRCLE →
POLLOKSHIELDS WEST
← INNER CIRCLE

STRATHBUNGO
JUNCTION

212ˣ

OUTER CIRCLE
INNER CIRCLE
WEST LINES
EAST LINES

537ˣ

317ˣ

RIGHT: Taken on 24th September 1960. Work has commenced on the building of the new signalbox. G. H. ROBIN/BY COURTESY OF THE MITCHELL LIBRARY, GLASGOW CITY COUNCIL

BELOW: The 6.12pm Inner Circle passes the old and new signalboxes on 31st July 1961, a week before the new box took over from the old. The junction signal has been moved to the south. W. A. C. SMITH/TRANSPORT TREASURY

FACING PAGE: The replacement power signalbox at Muirhouse Junction. J. KERNAHAN

BELOW: Display panel inside the 1961 Muirhouse power signalbox. J. KERNAHAN

On 18th September 1960 the part of the original Central Station extension line between Strathbungo North Junction and the junction at that time know as Muirhouse North Junction – a section latterly known as the East Kilbride loop – was closed. The junction signal was moved to the south after the track of the East Kilbride loop was lifted.

The replacement power signalbox at Muirhouse Junction opened 7th August 1961. Simplified layout brought into use (**BELOW**).

MUIRHOUSE JUNCTION

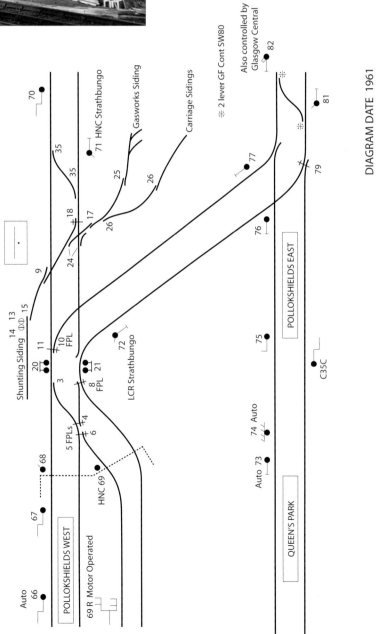

DIAGRAM DATE 1961

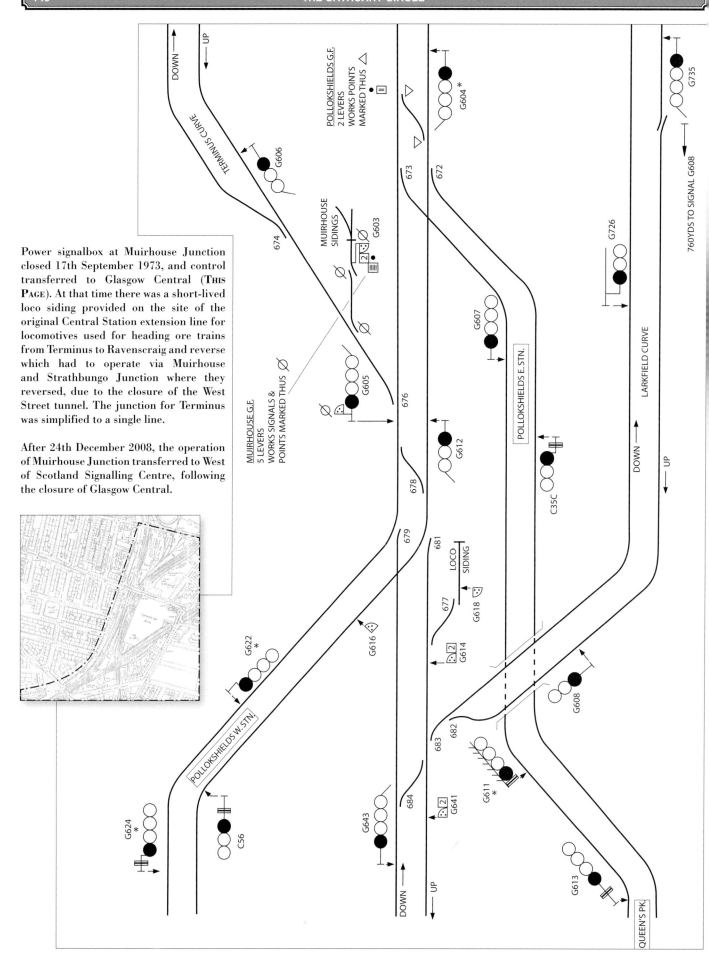

Power signalbox at Muirhouse Junction closed 17th September 1973, and control transferred to Glasgow Central (THIS PAGE). At that time there was a short-lived loco siding provided on the site of the original Central Station extension line for locomotives used for heading ore trains from Terminus to Ravenscraig and reverse which had to operate via Muirhouse and Strathbungo Junction where they reversed, due to the closure of the West Street tunnel. The junction for Terminus was simplified to a single line.

After 24th December 2008, the operation of Muirhouse Junction transferred to West of Scotland Signalling Centre, following the closure of Glasgow Central.

ABOVE: English Electric Class 20 No. 20109 in the temporary siding used for Terminus–Ravenscraig ore train engines on 8th May 1975. The 12.52 from Kirkhill is seen on the Outer Circle in the background, passing the remaining brick pillar which formerly supported the signal gantry removed in 1961.

W. A. C. SMITH/TRANSPORT TREASURY

BELOW: The norhern end of Muirhouse Junction as it became in 1973, with the junction to Terminus reduced to a single line.

APPENDIX 16
SNOOKER TAM OF THE CATHCART RAILWAY
BY R. W. CAMPBELL

Written in 1919, *Snooker Tam of the Cathcart Railway* is set in the fictional station of Kirkbride on the Cathcart Circle around the end of the First World War. It contains a reference to Crosshill station having been closed for 'nearly two years' and, as the station was closed as a wartime economy on 1st January 1917, the story can be accurately dated to late 1918. At this time, with so many men enlisted, the Cathcart Circle stations were being run by 'bits o' lassies and deevils o' boys'. While much of the story is somewhat far fetched, with tales of capture of Italian spies and 'sookin' sausages', the atmosphere of the human side of Circle station life is excellently captured. Life at 'the Central', Pollokshields and Cathcart blend with the antics of schoolboys, the affection with which railway staff were held by the passengers and the prophetic dream of railway nationalisation. James R. Smith started his employment with the Caledonian Railway at Pollokshields West in 1916 (see page 50) and recollected his happy memories of that time and of passengers' kindness and generosity. Possibly he was a real life 'Snooker Tam'.

Copies of the book can occasionally be found in second-hand bookshops, and on at least two occasions in the last fifty years parts have been dramatised by local groups. To give a flavour of the story and portray a little of station life nearly a century ago, five fairly representative chapters are reproduced here to bring the story of the Cathcart Circle to a close.

George Colligan inside the booking office at Shawlands. The clockface bore the name 'Caledonian Railway Co.'   P. AITKEN

SNOOKER TAM.

CHAPTER I.

SNOOKER TAM.

GOD made the country, man made the cities, and the railways made the suburbs. Suburbia was created for dividends, and dividends for Suburbia. In all cities – from 'Glesca' to Timbuctoo – there is found that proud section of the populace which refuses to live in a tenement and squabble about the washing-house key. We are all Tories, we are all snobs, even our Bolsheviks. Every man wants a main door and an electric bell. To be King of the Castle is a dream for which all men strive, especially those born north of the Tweed. It is the echo of our land hunger, our independence, and our pride. If we cannot get something in the baronial style, then we get the next best in villadom; hence the growth of Suburbia and the rise of the Cathcart Railway. This railway is as famous as the Grand Trunk Road or Watling Street. To be ignorant of the Cathcart Circle is akin to saying that the Thames is in Germany, and the Tweed in Alaska! After the 'Polis Force,' the Cathcart Railway is the greatest thing in 'Glesca.'

A wag has alleged that this railway was specially built 'for high heid yins in insurance offices, public-hooses, and drapers' shops.' No matter! It is a most convenient line, and the cheapest thing out of Lipton's. For fourpence you can ride round and round the Circle. Indeed, many a lover has found that it is better to invest fourpence in the Cathcart Circle than two shillings at the picture-house. Humorists call it the honeymoon line. It is a deadly trap for bachelors, and the hope of the pretty typists. All single men, on arriving in 'Glesca,' are advised to look for lodgings round the Circle. No wonder! At 'the five-thirty' can be seen everything from a Geisha to a Madonna. The Venus from Pollokshields rubs shoulders with the Gaby from Cathcart. Low blouses whisper romance, while the eyes have the story of Eve and the sauce of Byron. Calvin would lament the daring, but Prince Charlie would rejoice.

It is the Circle of Romance.

You will readily understand that everybody on the Cathcart Circle is a personality. The station-masters are experts in handling the crowd. And it's no use producing a leather card-case (empty) and shouting, 'Season.' It can't be done! 'Wee Mac,' the manager, has trained his flying squad to observe the God-fearing elders who 'slip' old concert tickets, and the respectable dons who always leave their money in their Sunday 'breeks,' and promise to pay 'in the mornin'.' There's nothing free on the Circle except an occasional ragman's flea or a suicide in the Mount Florida Tunnel. Only one whisky-bottle has been found by a passenger, which is direct proof of the remarkable observation of the staff. Next to the married men and the typist passengers, the staff is the most interesting gathering outside of Pickard's Waxworks. They can make cows laugh, and stop engines 'wi' a whistle.'

And this brings me to my story of one of the stations on the line. We shall call it Kirkbride. Kirkbride is quite a bonny place. All the houses are cut out like neat pats of butter; a tree in the front, three leeks at the side, and four daisies in the corner, in the style of garden cities. Everybody is thoroughly respectable. The residents willingly subscribe to the teetotal societies and get their Worcester Sauce from the licensed grocer. To prove their wonderful economy (now glorified by the war), the ladies go to bed while the silk blouse is being ironed. It is an unwritten law that you *never* call during ironing-hours. Everybody reads the *Record* and asks for 'a keek at the *Herald*.' The unfortunates who own a telephone become the unwilling proprietors of an exchange from which the neighbours order 'hauf-a-pun' o' haddies' or 'three neeps an' a carrot.' For all that, it is a jolly place, and one of the scenes of merry-making is the railway station. The station-master's name is Maister John M'Muckle, one of those kind old souls who live manfully on a hundred and fifty pounds a year, and so help to pay for the directors' oysters, Gold Flake, and Rolls-Fords. A decent man Maister M'Muckle, with a nod for every under-dog, and his bonnet off to every lady with the latest Treron fashions. Since 1914 Maister M'Muckle has not had a full-grown man on his staff. He has worked away, as he says himself, 'wi' bits o' lassies an' deevils o' boys. Oh man, it's an' awfu' war, is't no?'

One of the boys sent out by Maister M'Harrie, 'the super. o' the line,' was named Snooker Tam, on account of his nose, which was rather pointed. Snooker hailed from the Cowcaddens, where wife-beating is an industry and cadging is an art. But Snooker was a cut above the 'close-mooth' folks. He had always wanted to be a station-master and 'blaw a whustle.' As his father was alleged to be a 'polisman,' the 'whustle' instinct can be understood. The war gave Snooker his chance. Kirkbride provided him with a platform for his originality. The first thing he did on arriving at the station was to slip three round plumbers' washers into the automatic machine and get three packets of chocolates. No flies on Snooker Tam!

'Here, laddie.' said Maister M'Muckle; 'get the paste-pot an' shove up these bills aboot the Fair Holiday trains.'

'Ach! I'm no a bill-poster. I cam' oot here to be a high heid yin on the line.'

'What d' ye mean, ye rascal?'

'I jined the railway to wave a flag an' blaw ma whustle.'

'Get haud o' that paste-pot, or I'll mak' ye blaw the bluid oot yer nose.'

Snooker picked up the paste-pot and the bills, winking to Maggie M'Cheery, the ticket-girl, as he went out. Now, if you know anything about bills, you will realise that bill-posting is an art. These bills are generally printed in sections, either in halves or quarters. Great care has to be taken to keep the sections in order. Tam knew nothing about this. He was 'jist gaun to stick up bills.' This was the startling result:

G L A S	C A T
F A I	&
H O L I	D O G
A L T E R	S H O W
I N	A T
T R A I	B A R L I N N I E

It was unfortunate for the spotless reputation of Maister M'Muckle that the station filled up at this cruel hour with all the morning passengers, including Bailie M'Onie (a railway director) and Wullie

M'Footle, a bit of a wag, who was always clad in a short jacket and a pimple-sized bowler on his towsy head.

'Ha! ha! ha! Come here, boys, an' see the new bill-poster,' shouted Wullie to the gathering crowd of business men.

'That bates a',' remarked the bailie.

'Awa' an' bile yer heid!' ejaculated Snooker, picking up his bucket. At that moment Maister M'Muckle came out to meet the incoming train. His eye caught the bill, and it sent him purple. However, he passed by and saw the train out.

'Come here, ye rascal. What's this?' demanded the station-master.

'The bills,' muttered Tam.

'Bills! ye red-nebbit heathen! Affrontin' me afore yin o' the railway directors. Tak! it doon this meenit, or I'll gie ye the sack.'

'I didna ken,' mumbled Snooker, very much alarmed. He got off the bill in rapid time, and under the expert tuition of the station-master, who is the best billposter on the line, the glaring absurdity was righted.

'Oh man, you're an awfu' boy!' concluded Maister M'Muckle, with a twinkle in his eye, for, like all station-masters with small salaries, he had a sense of humour. 'Noo, get the brush an' clean oot the waitin'-rooms.'

Snooker grabbed the broom, and started to clean up the remnants of Woodbines, smoked by all the gentlemen of Kirkbride, who store them in silver-mounted cases, *monograms and all.*

Snooker stuck a fag-end in his jaw, and was sweeping away when Mrs Tummy Tumattoo, a well-known resident, arrived. This lady spoke English with the Kelvin-side accent, which is *most* refined.

'Here, boy, get my luggage into the train. There's three boxes, four portmanteaus, the parrot's cage, and a small bag *doon* in the corner of the platform.' The word 'doon' was an unfortunate slip, and convinced Snooker that she was one of those 'who pit it on a bit.'

'Are ye shiftin' yer ludgin's?' asked the boy.

'Don't be impertinent. I'm going to the coast. Put the things in the train.'

'Third class?' mumbled Snooker, going off for the barrow. It was a titanic struggle heaving up her bags and boxes. Snooker declared that the lady was shifting her coal-cellar in case she lost the coals while on her holidays. However, he managed the luggage, and having given the bad-tempered parrot a 'smack wi' his bunnit,' he looked into the carriage with the remark, 'It's a' in the van, missis.'

'Thank you. Here you are.' She handed him a penny.

'Keep it, missis, an' buy sugarally-water at Rothesay,' he said, tossing the penny through the window and banging the door.

As the train moved out, Mrs Tummy Tumattoo opened her mouth with rage, and let fall a brand-new set of ivories.

An obliging gentleman collected the débris. A dear pennyworth!

When Snooker slid on to his seat in the booking-office he remarked to bonny Maggie M'Cheery, 'Here, that auld wife offered me a penny.'

'Ach! that's naethin' on the Circle,' remarked Maggie.

'Hoo's that?'

'Yin o' thae toffs gied me a cough-drop for shiftin' hauf-a-ton o' bags an' boxes. War economy,' concluded Maggie, rubbing her nose with the back of her hand, and carrying on with the book-keeping.

During the day Tam had to perform many duties, from hosing down the lavatories to wheeling the barrow, from which he delivered egg-boxes, portmanteaus, and the half-pounds of ham, &c., ordered by the ladies 'to be sent out.' Nobody carries parcels in Kirkbride. To do so is a social sin, worse than 'eatin' black puddin's' with a dago, or sipping 'Johnnie Walker' with a Zulu. The unwritten laws of Suburbia are stricter than those of Mayfair.

Snooker enjoyed this experience, for Kirkbride has the jolliest 'slaveys' in 'Glesca.' They are frequently recruited from the Hielanman's Corner, which is at the end of Jamaica Brig. On any Thursday night between seven and ten you can see Flora, Jessie, or Jeannie 'chewin' the tartan' with 'polismen' and 'sodgers' (Hielanmen never work), and doing a 'hooch' when a recruiting-piper plays 'The Deil's in the Kitchen.' A lot of these 'deils' get into the Kirkbride kitchens, and many a grocer, flesher, or fruiterer's assistant has had to take unto himself a wife after calling for 'the orders.' To this cheerful system Tam had a pleasant introduction at the backdoor of Mrs M'Footle's brand-new mansion. The maid of all work, Flora M'Tavish, opened the door.

'Is this your hauf-pun' o' ham?'

'It is. She'll be a new boy on the job,' said Flora, using the feminine for the masculine, according to the Highlands.

'I'm no a she,' ejaculated Tam, putting his nose round the door.

'Whateffer will she be, then?'

'A he.'

'I thought she was a ferret, with a nose like that.'

'Ach! gie me a jeely piece, an' nane o' yer back chat,' demanded Snooker, sitting down on the jaw-box. Flora supplied him with all he desired, for it is an unwritten law that the 'slaveys' should feed 'the callers.' Lumps of bread and pieces of 'jeely' slipped over his throat with ease. When finished he commenced to admire Flora with almost a professional eye. She was a buxom lass, and quite bonny despite the soot on her nose.

'Gie me a kiss,' he said.

'Go away, boy.'

'Come on, noo, Flora, or I'll no come back.'

'If she will kiss, she'll kiss;' and Flora put out her lips.

Just as Tam was sealing the bargain the door opened, and in stalked Mrs M'Footle, a powerful-looking lady, fifteen stone, three feet broad, and a foot across the eyes.

'Get out, you young rascal! – For shame, Flora!'

Snooker fled to his barrow; and Flora, with that nerve characteristic of her sex, demanded to know 'why she couldn't kiss her boy cousin from Skye.'

'Kiss him ootside, then – no here,' shouted Mrs M'Footle, who always relapsed into her native doric when angry.

Meantime Snooker went on his rounds, wasting half-an-hour at each call. During this period Maister M'Muckle was awaiting his return, as his dinner-hour was 1 P.M. (sharp), and 'that deevil o' a boy hadna turned up to relieve him!' Maister M'Muckle was angry – real angry – a somewhat rare thing till the war started, and laddies became *men* on the railway. At last he turned up, his face covered with jam, and cookies bulging out of his trousers-pockets.

'Where hae ye been, laddie?' shouted the maister.

'Wi' the barry.'

'D—— ye, does it tak' ye a' day to deliver twa bags an' three parcels?'

'I didna ken the doors.'

'Na; but ye ken the jeely pieces. You've got a face like a jam-works, an' jeely hingin' frae yer nose.'

'Can we no speak to oor customers?'

'Ay, speak quick an' get off.'

'I thocht we had to be ceevil to get trade for the Circle.'

'What made ye think that?'

'Ma uncle's an insurance agent. He tak's tea at a' the hooses, an' kisses the weemin for orders. He's in the Proodenshul.'

'This is a railway, no the Proodenshul,' concluded Maister M'Muckle, going out for dinner. As the door closed, Snooker winked at Maggie and said, 'He's no a bad auld chap. Wud ye like a cookie?'

'Ay.'

They munched cookies till the maister returned. *Between bites they kissed!*

CHAPTER II.

SUBURBAN RIVALRY.

JEALOUSY has been part and parcel of human nature since the year one. It all started through Adam ordering a pair of fig-leaf trousers from the ancestors of Wattie Wulson, who kept the 'Coaliseeum' in the Garden of Eden. Eve promptly replied by demanding a banana skirt on the instalment plan from Antonius Andersonio, who kept a bazaar labelled 'The Poly.' From that day there has been trouble all over the world. Each household, village, town, and city competes with its neighbour in breeks, bustles, and bowlers; hence the growth of our huge drapery establishments, where you can buy anything from red flannelette nighties to margarine muslin blouses at elevenpence three-farthings per yard. (Don't forget the three-farthings.)

This rivalry has spread to the realms of house-building, gardens, clubs – indeed, every phase of our social life. You can see it everywhere from Kelvinside to Woolamooloo. The Cathcart Circle was, therefore, only human when torn with the all-absorbing question of 'Which is the Nuttiest – Kirkbride or Maxwell Park?' (pronounced 'Mexwell Park'). The more elderly men, tired with bringing up weans and skelping them, took but an onlooking part, but the youths and the maidens were as keen as 'Colman's' in this matter. The author dare not take any side. He can only reprint well-considered opinions. According to Wullie Wullocks and Argay Maclennan, two of the high priests in the gossip and grumbles business, Maxwell Park usually led, owing to the greater wealth achieved in 'Best Scotch' and War Bonds. This opinion is hotly contested in the drawing-rooms, tennis-clubs, and 'fitba'' organisations of Kirkbride. 'We are we, an' to Hong-kong wi' Mexwell Park!' This sums up the opposing view.

Now, this rivalry was easily noted by all observant passengers on 'The Circle.' If the flappers of Maxwell Park got into the train in the morning with fresh-air stockings, perforated blouses, and eau-de Cologne hankies, the Kirkbride flappers eclipsed this display the following day; and so it went on. But the boys – 'the deevils o' boys,' as Maister M'Muckle called them – printed their views on the carriage walls. Indeed, it was not safe for a member of the Plymouth Brethren to raise his eyes higher than the newspaper, lest he should see a message written by a sinful hand. Many of these messages would not pass the Press Bureau. Still, to obtain a glimpse of the controversy, here are samples of the scribbled odes:

CHANGE HERE FOR MEXWELL PARK,
MARGARINE, HARD COOKIES,
AND
INDIA RUBBER DICKIES.

The reply of a Maxwell Park boy written underneath :

WHA GET THEIR FAITHER'S AULD
WHITE SHIRTS CUT UP INTO
HANKIES ?

KIRKBRIDE.

These things were not true, of course, for it is well known that the 'Maypole' does a fine trade in best Danish. As for the hard cookies and the rubber dickies, these allegations must be left to the Solomons of the Court of Session. With regard to the origin of the Kirkbride hankies, this is an old Scots custom, and no man dare point the finger of scorn at such an economy in war-time. It has received the benediction of Bonar Law.

You will readily understand that this rivalry affected the railway staff. Kirkbride was out to beat Maxwell Park, and vice versâ. Maister M'Muckle quickly interested himself in the controversy. When he got wind of the fact that the station-master at Maxwell Park was planting some newfangled geranium, he promptly planted 'Sweet-william,'

'Tom Thumb,' and other scented varieties. Maister M'Muckle was a great man for 'scent.' But it was the station staff who really kept the war going. Snooker Tam early figured in the fray. When passing Maxwell Park one morning in the train he called out, 'Hi! hi!' to his rival, Jock Doo.

'What?' shouted Jock.

'That's yer breakfast,' said Tam, hitting him in the face with half-a-pound of soft black-soap.

'Yu!!! – Yu!!!–!! You!!!–!!!! Yu!' roared Jock; but the train went on, Tam leaning back on the seat with gusto, and occasionally blowing the fumes of a Woodbine in the style of a gilded D.S.O. But Jock Doo had his revenge. Jock could work the telegraph instrument, and that afternoon, when Snooker was away for dinner, the Kirkbride instrument went tick-tick-tick-a-tick-tick-tick, Maggie answered with a tick-tick, and the message came over the wires :

'Dere Maggie, – Your Tam is waukin' oot the wee lassie in the bookstall at Crosshill.

'He's a big baa lamb,
As soft as jeely-jam.
I'll nock him intae ham,
Wi' a dam! dam! dam!'

This was alarming news to Maggie, for she and Tam were already sweethearts; indeed, Tam had presented her with one of those silver rings discovered in sixpenny lucky-bags. Maggie, being naturally jealous, at once asked Jock Doo for his evidence. The instrument ticked back:

'I seen him eatin' joojoobs wi' her at the close-mooth last nicht.'

The sweet, trusting Maggie was roused to anger; in fact, she got so flustered that she gave a Gorbals Jew a first-class ticket instead of a third. He took it and smiled, for he was the first man who had ever diddled the Cathcart Railway. Tam entered shortly afterwards.

'Jings! it's cauld,' he said, sitting down at the fire.

'I'm no' speakin' to ye,' Maggie said, getting on with her books.

'Hoo's that?'

'Jist!'

'Ye're awfu' huffy.'

'Ay!' was the grim response.

'Whit wey?'

'I'm no speakin' to ye, I tell ye.'

'Dinna speak, then !'

'I'll speak if I like.'

'But whit are ye speakin' aboot?'

'You!'

'Me?'

'Ay.'

'Ach ! ye're daft.'

'I'm no daft,' she said, turning round on her stool and facing him.

'Ye said ye werena speakin', an' noo ye're speakin'; but I dinna ken what ye're speakin' aboot.'

'I ken, though!' she exclaimed, with fire in her eye.

'Ach! hae a joojoob,' he said, handing out a poke.

'Keep yer joojoobs!'

'Ach, awa'! ye've got the Spanish flu.'

'You'll get the flu if ye eat joojoobs at the close-mooth wi' lassies.'

'Whit lassies?' exclaimed Tam, aflame with righteous wrath, or seemingly so.

'Ye ken fine.'

'I've only wan lass.'

'It's no me, then.'

Crosshill by night, showing the signalbox on the platform.   BRITISH RAILWAYS

'Wha is it, then?'

'The Crosshill yin.'

'Crosshill?'

'Ay!'

'Oh?'

'Ay, oh!'

'Whit are ye "ay ohin" aboot?'

'Her!'

'Her?'

'Ay, her!'

'Whit her d' ye mean?'

'The book-stall yin.'

'Book-stall?' he said, scratching his head.

'She was eatin' yer joojoobs last nicht.'

'Last nicht?'

'Ay, last nicht.'

'No wi' me.'

'Wi' you!'

'Did ye see me ?'

'Na.'

'Wha telt ye?'

'Never mind!'

'Weel, ye're wrang, Maggie, for I wis at the Waxworks last nicht seein' the hairy man frae Woolamooloo. Somebody's been drawin' yer leg. They're jealous. I can prove it.'

'Oh!' she said, looking up.

'Ay, *oh!*' great emphasis on his 'oh.'

'Prove it, then.'

'Crosshill Station has been shut up for nearly twa years, so there's *nae* book-stall and *nae* lassie there,' he shouted triumphantly.

'Jings! Ye're right enough,' declared Maggie. 'I'm sorry, Tam. I'll no believe him again. Let's mak' it up.'

'Na!'

'Ach, come on, an' I'll gie ye a kiss.'

'Na.'

'Ach, dae,' she pleaded, with a tear in her eye.

'Tell me wha telt ye, then.'

'I canna dae that.'

'A' richt; I'm feenished wi' ye. I'll get anither lass.'

'It wis Jock Doo.'

'Jock Doo?'

'Ay!'

'When?'

'The day.'

'Did ye see him?'

'Na. He sent it ower the wire.'

Tam then related the incident of the morning, much to Maggie's glee.

'Come on, Tam; here's yer kiss.'

Just as they were sealing the contract, Maister M'Muckle entered the office.

'Here, stop!' he shouted.

'I wis jist takin' a spark oot o' Maggie's e'e,' mumbled Snooker.

'A spark!' exclaimed Maister M'Muckle.

'Ay!'

'Ye're gettin' ower auld in the horn at the sparkin' business. Hoo auld are ye, man?'

'Seventeen.'

'It's time ye were awa' to Constantinople.'

CHAPTER VIII.

'ALL SEASONS READY.'

There was no doubt about Jimmy M'Cloon's attention to the spirit of Romance. Post-cards, letters, or bits of his dull-coloured yellow hair arrived by every post. He was irrepressible. From infancy he had chanted:

'Bee baw babity,
Babity, babity, babity,
Bee baw babity,
Kiss a bonnie wee lassie.'

His ardour captivated the simple soul of bonny Maggie. It was the dawn of another world. She was whirled into all the joyful and sorrowful routine of love. She was fond of Jimmy, for Jimmy *always* had 'a quarter' of Birrell's or M'Coll's love lozenges. She was also fond of Tam; but Tam, unaware of the 'quarters,' was still dealing in pennyworths of 'black ba's' or eucalyptus-drops. He had not tumbled to this important matter – yet. Measured by their respective gifts, Jimmy was a winner, Tam a loser. She would have liked to have them both, but Tam was none of your second-fiddlers. He had no need to be; certainly not. No fewer than five of 'the wee slaveys' of the suburb made it their business to call daily to inquire if there were 'ony persels for the hoose.' Tam attended to their wants, much to Maggie's dislike, for she was queen of the booking-office, and resented any intrusions in her own domain. But Tam, being of the perspicacious order, quickly used these visits for stirring the green-eyed monster, and eventually worsting the exalted Jimmy M'Cloon. Like Foch, he was never in a hurry. The gradual assault on a boasted impregnability tells in the end. Meantime, the variety of his duties and the need of 'keepin' Puddin' doon' occupied all his attention. Not that Tam really disliked Puddin', but he had a vendetta against Pollokshaws. Like the battle of the Boyne to an Irish Maloney, Pollokshaws always roused Tam to scorn and fury. Vendettas in boy-life are usually caused by the most simple things; 'fitba',' stolen 'bools,' an unmerited 'skelp on the lug' are quite sufficient to implant in the youthful minds a hatred which lasts until they discard their knickerbockers for long trousers. In the case of Tam, it was difficult at first to discern the reason for his antipathy. But Puddin', skilled student of Sexton Blake, gradually pieced together little remarks and discovered the clue. And – would you believe it? – it all originated in a stolen drink of 'soor-dook.' According to Puddin', Tam had once attended a school picnic at Lochgoilhead. Each of the company received the usual 'poke,' consisting of a hot pie and a big round scone with three grains of sugar crying 'Lost!' on the top. The liquid refreshment was buttermilk, affectionately known in the best circles as 'soor-dook.' Tam got his tinnyful all right, but while he was indulging in a scramble for some spare scones, a tubby-nosed apprentice from Pollokshaws Bleach Works had bagged his tinny, soor-dook an' a'. There was a fight, of course; *but Tam didna win.* Hence the vendetta against Pollokshaws. For this crime poor Puddin' had to go through the hoop. Puddin', however, tried to live down the bad name of his well-known burgh. He exchanged a shilling gully-knife for a sixpenny blade, and offered a lace out of a Third Lanark football in return for a pipe-cover once used by Billy Hogg. He even assumed (in that stage) the literary education of Tam, and initiated him into all the blessings of his library – *Robinson Crusoe, Treasure Island, The Ha'penny Marvel, Union Jack, Boy's Friend,* and *Jumpin' Jake, the Iron-Chested Man of California.* These attentions certainly mitigated to a great extent the regrettable past; but now and again fuel was added to the hidden flames by the indiscreet action of a Pollokshaws message-boy who blandly offered a dusty old concert ticket faked up as a 'zone.' So there existed a veiled neutrality, pleasant enough on paydays, when their jaws were sticky with candy, but very much strained on Saturday evenings, when they read the junior football notes in the *Times, Citizen,* and *News.* However, like a man and his wife, these boys were united against all comers, as will be shown.

There has always been a standing feud between the High School boys and the laddies at the stations. This has its origin in social enmities, for the genteel are aye up against the gamin. And no doubt the high spirits of the High School had to be expended, either in breaking windows, cutting railway cushions, ringing rheumaticky ladies' doorbells, or, better still, baiting all the tow-headed boys who took the tickets at the gate. In this war the schoolboys were led by Conkie M'Beetle. Conkie had a nose like the King of Bulgaria, a tummy like Hindenburg, and a pair of calves like those you see attached to stout ladies paddling at Rothesay. At maths, he was dense, but at Rugger he could heave his way in and out of any scrum in which the Academy, Dollar, Greenock, or Ayr 'fancied their chance,' to use a local Rugby expression. The head of the scrum naturally led the assault on the boy-porters. Little things caused bloody battles. For example, the order issued by the railway company that everybody *must* show his season-ticket caused a terrific commotion on the Cathcart Circle. The manager was quite right, for his staff was reduced, and all his expert face-readers had gone to study pimple-headed Fritz, who at that time was endeavouring to take (without payment) season tickets to Calais, Paris, and the Leicester Lounge. Hence the order. Hence, too, the indignation of God-fearing passengers, who, somehow, imagined they were classed with those who drop buttons and bad pennies into the church offertory. But living, as they were, under the shadow of D.O.R.A., an Act by which you could be shot at dawn for saying Lloyd George or Milner blows his nose on a dirty hanky, they complied with a grunt. Not so the High School boys. Showing season tickets was much too democratic. To ask a boy clad in a chocolate cap, a chocolate blazer, and chocolate stockings with yellow rings to show his 'season,' somehow, appeared to them like asking the King for a reference. No; they would see the railway in blue blazes, Hong-kong, or Helabooloodoo before they would display their tickets for inspection by youths who were educated in Dobbie's Loan, New City Road, or the Saltmarket. But this was only a pretext for hostilities. Like the German-made assassination at Serajevo, it was the signal for war on the snub-nosed crew who wore corduroys, peak jackets, and C.R. 'bunnets.'

'Noo, laddies,' said Maister M'Muckle on the day the order was given, 'you'll mak' them a' show their seasons. Nae nonsense frae ony o' them.'

'Ay, Maister M'Muckle,' answered Tam; 'but whit aboot thae High Schule yins? They're aye jinkin' at the gate, an' the hauf o' them ride first-class wi' third-class tickets.'

'Dae yer duty, Tam,' was the brief reply.

'But whit if they fecht?'

'Fecht!' ejaculated the station-master. '*Defend the honour of the Company.*'

'Richt ye are!'

That was all that Tam wanted to know. Fecht! He and Puddin' were just spoiling for a battle with the tubby-tummied Conkie M'Beetle. The advent of the four-thirty was awaited with breathless interest. Puddin' was at one gate, Tam at the other. Conkie selected Puddin's gate, on the principle of the smaller the enemy, the less the resistance.

'All seasons ready!' shouted Puddin'.

'Seasons?' exclaimed Conkie.

'Ay.'

'What for?'

'Jist!' said Puddin', bracing himself.

'Oh!'

'Ay, oh!'

'Awa' and take a jump at yer face.'

'Show yer season,' demanded Puddin', closing the gate.

'Awa', man;' and Conkie heaved wee Puddin' aside and bolted out.

'I'll nab ye yet, ma lad.'

'Nab yer granny,' replied Conkie, putting his fingers to his nose.

'Whit a nose!' shouted Puddin'.

'Nae lip, Pollokshaws.'

'Wait till ma big brother gets ye.'

'We'll see,' said Conkie, heaving his bag up and turning home.

Puddin' returned to the booking-office to discuss a counter-attack with Tam.

'Whit are we gaun to dae wi' him?'

'Flatten him.'

'Ay; but he's ower big for me. It wud be like a bumbee hittin' a Zeppelin.'

'We'll baith tackle him.'

'When?'

'The morn.'

'A' richt; I'll haud, an' you punch.'

'That's it.'

Next day, when the train came in, unity of command was in being. The Allies were placidly awaiting the offensive. Conkie, however, was undaunted, for he had that blind courage always associated with those who are duds at maths, and useless at Greek. He walked forward as cool as a cucumber.

'Seasons,' roared Tam.

'Per-*haps*,' replied Conkie.

'There's nae per-*haps* aboot it.'

'Awa'.'

'I'll no awa'.'

'Here, cheese it.'

'I'll cheese ye. Ye havena got the wee fellah the day.'

'Get oot o' the road;' and Conkie tried to burst through.

Puddin', who had seen Yamaski Nogi-Pogi do Japanese wrestling at the Coliseum, promptly flopped down and collared the knees of the enemy. But Conkie let drive at Tam.

'Hit him in the belly-muscle,' roared Puddin'.

Tam, however, had planted an upper-cut on Conkie's nose, from which the blood of the High School flowed freely. The red stuff drawn by a bloater-eating democrat roused the pride and passions of the High School gladiator. With a kick he sent the Nogi-Pogi Puddin' flying, and tackled Tam with a rigour that was startling. It was a clean fight. No Lancashire kicking or Cumberland hugging; no female scratching or pounding below the belt; for a public-school boy always plays the game. Conkie was a bonny fechter, *and so was Tam*. The gamin knows the Queensberry Rules, and Tam fought like a gentleman.

'Biff!'

'Bang!'

'Uh!'

'Oo!'

At the end of five minutes both were blowing hard, but neither yielded. It promised to be a long affair, until Puddin' shouted, ' Here's a bobby!' Conkie picked up his bag and ran, and Tam adjourned to the office with a black eye and a very fat nose.

The policeman passed on with a grin; he, too, had been a boy.

'Good Tam,' said Maggie, patting him on the back; for, like all the lassies, she had the primitive love of human courage. This fight was really better than all the attentions of 'the wee slaveys' for the upsetting of Jimmy M'Cloon.

Maggie was swithering – swithering hard.

* * *

Next day, 'All seasons ready,' shouted Tam.

'There it's,' said Conkie, showing his ticket.

'You're learnin'.'

'Ay. … Here, you're no a bad sort. Come doon to the hoose for tea the nicht. Bring the wee fellah.'

'Richt ye are.'

That night, over ham and eggs, soda-scones, and cookies, the Conkie-Tam-Puddin' Alliance was born.

There's nothing mean about the High School.

Pollokshaws East station photographed from the signalbox.

G. H. ROBIN

CHAPTER XIII.

AT POLLOKSHIELDS.

THE relieving staff on the railway is a floating gang of bachelors who assume duty while the permanent staff are on holidays. You can usually tell a relief man. A relief station-master resembles a cross between an aspiring porter and a 'nippy' ticket-collector. He always coughs to hide his embarrassment when he comes on to the platform, and when he waves the flag to the guard he does it in a way which suggests an apology for his existence. In the booking-office he steps in an uncertain manner, afraid to exercise the majesty of his rank, and, to keep the peace, will even descend to smoking a Woodbine with a boy-porter. The reason for this timidity is lack of permanent rank, and the disadvantages of being a temporary gent. Another reason given by the porters is that relief station-masters are usually 'pushin' yins,' those who want to break the laws of seniority, and by the aid of a smooth tongue and a director's kick in the —— get hold of this job, preparatory to jumping the permanent pitch of a station-master who, *for a moment*, forgets that his body, soul, breeks, and a' are the sole property of the Company, and indulges in a long-hidden hauf-mutchkin – *jist to show his independence*. It's a queer world the railway, and the uncertainty of tenure is the reason which makes all ranks freeze on to their jobs like limpets.

This, by the way, is simply a preliminary blether to introduce the question of relieving duty, a task which, by the hand of Fate, devolved on Snooker Tam.

'Tam,' said the maister one morning.

'Ay.'

'You're for relievin' duty at Pollokshields.'

'Whit's up?'

'Wee Tam M'Jink's got the measles.'

'But I thocht I wis permanent here?'

'Man, there's naethin' permanent on the railway except the permanent wey, and even the sleepers get the seck for speakin' back to the engines. Dae whut ye're telt.'

'But wull I get back here?' whimpered Tam, his eyes drifting to Maggie, who was also ill at ease.

'Ay, ay. Off ye go.'

Tam went out to the door like Napoleon after Waterloo. Jumping into the train with a heavy heart, he flung himself back on the cushions to muse on Maggie, the five wee slaveys, and even Puddin', whom he was leaving behind. No doubt there would be hospitable back-doors in Pollokshields, but the bird in the hand is worth two in the bush, and he knew that Jimmy M'Cloon would now have a clear coast and a great opportunity to become the lifelong idol of Maggie. Besides, that youth Puddin' was stirring himself. Puddin', he observed, was now wearing a new rubber dicky and a vermilion tie. He had been buying sweeties of late instead of *The Boys' Friend*; in short, Puddin' was feeling his feet, and beginning to understand that the lads were meant to chase the lassies. 'It wis a bit thick,' concluded Tam as the train stopped at Pollokshields.

You must understand that Pollokshields is a most important station. This opinion is not endorsed in Newlands, Maxwell Park, or Kelvinside. Nevertheless, it is important. The failure to recognise the social status of any citizen of Pollokshields entails social ostracism

CR 'Dunalastair IV' 4-4-0, at the time LMS No. 14453, leaving Pollokshields West in June 1948 with an Inner Circle train. On the signalpost the Pollokshields West starting signal has been removed, but the position of the Maxwell Park distant has not been altered. The site of the signalbox is adjacent to the third coach of the train.

G. H. ROBIN

and an absence of Pollokshields visiting-cards (4 × 4) on your hall table. As a matter of fact, Pollokshields claims all the ancient glories of faded Park Circus, and avers that all those who live within its bounds wipe their lips with napkins and sleep in pyjamas – even the ladies. The ladies *never* carry their parcels, and all message-boys *must* go round to the back-door. Surely this reveals that Pollokshields is the haunt of the mighty, no matter what other suburbs say; but, to hold the balance even, we must give the Newlands point of view. Here it is as expressed in visiting-cards :

MRS PRIM POLITELY.

At Home,
2 P.M.–2.20 P.M.,   MARBLE AVENUE,
1st Wednesday.   POLLOKSHIELDS.

MRS CHEEREMUP.

At Home   PLENTYVILLE,
always.   NEWLANDS.

The Newlands card shows the cosmopolitan meet-everybody generosity of the *nouveau riche*. So says Pollokshields, *not* the author – Heavens, no! He dare not enter into this terrible controversy. However, Pollokshields is interesting. It understands the fashions, can value 'form,' and no lady will be found in red stockings, yellow skirt, or a corned-beef coloured bonnet. Indeed, some of the prettiest girls come from Pollokshields, and any one who has seen its famous tennis-club will agree that in feminine productions Pollokshields has 'the goods.' There is also dignity in its pose. The stately demeanour of its avenues somehow stops messengers from whistling 'Annie Roonie,' and causes Ford cars to scoot through like blazes, lest they be outdone by a local nickel-plated, blue enamelled, flower-bedecked Rolls-Royce. *They have got 'the hard stuff' in Pollokshields.*

Now, there's a reason for everything on the railway, even the weighing of your luggage. Just as you buy boots to fit your feet, so does the railway company choose station-masters to fit the various kinds of stations. This procedure is based on the principle, for Gallowgate, a knockout; for Pollokshields, a polished 'How-d'ye-do-sir?' sort of man. And, as the porters say, 'they send them [the porters] there to learn hoo to lift their bunnets.' The station-masters of Pollokshields have always been men of the world – able to distinguish between those who are likely to lunch with the directors and those who are not. They have the grand manner akin to that of the gentleman who wears a gold-braided top-hat in the Central. When they step abroad they breathe the air of majesty, and when the top-hat (or bonnet) comes off, it is done in the style of a Spanish senor.

You will at once say, 'What the devil has all this got to do with Tam?' Everything! It was a new world. From a happy, hail-fellow-well-met booking-office at Kirkbride he was plunged into the austere dignities of Pollokshields. There were no secret 'draws' at Woodbines in that department which is usually at the end of the station buildings. He had to get a move on, scrub his rubber dicky, knock the egg-dreeps off his tartan tie, and sleep on his trousers to get a crease on them. The skip of his bonnet had to be polished with beeswax, while he had to blaw his breath on his buttons and rub them hard to get them as clean as the sodgers'. A revolution! From a tow-headed gum-chewer he was compelled to be a well-scrubbed automaton who had to salute

the 'heid yins' and see all 'the Gorbals yins' off the premises – *at once. There's no mixed company in Pollokshields.*

'Here, boy,' said the new maister.

'Whit?'

'Whit are ye whittin aboot? Is that the wey ye answer yer betters?'

'I didna ken, I'm only an apprentice.'

'Say "sir," an' move slippy. Awa' wi' that parcel to Gold Plate Avenue.'

'Rieht ye are.' Tam couldn't handle the 'sir.' It stuck in his gills. His forebears had voted for Gladstone and Bradlaugh. But he went off quickly, eager to explore the back-doors of his new town. *En route* he was particularly struck with the many charming ladies in tailor modes, and for once he longed to be 'a toff' and give them 'the nod.' On entering Gold Plate Avenue he drew his breath. He had never seen such large houses, and wondered if they were museums. At last he reached his destination, a magnificent place redolent of 50 per cent. from rubber, tea, or oil. His quick eye caught a notice:

ALL MESSAGE-BOYS *MUST* GO ROUND TO THE BACK-DOOR.

'Jings! They don't hauf pit it on oot here!' he mumbled, blundering through the gate and knocking at the back-door.

True to tradition, he was kept waiting for fifteen minutes. This is an unwritten law, and one designed to impress all democrats. It was invented by the superior Curzons. Then the door opened, and a haughty, perjink sort of maid appeared.

'Here, Annie; here's yer percel.'

'Annie! Wha are ye Anniein' at?'

'I thocht that wis yer name.'

'Dinna think, then.'

'Ye're awfu' sniffy.'

'You're very cheeky.'

'Ach, awa'!'

'You awa'.'

'Hiv ye no a sangwidge an' a cup o' Mazawatee?'

'No.'

'Ye're gey funny oot here.'

'Whit station wis you at before?'

'Kirkbride.'

'I tho't that;' and the door banged in such a way that it blew his bonnet off. He picked it up, knocked the Pollokshields dust off, and with a grin adjusted it on his head and went out, banging the gate in such a way that an old pedestrian *jumped* and let fall a set of ivories out of his mouth.

'Sorry, maister,' said Tam, lifting a beautiful plate of incisors and molars and handing it to him.

'Learn to shut a gate properly, my boy,' was the short retort.

'Ach, awa'!' and Tam strolled off, very much annoyed with his first back-door experience in Pollokshields.

But when not worrying about Maggie, Puddin', or Jimmy M'Cloon, he found much to enliven him in Pollokshields. The robust old gentlemen who dealt in tobacco, rubber, oil, ships, boilers, and Highland Dew were a class apart. Dignified, breathing pound-notes, and handling bundles of 'fivers' when taking a tuppeny ticket. Generous, too, for they threw their shillings around as if they were farthings. 'The men make the city,' and they were typical of the proud old bailies who used to walk 'the plainstanes' and risked their Scots pounds in the clippers that brought wealth and fame to the Clyde. As for their wives, Tam was impressed by the stout, bustling ladies, clad in silks and ermine, many of whom had helped the guidmen to mak' their siller in ham, beef, or coal. If they did reveal their origin by asking for a first-*cless* ticket, that to Tam was simply the hall-mark of greatness. They had worked for their position, and Tam only respected those who had. After all, it is these hearty women who are the mothers of men, the good counsellors of rising business Napoleons, and the steady friends in black adversity, as they are the cheerful companions in success. Tam took to the old ladies, for they were mothers; and mothers of all degrees always love boys, be they ever so poor. Many a sixpence and big fat orange were pushed into his hand. As he said himself, 'The auld yins are no mean, onywey.'

But the youth of Pollokshields created mixed feelings within his breast. Somehow the chocolate-coloured bonnet of the High School still roused his ire. The only explanation that Tam gave was that 'they were aye pittin' it on.' But the prejudice really arose through the High School monopoly of all the pretty flappers in pigtails. Being just a boy-porter, he had no innings, and he did resent these pretty darlings jumping into dark first-class carriages with youthful Byrons and 'no askin' *him* in.' Sheer jealousy! However, he had a great admiration for all the pretty young ladies who, clad in smart tailors' modes, white gloves (mustn't forget the white gloves), coquettish hats, neat and none of your d—— nonsense footwear, with a Drooko umbrella and a ten-pound crocodile bag, took the train on Saturday mornings for the time-honoured Buchanan–Renfield–Sauchiehall Street parade. If you happen to be 'a blood,' you will know all about this social event. These well-groomed, healthy-skinned, and hefty wenches roused him to poetic ardour. Indeed, he even winked at the more daring of the tribe. Being public-school girls, they laughed; and if Tam had been five years older, with an R. W. Forsyth's tweed suit on his back, he would have 'got off,' for they have a quiet longing for the Devil in Pollokshields.

'The bloods,' of course, got a mixed reception from him. Tam thought they were 'too toffy,' and *the yawn*, cultivated at Dollar, Blair Lodge, Glenalmond, Oxford, or Cambridge, left him cold. These youths could give him his orders. Tam hated orders. He liked 'to be asked, no pushed.' But Tam was an unreasoning democrat, secretly jealous of jaunty bowlers, tight-waisted jackets, and turned-up trousers. Between you and me, Tam wanted to be one of 'The Boys,' one of those gay youths who work from ten to eleven and three to four, and between-times drink coffee in Craig's, or tell the old old tale in the lounge of the picture-house. But he copied them, and, by saving up his tips, got a ready-made swanky Harris-tweed outfit, a chase-me-Charlie Homburg hat, American bulb-toed boots, gloves (one shilling and elevenpence three-farthings), and a Fair Holiday cane at sixpence (sixpence halfpenny with a silver mount). At last he was 'one of them,' and on the first Sunday out there was a terrific commotion amongst the wee slaveys who take the air in Queen's Park. When the bold Lothario walked through, swinging his cane and blowing reek from a Woodbine, the eyes of the wee Maggies and Marys opened wide.

'By jings, that's a smert yin!'

'The goods.'

'An awfu' nut.'

Tam had his ears cocked for all these things; indeed, like Beau Brummell, he expected them. This advent into social greatness lifted him to the heights of daring and romance. And then he got a *bump*.

Ahead was Puddin', his hefty figure dressed in a nutty Norfolk suit, while his red face was surmounted by a brand-new half-crown straw hat. He was smoking a cheroot, and now and again flicking off the ash with his little finger in the style of a wealthy Jew. Smugness personified.

Maggie, more sweet than ever, was walking by his side.

'Heavens! ... Jings! ... HELLP!' muttered Tam, who, as yet, was not observed by the devoted couple. It was an awkward moment, a *desperate* fix; but with the readiness of a courtier he gave 'the nod' to a charming little nursemaid, hooked her arm, and walked past blushing Maggie and the now apoplectic Puddin', like Duggy Haig 'cutting' Hindenburg in Mons.

'Oh my! I'm frichtened,' declared Maggie.

'I'm no,' said Puddin'.

'It's your fau't.'

'You're a fine yin, efter me buyin' thae joojoobs. Am I no as guid as him?'

'Come on; the folk are lookin',' said Maggie, pulling the angry Puddin' on.

'A' richt; but, mind ye, ye'll no get me to buy ye cookies an' tea at Rouken Glen again. Ye're only playin' wi' Jimmy M'Cloon and me. It's Tam ye want!'

'Mebbe! But here's the caur. Bye-bye;' and off she ran.

'That bates a'!' said Puddin', scratching his head. 'Hang them a'! I'm feenished wi' lassies. I wush I had stayed at hame an' read *Comic Cuts*.' He turned away towards Pollokshaws with just a feeling of something going to happen.

He was beginning to feel Tam's fist on his nose.

The stairway from the street level building to the platform at Crosshill shortly after the installation of electric lighting. The lattice ironwork on the bridge and stair is still easily seen and the street-level building (page 129) has not yet been demolished. BRITISH RAILWAYS

CHAPTER XIX.

THE CLAIMS DEPARTMENT.

SUPERINTENDENT, CLAIMS DEPARTMENT.

DEAR SIR,—I have been instructed by Mrs I. M. Pertinent to represent her claim on your Company for the sum of £50 expended on medical advice and treatment for a small Yorkshire Terrier which contracted a chill while waiting for the London express. An early settlement will avoid trouble. Failing a mutual agreement, action will be taken in a Court of Law.—Yours truly,

SLINKEM AND SLINKEM,
Solicitors.

SUPERINTENDENT, CLAIMS DEPARTMENT.

DEAR SIR,—While travelling with the 3.20 P.M. the other day a spark from the engine alighted on my white fox fur, burning a little round hole. I therefore claim £10 as compensation.—Yours faithfully,

MILLY DOOEMIN.

SUPERINTENDENT, CLAIMS DEPARTMENT.

DEAR SIR,—My client, Mr Rufus Shonkostein, Passover Villa, Wee Jerusalem, Glasgow, has instructed me to claim damages for the loss of two heads off the brass nails on his *papier-maché* trunk. This trunk is an heirloom from his Polish father; the loss is, therefore, regretted. As my client is willing to settle the matter for a new leather one by Reid & Todd, I hope there will be no undue discussion about the matter.

I also assume you will pay the costs involved – i.e. 6s. 8d. for this letter, 1½d. for stamp, and 2d. for notepaper. (No charge for posting.)

Awaiting a prompt reply,—I am, yours truly,

HERMANN IBOLSKI,
Notary Public, Barrister-at-Law,
Legal Adviser to the Rabbis at the
Meat Market.

DERE SUR,—I wis in the fower fifteen frae Poalukshaws tae the Central, an' I lost ma bag. Gawd strooth! The weans mulk bottle wis in it, an' a hauf-pun o' Masseys Irish as weel as ma ticket for the blanket manauge. Maggie McGoogan wis wi' me an' can prove it. O, an' I forgot there wis a hauf-mutchkin o' 'The best.' Ma man's batin' me fur lossin' the hauf-mutchkin. I'm no carin' aboot ma bag or the wean's bottle, but if ye send the price o' the hauf-mutchkin, I'll dance at yer waddin'.—Yoors trooly,

Aggie Cuhoon,
Mull Vennel (3 up).

DEAR SIR,—Last week I sent a cage o' cock canaries frae Shawlands tae Hamilton. They were a' prize yins, an' the big cock lifted a First at the Rouken Glen Whustlers Show. But when the cage got tae Hamilton there wis nae cocks – *they were a' hens*, an' the man that bocht them frae me says they canna whustle, an' can only cheep for their meat. That's queer, is it no? Hoo did the cocks turn into hens between Shawlands and Hamilton? An' this mornin' he writes an' says they're still hens, but *no canary hens*, jist yellow yites painted wi' pent. I ken fine they're a lot o' canary men in Hamilton. An' it strikes me that yin o' them chinged the cocks into hens, an' no canary hens at that. Seein' that I mak' ma leevin' oot o' canaries, *specially cock canaries*, I wid be obliged if you would look efter this and get me my cage o' cock canaries back, *specially the big cock* that lifted the First at the Rouken Glen Whustlers Show.

I've drooned the yellow yites.—Yours, very much upset,

WULLIE M'GINTY,
Cock Canary Dealer,
Ham Close, Shawlands.

CORRESPONDENCE WITH MR ARTHUR NICKEM.

(1.)

SUPERINTENDENT, CLAIMS DEPARTMENT.

DEAR SIR,—I travelled in the ill-fated express which came to grief near Bleattock and went on fire. I have lost my cowhide trunk, inside of which was a presentation gold watch, also a golf-bag with three New Auchterlony mashies, a shell-case of a six-inch which I was taking home as a souvenir, and a deed-box with some family papers. This is a great loss, and I therefore claim compensation.

No reasonable sum refused.—Yours truly,

ARTHUR NICKEM.

(2.)

ARTHUR NICKEM, ESQ.

DEAR SIR,—We have examined your claim, also the débris of the express. In the remains of a leather bag we have discovered a watch – *a brass watch, value ten and six.* You may have this article on calling at this office.—Yours truly,

WALTER WATCHALL,
Superintendent.

(3.)

SUPERINTENDENT, CLAIMS DEPARTMENT.

DEAR SIR,—I *never* wear brass, and what about golf-clubs, shell-case, deed-box, &c.?—Yours truly,

ARTHUR NICKEM.

(4.)

ARTHUR NICKEM, ESQ.

DEAR SIR,—We have discovered the heads of several Braid putters and cleeks, but no Auchterlony mashies. Seeing that these heads have survived the fire, we can only conclude that you must have been mistaken about having three Auchterlony mashies on the train.—Yours truly,

WALTER WATCHALL,
Superintendent.

(5.)

SUPERINTENDENT, CLAIMS DEPARTMENT.

DEAR SIR,—I may have been mistaken about the Auchterlony mashies, but you do not mention shell-case or deed-box.— Yours truly,

ARTHUR NICKEM.

(6.)

ARTHUR NICKEM, ESQ.

DEAR SIR,—With reference to the shell-case, we have discovered the case of a fifteen-inch shell, not of a six-inch. As you have distinctly mentioned a six-inch case, we conclude there was no six-inch shell-case on this train. In any case, it is an offence under D.O.R.A. to have such a thing in your possession.—Yours truly,

WALTER WATCHALL,
Superintendent.

(7.)

SUPERINTENDENT, CLAIMS DEPARTMENT.

DEAR SIR,—There *was* a six-inch shell-case on the train, but I imagine it has got melted in the fire. But do inform me per return about the family deed-box and papers.

This is most important, and *I am determined to have satisfaction.*—Yours truly,

ARTHUR NICKEM.

(8.)

ARTHUR NICKEM, ESQ.

DEAR SIR,—We have now had an opportunity of examining thoroughly the whole of the débris. No deed-box has been discovered, but we have found a *band-box* containing pawn-tickets, ladies' photographs, a beer-bottle, also a bundle of correspondence addressed to you. This correspondence is from the Claims Departments of *several* Railway Companies, showing that this is your *unlawful* means of livelihood. Under the circumstances we believe your present claim to be *fraudulent*, and have asked the Judicial authorities *to issue a warrant for your arrest.*—Yours truly,

WALTER WATCHALL,
Superintendent.

(9.)

SUPERINTENDENT, CLAIMS DEPARTMENT.

DEAR SIR,—Sorry we cannot do business. I hope to have better luck with the N.B.—Yours hopefully,

ARTHUR NICKEM,
Claims Specialist.

CR '439' Class 0-4-4T No. 55207 sits at the buffers at Platform 8 in Glasgow Central station having arrived from a trip round the Circle on 12th June 1954. The water tower used for replenishing the tanks on the once intense service can be seen beside the engine. G. H. ROBIN

BIBLIOGRAPHY

The following have been consulted.

PRIMARY SOURCES

Minutes of
   Cathcart District Railway Company
   Caledonian Railway Company
   Lanarkshire & Ayrshire Railway Company
   Glasgow & South Western Railway Company
   Glasgow & Kilmarnock Joint Line Committee
   London Midland & Scottish Railway Scottish Committee

Cathcart District Railway Company
   Secretary's Letter Books
   Annual Reports and Accounts

Miscellaneous Railway Acts and Parliamentary Plans
Ministry of Transport and Department of the Environment Accident
   Reports
Caledonian Railway Working Timetables and Appendices

BOOKS

Why Cathcart? by Jean Marshall (1969)
Cathcart Memories by Alexander Gartshore (1938)
Glasgow by A. Macgill (1935)

The People's History of Glasgow by John McDowall (1899)
Jubilee of the Glasgow Tramways 1872–1922
The McIntosh Locomotives of the Caledonian Railway (1948)
The North British Railway by C. Hamilton Ellis (1955)
Locomotives at the Grouping by H. C. Casserley and S. W. Johnston
   (1966)
The Glasgow and South Western Railway by C. Highet (1955)
The Glasgow and South Western Railway, Stephenson Locomotive
   Society (1950)
Forty Years of Caledonian Locomotives 1882–1922 by H. J. Campbell
   Cornwell (1974)

NEWSPAPERS AND PERIODICALS

Pollokshaws News
Southern Press
North British Daily Mail
Evening News
Glasgow Herald
Edinburgh Gazette
The Bulletin
Evening Citizen
Scots Law Times
Trains Illustrated
Railway World
Railway Magazine

Electric Multiple Unit 050 passes Muirhouse Junction with an Outer Circle train heading for Glasgow Central.   H. STEVENSON